Power in Performance

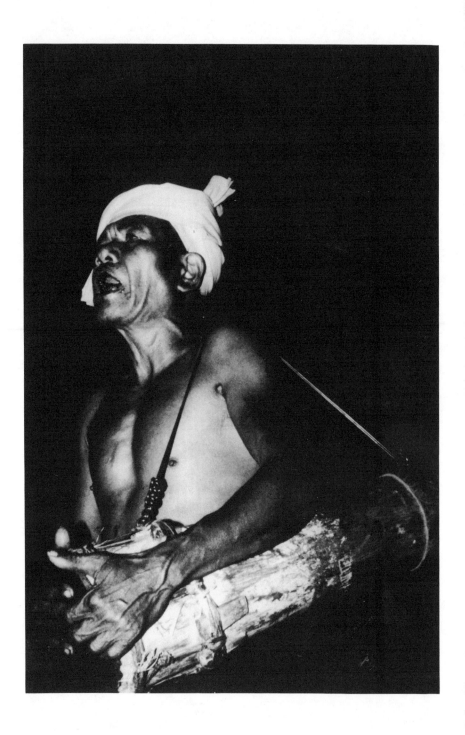

Power in Performance

The Creation of Textual Authority in Weyewa Ritual Speech

JOEL C. KUIPERS

University of Pennsylvania Press

Philadelphia

University of Pennsylvania Press
CONDUCT AND COMMUNICATION SERIES

Erving Goffman and Dell Hymes, Founding Editors
Dell Hymes, Gillian Sankoff, and Henry Glassie, General Editors

A complete listing of the books in this series
appears at the back of this volume

Frontispiece: A 'singer' (*a zaizo*) beats a hand drum during his all-night performance
of a placation rite.

Copyright © 1990 by the University of Pennsylvania Press
Printed in the United States of America

Library of Congress Cataloging-in Publication Data

Kuipers, Joel Corneal.
    Power in performance : the creation of textual authority in Weyewa
ritual speech / Joel C. Kuipers.
        p.   cm. — (University of Pennsylvania Press conduct and
communication series)
    Includes bibliographical references (p.) and index.
    ISBN 0-8122-8245-0
    1. Wewewa (Indonesian people)—Rites and ceremonies.   2. Wewewa
(Indonesian people)—Folklore.   3. Folklore—Indonesia—Sumba
Island—Performance.   4. Wewewa dialect—Social aspects—Indonesia—
Sumba Island.   5. Wewewa dialect—Texts.   I. Title.   II. Series.
DS632.W48K85   1990
306'.0899922—dc20   90-12529
                                                              CIP

Contents

Tables and Illustrations

Figures

Plates

Frontispiece: A 'singer' (*a zaizo*) performs the words of the ancestors in an all-night placation rite

Preface

On the island of Sumba in eastern Indonesia, a vibrant form of ritual speech is required in all ceremonial events. This study, based on over two years of ethnographic fieldwork among the Weyewa of western Sumba, provides an analysis of such verbal specialization in its rich social and cultural context. While learning the Weyewa language, I saw, recorded, and took part in many rites of divination, placation, and fulfillment. The transcriptions from a selected set of such events, along with Weyewa commentary on these texts, constitute the essential data on which much of this analysis is based.

Conceived as 'words of the ancestors,'[1] this couplet style of speaking takes shape in a variety of performance genres. The most sacred and closely guarded of these transmit the ancestral 'voice' in formal, poetic, but intelligible monologues that narrate the history of promises, obligations, and commitments to ongoing relationships of ceremonial exchange. According to Weyewa ritual ideology, since descendants are prone to change, innovate, and forget, they often neglect the ceremonial responsibilities these words engender. Therefore, most ritual discourse necessarily consists of genres devoted to the recovery and construction of these 'words' through creative dialogues, exuberant oratory, and elegant narratives. This study is concerned with the ideological, interactional and poetic process of "entextualization" by which these authoritative performances take shape.

I studied the words and voices that make up this process at a particular moment in a history of exchanges. These partly collusional, partly mystifying "webs of significance" tended to be represented in dyadic form as a relation not only between ancestors and their descendants, but also between teachers and students, 'trunks' and 'tips,' wife-givers and wife-takers, government and constituents, Sumbanese and 'white foreigners' (*dawa kaka*; literally 'white Javanese'). As Elizabeth Traube (1986) discovered during her research among the Mambai of Timor, fieldwork in eastern Indonesia can be viewed as a negotiated process of exchanges only partially guided by the wishes of the ethnographer; my presence over the course of more than two years of fieldwork was assimilated at various times to a role within these structures of reciprocity.

Since no other anthropologists had lived among the Weyewa for any extended period of time when I arrived in 1978,[2] I mistakenly believed at first that my Weyewa friends had few preconceptions about what "anthropological research" was all about and that I would have a free hand in shaping the circum-stances of our interaction. But as Triloki Pandey discovered among the Zuni, anthropological research can be guided by the history of transactions between the people being studied and prior researchers (1972). Informants have concep-tions about what the ethnographer should be doing, based partly on their expe-rience of, or hearsay about, previous investigators. Dell Hymes, for instance, was once asked by his Wasco friend Philip Kathlamet, "Can you take words apart like [Edward] Sapir?" (1981:210).

Up until the middle 1980s, visits by white foreigners to the Weyewa region were sufficiently infrequent that they were the focus of considerable curiosity, speculation about intentions and not a little confusion. When I first visited the island in July 1978, I found that several models of interpretation were circulat-ing, constructed out of past experiences and oral tradition. Some of these were legacies of the Dutch colonial officers, who were variously represented as horse-traders (Wielenga 1916:302) and white-skinned slave traders (see Needham 1983), but attempted to represent themselves with parental imagery. The contro-leur van der Feltz in the 1860s, for instance, sought to dispel the mercantile image by marching into a village, and, as he tells it,

> after I had offered a proper salute of gunfire to the various rajas, I told them that in the name of the Government, I had brought them a flag and a scepter, along with a *baba* [herd horse], which one after another were placed in the hands of Oeboe Ngebie [a raja]. I impressed upon him that the flag was a sign of the good will of the Government towards Soemba, and that they must cleave unto it as a child unto its father (in Wielenga 1916:355; translation mine).

This kind of paternalism eventually translated into a role in dispute mediation, loan brokering, and law enforcement. To a certain degree, resident Westerners seem still to be associated with these activities; thus on a number of occasions, although I never indicated any interest or expertise in these directions, my ser-vices were solicited for these duties. While I never became seriously involved personally in mediating a dispute, it was often tempting, since litigation may informally draw for its authority on the sacred genres of speech that I sought.

As the Dutch consolidated their power through military force beginning in 1906, the complementarity but relative equality of the mercantile idiom of in-teraction soon gave way to more asymmetrical and hierarchical forms of relation-ship: paternalism eventually led to a class- and race-based difference in which the Dutch were commonly addressed as *marómba* 'aristocrat.' The Dutch mis-sionary-linguist Louis Onvlee, for instance, was known as Marómba Ndende Kadu 'Noble of Standing Horn,' and a famous Dutch military commander, Lieutenant Berendsen, is today referred to as *Marómba Winni Mbolu* 'Winni Mbolu's Noble,' after a Sumbanese woman he took as his concubine. The term *marómba* had almost gone out of usage by the time of my fieldwork, for it was rarely applied to me (or anyone else); during my initial fieldwork I was addressed as *Pak Yoel* 'Mr. Joel,' and later with the teknonym *Ama Mbere* 'father of Berendt.' Nonetheless, despite initial awkwardness, I grew accustomed to receiving a seat of honor at feasts, eating along with the most privileged guests, and being treated with the deference and respect Weyewa accord to people of high rank.

During the period following World War II, Indonesian independence and the brief flowering of the Indonesian Communist party (PKI) changed forever the way that Weyewa and other Sumbanese looked on class privilege, social hierarchy, and white foreigners. Although the Dutch presence on Sumba was small and relatively benign in comparison to Java, and left few bitter memories among Weyewa (but see Hoskins 1987), cries of *feodal!* (feudalism!) still retain some currency as a way of criticizing a "traditional" hierarchic social order sanctioned by the Dutch. Since the mid-1960s, a new hierarchic scheme has been developing, organized along rural/urban and pagan/Christian lines, informed by an ideology of upward mobility through education.

In my first few encounters with Sumbanese, before I ever reached the island, my presence was assimilated to a role in the educational system of exchange. Before beginning fieldwork on Sumba in the fall of 1978, I spent nearly three months in Malang, East Java, attending an advanced Indonesian Language Study Program, during which time Mathias Malo, a native speaker of a Sumbanese language working in Malang as an attorney, generously helped me with my initial efforts to acquaint myself with his language. I did this by composing simple conversations in Indonesian, which Mathias then translated into Weyewa. By memorizing these phrases and by going over transcriptions of some taped speech events obtained during a brief preliminary visit to Sumba in July, I was able to acquire a rudimentary knowledge of the structure and morphology of this language before actually beginning fieldwork. Eventually, almost all my fieldwork and interviews were conducted exclusively in the Weyewa language.

From these encounters it soon became clear that if I was to seek knowledge about ritual speech, I could do so as a 'college student' (*mahasiswa*), which implied that others would 'teach' me. Furthermore, education was something authorized by the government, and my letters of permission from the government made it clear that research was a legitimate part of this. Most of these initial encounters were with relatively acculturated and well-to-do individuals who either were themselves college students, or had been, or were familiar with the category. For these teaching services, I reciprocated with small gifts, but usually not money, which I was told would be inappropriate for persons of educated status.

When, after boarding an old DC 3 airplane, I arrived on the bare meadow of West Sumba's airfield, I was still undecided as to which of the several closely related but mutually unintelligible languages I would study. While conducting a preliminary survey, I stayed at first with some Chinese friends of Mathias Malo in Waikabubak, the capital of West Sumba. I finally settled on the Weyewa speakers because there had as yet been no detailed ethnographic treatment of this area, Christianity had had relatively little impact on the indigenous form of religious practice called *marapu*, the region was centrally located, and the use of 'ritual speech' (*tenda*) seemed particularly lively there.

With the assistance of John L. Keremata, a well-known Weyewa school-teacher living in Waikabubak, I was able to find a small, unoccupied house of bamboo construction conveniently located at the base of an important village named Elopada, formerly inhabited by the late raja, Bulu Engge. Since the Dutch missionary Onvlee had lived in his own home, and not in the home of another family, it made sense to Keremata and others that I should have my own place, too. It was a simple but comfortable structure, one that permitted me to live in a manner not so very different from my Weyewa friends. Finding a place of my own turned out well in retrospect, since my house came to be a scene of many all-night discussions with ritual specialists, something of a hangout for visitors and friends on their way to the bi-weekly Elopada *parengga* 'market' (lit. 'meeting'), and a frequent stopping point for casual betel-chewing and curiosity seekers, all of which are advantages to an ethnographer, but which might be seen as inconveniences to a large family. A young Weyewa couple, Rina Dairo and John Mbili, along with their daughter, Albina, and their nephew, Tamu Ama, did move in with me, however, to set up and keep house for me.

Keremata also helped me find able, diligent, and reliable assistants who lived near my house. Three of these "assistants" (from the Indonesian *asisten*, a term they adopted for lack of a better way to describe this complex relationship) were very important in my fieldwork. During periods of regular research, they agreed that wages approximating those of an elementary schoolteacher's monthly salary—about fifty dollars a month in 1978–1980—would be appropriate. All native speakers of Weyewa, and members of a literate elite (but not wealthy by Weyewa standards), these three men and I gradually evolved a division of labor in the analysis of ritual speech that has worked quite well: we have transcribed and analyzed well over 3,000 pages of linguistic material over nearly two years of collaboration. Often (though not always) accompanied by one or another of them, I would tape-record a speaking event and make notes and drawings on the social circumstances in which it occurred. Then Mbora Paila, a technically in-clined, diligent former state agriculture department employee, transcribed the tapes into notebooks. Enos Boeloe, a well-liked and socially prominent retired minister and former linguistic assistant to Onvlee, checked the transcriptions against the tape, and for the first few months of our work he also did interlinear Indonesian translations of the ritual speech transcriptions. I would then check and annotate the materials. Finally, often with the help of the clients and prac-titioners involved in the recorded event, I also would work with Petrus Malo Umbu Pati, a brilliant, outspoken, former school administrator, who helped me to understand the meanings behind the words and the larger contexts of ideology and action in which they occurred.

The only model of anthropological investigation known to some of my friends was the extensive and distinguished linguistic and ethnological research of the Dutch linguist-missionary Louis Onvlee. Onvlee lived until the 1950s outside the tiny but polyglot government administrative center in Waikabubak, studying Weyewa and the closely related language of the neighboring Loli folk, some twenty kilometers away. Since his work mainly concerned translating the Bible into Weyewa, many people associated my concern with speech with his linguistic investigations. More importantly, however, Onvlee was also associated with the Dutch government administration, gathering data to settle land disputes; indeed he had travelled to Weyewa in this capacity (Onvlee 1973:57). Many were the times I would walk into a village I had never visited before to hear my presence explained as *nya nggobba-na Marómba Ndende Kadu* 'he is the counterpart of Professor Onvlee' (lit. the 'Nobleman from Standing Horn,' the name of the place where Onvlee and his wife lived).

The apparently universal admiration for Onvlee and his work did much to facilitate my entry into the field. Enos Boeloe, one of his well-trained assistants became my close and loyal friend and research co-worker. When I took notes on what people said and recorded their speech, this was sometimes accepted because people had seen or heard of how the *Dokter Bahasa* 'Doctor of Language' similarly objectified their language. It should be noted here that Onvlee did not have the use of a tape recorder during most of his research in Sumba, from 1926 to 1955.

But in time the reality emerged that I was not Onvlee, and my methods and goals were different. To many of my Weyewa friends, roughly 80 percent of whom remained stout adherents to their indigenous form of religious practice and belief, an important and nagging concern was whether I was really a missionary, interested in their language as a tool for saving souls. Some weeks after I arrived, I held a feast with the goal of explaining my motives and assuring them that I was interested in studying their language, particularly 'ritual speech.' Each ritual leader who attended went home with a chunk of pig meat (*wawi kaza* 'community pig'; see Onvlee 1980:156), a gift that carried with it a customary obligation to assist and reciprocate at some future date.

This feast indeed resulted in many invitations to attend more feasts, but did not necessarily remove their doubts. If there was a turning point in my field research, it was one night when I went, unaccompanied by any assistants, to record an all-night placation rite. Many of the ritual spokesmen who had been at my feast were there, and they questioned me closely about my purposes. Was I trying to convert them? Was I trying to gather data to settle land disputes? My negatives met with polite, but cool responses.

Later that evening, however, I did something they did not expect that seemed to banish some suspicions. During the first hour or so the *zaizo* rite of placation (discussed in Chapter Six), participation is relatively unrestricted, and anyone who wishes to do so may address a singer in ritual speech and offer a blessing, a clarification of a point, or a greeting. I had been practicing ritual speaking at home, with the help of several experts, and I decided to take this opportunity to greet the speakers, explain in a formal fashion the purpose of my attendance, and offer a short, customary blessing on the proceedings. Though my speech in reality was a rather modest, brief little effort, several of my Weyewa friends were extremely impressed. I continued this practice at other ritual events, and these small forays into public speaking went a long way toward demonstrating my sincerity. Over time, it came to be customary, whenever I attended a ritual speech event such as a *zaizo*, for me to make some brief statement in ritual speech.

In general, I felt (or was made to feel) that most Weyewa welcomed my interest in their culture and saw me as having a legitimate right to know. My camera, tape recorder, and notebooks were usually perceived as opportunities rather than threats. In fact, tape players were becoming an increasingly popular commodity during my stay on the island—more popular than radio—and ritual speech was a frequent subject of these recordings. Most ritual speech performers seemed to delight in receiving copies of photographs of themselves and hearing their voices played back on the tape recorder. On market days, lines occasionally formed outside my house of people interested in having a personal song, folktale or some other verbal genre recorded and played back to them on tape.

For reasons that will become increasingly clear over the course of this analysis, an in-depth field study of ritual speech requires a practical understanding of a complex hierarchy of exchange and reciprocity in Weyewa ceremonial ideology. Put simply, not all ritual speech forms are of equal exchange value. While personal songs and some folktales were often freely performed, many were the times I asked about particular forms of speaking and was told that they 'are not easily spoken' (*nda pa-tekki awa*), and are 'sacred' (*erri*). I was often told that performing certain genres without proper ritual preparations, out of context, or in an insincere fashion is forbidden. Violations of these taboos are a cause for misfortune, and the more sacred the genre the more serious the punishment inflicted on the offender.

The meaning of such statements about the sacredness of discourse is only partly interpretable in the context of cosmology and symbolic structure. They are also declarations of the value of one's knowledge of ritual lore, and the relationship to the questioner. In many cases, the speaker would proceed to suggest that a ceremony of 'betel and areca nut' offering (*pa-mama*) could be performed, after which the 'sacred' words could then be released. While none of the dozens of rites of misfortune that I attended were ever performed on this basis, or for me as the primary audience, I have recorded a number of traditional myths mediated by this kind of exchange. In practice, this involves minimally sacrificing a chicken and offering a certain amount of money or goods to the speaker on a plate containing betel and areca chewing ingredients. In response, the speaker accepts the offering on behalf of the ancestors whose words he purports to represent by tossing a small amount of the dried areca nut from the plate to the east and west, and informing the ancestral spirits in ritual speech of his intentions to speak in their 'voice.'

This *pa-mama* ceremony for gaining permission to perform certain genres is commonly used by Weyewa among themselves. When a man wishes to stage a celebration ceremony, for instance, he may first need to know more about the family relations among the potential participants. In order to obtain this knowledge, he may request the performance of a sacred genealogical narrative by an expert. The speaker is then compensated with a 'red rooster' (*mawailo woka*), and perhaps some money and other goods. While many songs, folktales, or general genealogical knowledge may be obtained in this way, the most sacred *kanungga* narratives (described in Chapter Seven) cannot be performed outside of their appropriate context.

But the legitimacy of such inquiry consists in more than the performance of a simple mechanical ritual of *pa-mama*. Many Weyewa passionately believe that such work is vitally important to recovering the lost or forgotten 'word' of the ancestors. Most adult Weyewa are quite aware that their culture has undergone profound transformations since World War Two, and the future holds out the promise of even more change. The goals of my research, and the goal of the rituals of misfortune described in this book were thus described by Weyewa in curiously parallel terms: as a way of recovering the word, fixing it and returning it to its full plenitude (cf. Traube 1986:ix). Many times ritual leaders would point to my notepad and tape recorder during a break in performance or after an event, and admonish me—even implore me—to "get it right" for the sake of posterity and to "listen to what is true; do not report lies."

The instruction to "get it right" is a humbling one, considering the multiple, shifting, and competing epistemological frameworks of evaluation, not only within the Western social disciplines within which I write (see Geertz 1983b), but within Weyewa culture (see Chapter Two and the Epilogue). Despite my efforts to follow the categories and the analytical strategies of my Weyewa teachers by focussing on the locally salient but highly polysemic category of 'words,' I have perhaps done some violence to the wishes of some of my more conservative informants by not limiting my analysis to the ideal and changeless symbolic order that they so hoped their words embodied, but also including verbatim transcriptions exhibiting the emergent, situated, and at times improvisational characteristics of their discourse in the context of the cultural activities in which they took place. On the other hand, by concentrating on the relationship of speaking to the Weyewa struggle for coherence in their ritual life, I may have represented these verbal activities as more systematic than they might have appeared had I chosen another framework for presentation. With this study, I cannot claim to have fulfilled Weyewa hopes for an authoritative, debate-silencing monologue that restores the true 'word of the ancestors'; rather, I hope I have, as Weyewa ritualists like to say, "assembled the lips in pairs, brought together all the faces," so that a dialogue can begin.

Notes

1. Single quotes enclose glosses of Weyewa terms.
2. Akiko Ono (1976) had conducted a number of short visits to Weyewa in the 1970s.

Orthographic Notes

Bringing Weyewa ritual speech to the printed page demands close attention to the techniques of translation and transcription. Dennis Tedlock (1983) has remarked that the task of transforming the spoken arts of non-Western cultures into written texts requires crossing cultural gulfs much larger than those faced by translators who move from one Indo-European tradition to another. Dell Hymes (1981) has also criticized the often clumsy, so-called "literal" and "scientific" translations of some early ethnographers, as "a mark of naivete, not objectivity." As Hymes and many folklorists are urging, translators must render texts in a way that offers a tribute to the beauty of the original art. During the course of many discussions with Weyewa consultants, I have struggled to find more elegant, valid, and efficient methods for handling the richness of Weyewa texts.

Over the past two decades, with the advent of portable tape recorders, it has become possible to bring greater detail and accuracy to transcriptions of speech events (see Fine 1984, Ochs 1979). The result has been greater recognition of "unsuspected designs" in the speaker's expert use of intonational, pitch, pause, and rhythmic resources in the organization of texts. In the many Weyewa texts I recorded, repetitive phrases and embedded quotations—sometimes ignored or dropped from translations—often provided crucial clues to text structure and speaker's intent.

In general, I have placed Weyewa text lines flush to the left margin of the page. Poetic lines of couplets, defined by rhythmic and semantic parallelism, are made typographically parallel through equal levels of indentation. When the spoken line is too long for the page, the remaining portions of the poetic line are further indented in a parallel fashion. For example, in the couplet,

oruta koki	gather the monkeys	1
ta kalunga	in the field	2
ka ta mandi'i teppe,	so that we can sit on the mat,	3
wandora-na wawi	summon the pigs	4
ta maredda	in the meadow	5
kai terrena pa-mama;	so that you get the quid;	6

lines one through three and four through six are each part of a single poetic line, but on the page appear as three typographical lines apiece. To show that, for instance, line 2 of this preceding text does not constitute a new poetic line but rather a continuation, it is further indented from the margin. Ratified changes in actual speaking participation reflecting semantic contributions are represented by new lines flushed left and extra vertical spacing. Interjected "back channel cues" or overlapping commentary not affecting the general participation and line structure are indented (e.g., "it is true," "aha!" "oooo") with square brackets indicating the position of overlap. For instance, in the 'blessing songs' considered in Chapter Seven, when a chorus continues the line of a singer by extending his final vowel ("oooo"), I represent it as follows:

ngara ndukka anaaaa nggenggeooo   all the spider children ooo
                    [
chorus: *ooooo!*   *ooooo!*

Couplets are not the only units of text structure in Weyewa ritual speech. For lack of a consistently applied Weyewa cover term, I have borrowed Hymes's phrase "stanza" to describe a diverse group of supra-couplet structures which emerge in different ways and in different shapes in various Weyewa genres examined in this book (cf. Hymes 1981).[1] For instance, in divinatory discourse, groups of couplets are linked together by thematic content, anaphoric and sometimes cataphoric co-reference, and are formally bounded by "discourse markers." In divination, these include *takka* 'but,' *ne ba hinna* 'now' and various "locutives" e.g., 'you say,' 'I say,' '[he, she, it] says,' etc. (see Chapter Four). In such cases, discourse markers cueing the stanza boundaries are flushed left, while groups of couplets are indented to reflect their status as continuations. Since the stanzas in sung genres such as *zaizo* placation songs (Chapter Six) and in 'blessing songs' (Chapter Seven) tend be strophic in character—in that the repeated musical pattern coincides with stanza boundaries—there are usually fewer discourse particles marking the structural units of the song. In such cases, initial lines are flushed left, while subsequent couplets in the stanza are indented to indicate that they are a continuation of a single stanza.

Although writers such as Dennis Tedlock (1983) and Dell Hymes (1981) have disagreed about the significance of certain aspects of discourse structure, they agree that unless more attention is paid by ethnographers to the significance of such textual cues, including pauses, and repetitive discourse markers, and the role they play in segmenting the discourse into units such as stanzas, scenes, and the like, much of the meaning of such native texts will have been "in vain" (Hymes 1981; see also Woodbury 1985). The repetition of such markers guide us to a clearer understanding of not only what the speaker had in mind, but the genre conventions as well.

Weyewa Orthography

Appreciation of the rhythmic and syntactic structures of Weyewa ritual speaking requires a grasp of the phonological and morphological characteristics of the Weyewa language and the method used here for representing it orthographically.

The phonemes of the Weyewa language are five vowels /i, e, u, o, a/, three nasal consonants /m, n, ng/, nine stops /mb, b, p, nd, d, t, ngg, k, ' (glottal stop)/, one spirant /z/, two semi-consonants /w, y/, two lateral consonants /l, r/, one affricate /c/, and consonant length. There are four diphthongs /au, ai, ou, ei/. Phonemes are enclosed in forward slashes.

While the phonetic quality of the Weyewa consonants exhibits relatively little variation, vowel qualities vary allophonically. The table offers a brief description of the phonetic significance of the consonant symbols used in the orthography. Phonetic representations are enclosed in brackets.

Symbol	Description
Nasal Consonants	
/m/	bilabial nasal
/n/	alveolar nasal
/ng/	velar nasal
Stops	
/mb/	prenasalized bilabial voiced stop
/b/	preglottalized, implosive bilabial voiced stop
/p/	bilabial voiceless stop
/nd/	prenasalized voiced alveolar stop
/d/	preglottalized, implosive voiced alveopalatal stop (see Onvlee 1950)
/t/	voiceless alveolar stop
/ngg/	prenasalized voiced velar stop
/k/	voiceless velar stop
/'/	glottal stop
Spirants	
/z/	alveopalatal spirant (voicing varies dialectally)
Semiconsonants	
/w/	labiodental voiced semiconsonant
/y/	palatal semiconsonant
Laterals	
/l/	apico-alveolar lateral
/r/	alveolar lateral
Affricate	
/c/	voiceless alveopalatal affricate

The pronunciation of the first position vowels varies in relation to the following consonant. In order to demonstrate contrasts in the following minimal pairs, the vocoid symbols listed below will be taken to have the following meanings:

[i] = high front unrounded
[I] = lower high front unrounded
[e] = mid front unrounded
[ɛ] = lower mid front unrounded
[a] = mid central unrounded
[ə] = low central unrounded
[u] = high back rounded
[U] = lower high back rounded
[o] = mid back rounded
[ʌ] = lower mid back rounded

1. /i/ in first position is realized as [i] before single consonants:
   [ti lu]   /tilu/   'ear'
   [I] before doubled consonants:
   [tɪl lu]   /tillu/   'middle'
   However, in final position, whether preceded by a single or a doubled consonant, the pronunciation is always [i]. For example, when preceded by a single consonant:
   [ni ri]   /niri/   'edge'
   or preceded by a doubled consonant:
   [lɪm mi]   /limmi/   'you (pl) say'
   the final vowel is realized as [i].

2. /e/ in the first position is realized as [e] before single consonants:
   [ne we]   /newe/   'traditional story'
   [ɛ] before doubled consonants:
   [nɛw we]   /newwe/   'here'
   This particular minimal pair also illustrates how the vowel in the final position is realized as [e].

3. /a/ in the first position is realized as [a] before single consonants:
   [wa no]   /wano/   'to wash'
   [ə] before doubled consonants;
   [wən no]   /wanno/   'village'
   In final position, /a/ is realized as [a]:
   [po la]   /pola/   'stalk'
   [pʌl la]   /polla/   'sour'

4. /u/ in the first position is realized as [u] before single consonants:
   [tu ra]   /tura/   'to open, begin (a swidden)'
   [U] before doubled consonants
   [tUr ra]   /turra/   'cataract'

In final position, /u/ is realized as [u] regardless of the preceding consonant:

[mbu lu] /Mbulu/ 'man's name'
[Ul lu] /ullu/ 'to go before'

5. /o/ in the first position is realized as [o] before single consonants

[o ma] /oma/ 'garden'

[ʌ] before doubled consonants

[ʌm ma] /omma/ 'money, ear pendant'

In final position, /o/ is realized as [o] regardless of the preceding consonant:

[wa no] /wano/ 'to wash'
[wən no] /wanno/ 'village'

Where there is variation among the consonants, it is often a result of dialect differences. For example, /w/ is realized as [w] in some portions of the Weyewa speaking world, as [v] in others, and occasionally as [gh] in the Laura and Tana Righu districts. /z/ is realized variously as [s] (near Loli) and as [θ] (in Tana Righu).

The canonical shape of Weyewa words is CVC(C)V: intervocalic doubling of consonants always involves gemination. Other frequently occurring shapes include (C = consonant, Dp = diphthong, V = vowel):

Shape	Example	Gloss
CDp	ndou	'year'
V	i	'contents'
CDpCV	touda	'three'
CVVCV	duada	'two'
CVCDpCV	mandauta	'to fear'
DpCV	aura	'to swear'

Any of the vowel phonemes may occur in either of the positions. Consonant length only occurs intervocalically. The glottal stop does not occur phonemically in initial position. Stress is rather pronounced, and falls most often on the penultimate syllable of the root word. Since stress placement is not affected by affixation, the root word will be separated from prefixes and suffixes with hyphens to assist the reader in identifying it. The Weyewa prefixes are *pa-, ka-, ma-*, and genitive and modal suffixes are *-na, -ngge, -langge, -po, -ba, -do*, and *-ki*; pronominal suffixes are *-ngga, -nggu, -na, -ni, -ma, -nda, -mi(nggi)*, and *-da*. Thus *kawukku* 'knot, binding' becomes *pa-kawukku-na* 'that which is bound.' There are of course, exceptions to the stress placement pattern: For example, *wátara* 'corn.' For purposes of this work, there is no need to devote a special accent mark to indicate these cases.

The accent mark will instead be used to mark vowels preceding doubled consonants represented with digraphs. While many readers will perhaps want to take the wisdom of this procedure on faith, for those interested in a phonological and orthographic explanation, a more in depth discussion will be required.

During the first few months of research, in transcriptions and in my field notes, both Mbora Paila and I used the orthography we learned from Enos Boeloe, who in turn had learned it from Professor Onvlee, who used it in translating the New Testament (Onvlee, Boeloe, and Mbili, eds. 1970) and a book of Old Testament Bible stories (Onvlee, Boeloe, and Mbili, eds. 1938) into Weyewa. Onvlee's writing system was very clever in many ways, using a basic Latin character set that could be found on almost any European typewriter. For instance, the Weyewa language (as well as many other Sumbanese languages) has a significant distinction between implosive and/or glottalized versus non-glottalized b and d sounds (labial and dental stops; see Onvlee 1950). Instead of writing them ?b versus b, and ?d versus d, or b' versus b, which might look a little odd and require a special typewriter, he wrote them b versus mb and d versus nd respectively. This becomes especially important in the case of doubled intervocal consonants, since representing *hidda* 'they' as *hid'd'a* is very unattractive.

The trickiest choice regarding the orthography, however, turns on the issue of whether Weyewa words can permit a syllable that ends in a consonant. This is not a minor issue, nor one that is simple to resolve. It is not trivial for the fieldworker who is planning to produce and analyze hundreds, even thousands, of pages of transcriptions, and who is not at all happy about the prospect of correcting thousands of spelling errors. It is also important to have an orthography that assistants feel comfortable using, and that is easy to learn. The easiest writing systems to learn are the ones that correspond most closely to the native ear.

This whole issue of how Weyewa syllables end arose after a few weeks in the field, when I visited a proud and semi-literate owner of a gong on which he had inscribed his village name, spelled *Nggollu Winno* 'corral of areca palms.' The spelling should have been *Nggólu Wíno*, according to Onvlee. I pointed this out to Mbora Paila, who replied that these people were uneducated, and he said that when uneducated Weyewa try to write their language they often make the mistake of writing two consonants where there "should" be only one. I later noticed other such peculiarities, checking government census records: a hamlet called 'grass village' was written *wanno wittu* and not *wáno wítu*. What was interesting was that these errors always occurred in the same place in the word: in the middle of the word, between vowels. I never saw anyone try to double a consonant at the beginning of a word.

That these "errors" should be so systematic intrigued me. Onvlee's writing system, as he describes it, rests on the premise that "in Sumbanese, there are no closed syllables and thus no consonant clusters in the middle of the words" (1973:166). After looking through many pages of inconsistent writing, I decided to examine the Weyewa sound system more closely. It turns out that Weyewa words do indeed have syllables that end in consonants. The evidence comes in part from listening to Weyewa pronounce words for emphasis, which they often do in narration in colloquial and ritual speech. For instance, a diviner offering a chicken to the spirits says *nak:::ka manu* 'thiiiiis chicken' and the first syllable of the word *nakka* (as I write it) ends in a k: (*nak*) with the next syllable beginning with a k: (*-ka* [*manu*]). When they pronounce the words slowly (an artificial exercise to be sure), the presence of two consonants "in the middle of the words" is in fact easy to hear.

The arguments in favor of modifying Onvlee's orthography—the professed ease in writing, the evidence of closed syllables—were later joined by an argument based on phonological "economy." Choosing vowel length or stress as the phonemic and hence "determining" factor in this arrangement is less "economical" than choosing consonant length. This is because, if vowel length were judged to be phonemic, an extra rule would be required to specify that only "long" vowels occur in monosyllabic words, for example, in *pu* 'heart' and *du* 'connection.' Since there is no good phonetic reason for this distributional restriction (e.g., if long vowels were easier to pronounce in monosyllables), then it can be taken as evidence relevant to the phonemics of the language. The same argument applies to fortis and lenis stress. Extra rules would have to be brought forth to explain why only lenis stress occurs in monosyllables, while both fortis and lenis stress can occur in other syllabic shapes. On the other hand, if consonant length is taken as phonemic, a simple, general rule applies to all cases: lengthened consonants only occur intervocalically.

But if doubled consonants occur intervocalically, what should we do about the phonemes represented with digraphs? For example, 'water buffalo' becomes *karambmbo*, which is unsightly and virtually unreadable. The solution adopted here, which arose in discussions with my French colleague Brigitte Renard-Clamagirand during the summer of 1988, is to use an accent on all vowels preceding doubled digraphs. Thus *karambmbo* becomes *karámbo* 'water buffalo.'

A final note on English usage. When I use male-gendered pronouns in the text, I do *not* mean that these should be understood generically, but rather specifically as having male referents. When female referents are intended, I will so indicate with female gendered pronouns.

Notes

1. When speaking of sung verses, Weyewa sometimes refer to these units as *nauta* 'steps,' connoting the generally falling intonational structure. Another similar label for such units is *kateki* 'step,' more often applied to spoken verse. In a Weyewa translation of the New Testament, the segmentation of the text structure used visual rather than kinetic metaphors: individual verses were called *mata*, literally 'eyes,' while chapters were labeled *kawukku*, literally 'knot, bamboo internode.'

Acknowledgments

In the "field" and after, I had help in producing this book. My Weyewa assistants, Petrus Malo Umbu Pati, Ds. Enos Boeloe, and Mbora Paila already mentioned in the preface, offered invaluable assistance in collecting, interpreting and organizing the data, as well as offering hospitality and encouragement. As 'wellsprings' of ancestral words and insightful explanations, Mbulu Renda, Rato Kaduku (Umbu Tawila), Lende Mbatu, Malo Pare, Ngongo Pandaka, D.D. Bobo, and S.D. Bili never seemed to run dry. I am grateful to them and to many others who, for reasons of the delicacy of the subject matter, appear in the text as pseudonyms, or who wished to remain anonymous. I apologize to them in advance for any errors and misinterpretations which remain in the text despite their best efforts: *kaballa nda pa-ate-wangga, kapingge nda pa-rutto-wangga*.

I wish to thank my parents, Jack Kuipers and Lois B. Kuipers, for being a constant source of encouragement and moral support during my graduate studies and beyond.

Although my wife and partner Teresa Anne Murphy has never set foot on the island of Sumba, she journeys through these chapters with me as my closest companion. Despite her own pressing professional obligations, she has been my single most constant interlocutor in these pages. She has always found time to read and re-read drafts, offering advice and encouragement. If audiences are in some sense "co-authors," then certainly the voice in this book is partly hers.

Like any other book, this work incorporates the words of intellectual colleagues in ways that surpass proper acknowledgment. While there are no doubt others I have neglected to mention, some of the individuals to whom I am indebted include: Sander Adelaar, John Bowen, Charles Briggs, Steven Caton, Wallace Chafe, Harold Conklin, Shelly Errington, James J. Fox, Rufus Hendon, Janet Hoskins, Dell Hymes, Judith Irvine, Ward Keeler, Webb Keane, John Kirkpatrick, David Konstan, Susan McKinnon, Rodney Needham, Brigitte Renard-Clamagirand, Jos Platenkamp, James Scott, Michael Silverstein, Elizabeth Traube, Bill Watson. Special thanks are due to Dell Hymes and Judith Irvine for particularly thorough readings of earlier drafts. Over the years, all have tried in various ways to help me improve the ideas in this book, and cannot be blamed when I have failed to understand or follow their advice.

The research for this book was carried out with the sponsorship of the Pusat Penelitian of the Universitas Nusa Cendana in Kupang, Timor, and the Indonesian Institute of Sciences (LIPI). Financial support came from the Yale University Concilium on International and Area Studies Dissertation Research Grant, Yale University Council on Southeast Asian Studies, Sigma Xi, Institute for Intercultural Studies, The Social Science Research Council, National Endowment for the Humanities Summer Stipend, National Endowment for the Humanities Fellowship for College Teachers, and the Fulbright–CIES Research Scholars Program. Publication was supported by the George Washington University Publication Fund. I am deeply grateful for this support.

1

Power in Performance

In December of 1987, officials of the Indonesian government on the island of Sumba banned a variety of ritual speaking events as 'wasteful' and 'backward.'[1] The whole series of ceremonial performances by which men construct the most sacred and authoritative texts in their culture is now against the law. This book is about those outlawed performances. I began studying them more than a decade ago, but I have had no difficulty continuing my research since the ban. As one official in the Department of Education and Culture informed me, I am studying linguistic and literary forms: "grammar and poetry." The poetic couplets on which this ritual style is based are not restricted. On the contrary, the regional government expressed interest in my preparing a ritual speech textbook for elementary school children. Nor are the myths banned that these performances enact; again, the local representatives of the Department of Education and Culture showed a real interest in printing some of these texts for educational purposes, in order to develop a national folklore, an emerging category of state culture.

What are banned are the *performances*. The (written) texts are safe but the performances dangerous. Why? What happens when people actually *use* language in situated action? What becomes of the formal structures and abstract patterns of discourse when they are put into play? Many Weyewa argue that while the official purpose of the ban is to prevent excessive ritual slaughter of cattle, it is the verbal and ritual *enactments* that bother officials the most; after all, Weyewa elders observe, the state-sponsored ceremonies are often equally 'wasteful' in financial terms. Moreover, the government leaders themselves continue to engage in costly displays of wealth, in the form of lavish house-building, birthday parties, marriage ceremonies, and the like. But since the officials perform these activities in the framework of legitimate religions such as Christianity or Islam, they do not challenge the authority of the government.

For Weyewa, authentic performances of the 'words of the ancestors' are the ultimate expression of an indigenous system of religious and social authority. Even by eastern Indonesian standards, where this phenomenon of 'speaking in pairs' entails far-reaching political, economic, and emotional commitments, Weyewa seem particularly obsessed with these words as the essential concern of their ritual activities. For them, complete saturation in the words of the ancestors is an important goal guiding the stages of a prolonged ritual process of atonement and exchange between the ancestors and their descendants, between wife-givers and wife-takers, and ultimately between life and death. When neglectful humans fail to heed the 'voice' of their forebears, misfortune strikes and the living descendants must initiate a cultural process of restoring the true 'voice' or 'word' of the ancestors. They re-engage this ancient discourse, not through trance or possession, but through a series of rites of divination, placation and fulfillment. While this process of contrition can become a "path to riches and renown,"[2] it is also one that exhibits a clear sociolinguistic trajectory. In Weyewa terms, this means moving from a squabbling debate to an utterly unified and monologic *performance* of the words of the ancestors. It is these final climactic speaking events that are now against the law.

Long ago, Weyewa say, the ancestors gave their living descendants their 'word, voice' (*li'i*). The lexeme *li'i* exhibits a tension between two related senses, one emphasizing prolonged moral obligation and the other focused on immediate performance. In the first sense, *li'i* refers to a message, a mandate, a promise, and a duty; it is a temporally structured network of (deferred) obligations. For example, a common way of describing a promise to exchange something in the future is *katukku li'i* 'to plant the word'—a reference to the customary act of erecting a pole to signify the declaration of a promise. More generally, *li'i inna, li'i ama* 'words of the Mother, words of the Father' refers to a set of (verbal) instructions that are handed down from generation to generation, and that descendants should fulfill. In its widest application, *li'i* refers to 'Weyewa tradition': all the customary, changeless, and ancient obligations and responsibilities that those words engender. In this sense, *li'i* is associated with a fixity which endures over time, as expressed in the couplet referring to traditional custom: 'stone that does not move, earth that does not change' (*watu nda ndikki, tana nda ngero*). *Li'i* also refers to the 'voice' as a feature of oral performance. This sense of 'voice' often assumes an audience and highlights aspects of delivery: it may be described with adjectives such as 'hoarse,' 'thin,' 'powerful,' 'broken,' 'flowing,' 'soft,' and 'deep.' In this sense, the 'voice' is individualizing and particularizing and reflects a distinct speaking personality. For instance, when a ritual spokesman presents his point of view in a ceremony, it is called 'to put forth the voice' (*tau-na li'i*). 'Voice' also encompasses features of performance organization, such as rhythm, melody, and harmony. The verses of a song, for instance, are called 'steps of the voice.' If ritual actors fail to coordinate their performances properly, in either rhythm or meaning, the offense is represented as a vocal problem: 'their voices were out of step'; or 'their voices were like untuned gongs.'

The dual senses of *li'i*—as promise and performance—fuse in the Weyewa style of dyadic 'ritual speech' (*panewe tenda*; see Fox, ed. 1988). The paired structure of the couplets is mirrored in a fundamental and productive aesthetic principle of Weyewa ritual ideology by which social arrangements, objects, and events of all kinds are symbolically represented as pairs (e.g., 'inside/outside,' 'mother/father,' 'left/right,' 'elder/younger,' 'trunk/tip') constituting a pervasive scheme of dual classification. When the 'word' is neglected and misfortune ensues, specialist performers of ritual speech recover it through a culturally recognized 'path' of atonement and feasting. They begin with divination, then re-state the neglected promises or 'words' in placation rites, and finally fulfill these promises in celebration and housebuilding feasts. As both the special medium for describing the *li'i marapu* 'words of the ancestors' and the vocal instantiation of it, ritual speech represents a "performative" evocation of what is held to be an enduring, ancestrally established order.

The privileged character of Weyewa ritual speech is not legitimized with reference to some unspoken, silent natural order. Weyewa do not view the performances of ceremonial 'words' as impoverished or (to borrow from Saussure [1959]) incomprehensible *signifiers* that refer ultimately to a prior, privileged natural order of *signifieds*. Ritual speech is not a noisy necessity of latter-day priests designed to obscure a more ancient but non-speaking ancestral order (compare Traube 1980:298; Traube 1986:16–19), but rather a way of achieving a kind of semiotic communion between the verbal acts of the ancient spiritual custodians of tradition and their living descendants.[3] Ritual events restore order in and through exchange between speaking parties, not by transcending the 'words' in favor of pre-verbal referents. In this sense, for Weyewa, if the 'word' is the "beginning," it is the "end" as well.

Among Weyewa, the concept of an ideal, traditional, harmonious ritual order of exchanges—the "flow of life" (Fox, ed. 1980) depends on a deal, a 'word,' negotiated verbally, usually between the living and the spirits of the dead as holders of tradition. It has remarkably little to do with a presumed "natural" order, be it a seasonal round or the human life cycle. Compared to other Sumbanese societies, Weyewa possess few calendrical rituals of any significance, such as the yearly *nyale* 'seaworm' festivals of horseback jousting performed by the coastal dwelling Kodi, Wanukakan, Laboyan, and Nggaura ethnolinguistic groups. Nor do they possess elaborate rituals of the life cycle: birth is a muted event, ritually speaking; puberty is virtually unmarked in either sex; even marriage and death rituals, while economically and ritually important, are not accompanied by the kind of extended, focused, and highly ritualized verbal display that one finds in rites of misfortune.

Where Weyewa ritual life finds its specific focus is not in the predictable changes of the annual cycle or the life cycle, but rather in the sudden changes brought on by calamity (*podda*). Their concerns with calamity and change are deeply interconnected: the preoccupation with misfortune is a way of talking about the transient, fleeting nature of valued cultural knowledge. Weyewa often interpret calamities as resulting from the individualistic pursuit of novelty and innovations rather than following the traditional and ancient teachings or words of the ancestors. I do not mean that all calamity represents a social change; events such as fires, floods, or sudden deaths do not necessarily result in deep transformations to the basic character of society. Nor are all social changes regarded as calamities by Weyewa: high-yield, pest-free varieties of rice and simple medical care, for example, have been available since the early 1980s and have met with widespread acceptance. But when calamities do occur, they are ritually interpreted as a result of someone's neglecting the word and breaking a promise. This happens because people forget, wander away, pursue individual interests, and fail to reproduce the word, thereby threatening conventional norms. It is only through the authentic performance of the 'words of the ancestors' that political, economic, and social order can be restored.

Analysis of Ritual Speech Performances as Entextualization

The Weyewa preoccupation with the fleeting and transient nature of the 'word' amounts to a concern over how to "fix" meaning, a process which Ricoeur has called "inscription" (Ricoeur 1976:26–29; Ricoeur 1981). By this he means something considerably more than the literary activity of writing with a pen, or the artistic one of etching into bark, steel, or stone; he means the whole process whereby the evanescent character of meaning is stabilized, established, and controlled. The result of this transformation from flowing talk to fixed text is something relatively detached, externalized and objectified, which can be appropriated, guarded, or exchanged.

The Weyewa ritual process of recovering and restoring the 'words of the ancestors' offers a particularly clear example in which to explore the process of extracting, objectifying, and incorporating words in its sociocultural context. As a way of calling attention to the relation between social practices and discourse structures, I refer to it as *entextualization*, by which I mean a process in which a speech event (or series of speech events) is marked by increasing thoroughness of poetic and rhetorical patterning and growing levels of (apparent) detachment from the immediate pragmatic context (cf. Bauman 1987b; Briggs 1988; Kuipers 1989).[4] The end result is a relatively coherent text conceived "inter-textually" as an authoritative version of one that existed before, or elsewhere. It is not regarded as merely a novel, spontaneous creation by an individual performer in the "here and now," even though in many ways it is. Drawing on a variety of rhetorical disclaimers, poetic allusions, and cohesive devices, such textualized performances deny their situated character.

This approach to the study of inscription departs in some important ways from that of those who study only written models of text production. Many of these writers dwell upon the psychological implications of the inscribed text, and on its role in the transformation of consciousness or a cultural *ethos* (see especially Ong 1984; see also Bell 1988; Harris 1984; McCanles 1982; Marvin 1984; Olson 1977; but see Becker 1979; Geertz 1983b:30–33). Several authors in the recent volume *Writing Culture*, for instance, emphasize the essential, disjunctive, and hegemonic role of writing in ethnographic "textualization," which they argue consists of a process of translating "experience into text" or "inscription" (Clifford 1986:115; Marcus 1986:184–185; Tyler 1986:127; Tyler 1987; see Clifford and Marcus, eds. 1986).

But as studies such as that of Scribner and Cole (1981) have warned us, writing (here used in the narrow sense of the term) does not necessarily transform consciousness, but must be analyzed in its cultural context of use (see also Heath 1983). This advice applies well to the study of "inscription" more generally. Indeed, efforts to entextualize meanings are themselves cultural performances, which as Bauman, Hymes, Sherzer, and others have shown, are best analyzed in terms of such ethnographic components as the setting, participants, act sequence, and the like (see Bauman 1986; Hymes 1974; Sherzer 1983).

If entextualization does not necessarily produce certain mental states, neither does it produce particular social ones. Thus, as Irvine has observed about Bloch's (1975) efforts to link formalized (and in these terms, "entexted") language in Malagasy with social control, rigidly structured verbal behaviors need not *in and of themselves* be linked with positional identities of social authority or a heightened situational focus (Irvine 1979). Highly structured formal language may indeed sometimes be a relatively marginal part of a larger main event, as in the case of background music performed in a crowded restaurant, where conversation and eating are the situational foci. Like formality in language, entextualization must not be reified as a "thing" with certain inherent properties or states, but treated as a useful analytical concept with which to make sense of ethnographic data.

In certain societies, where an encompassing and powerful religious ideology harks back to an earlier period of revelation and cultural grandeur, in which privileged spiritual knowledge was believed to have been communicated in special style of language, then the concept of entextualization is useful in characterizing the extraordinary convergence of textual structures and ideological authority (cf. Tambiah 1985). Examples are not hard to find. Within the *puru k'op* style of ritual speaking inherited from the sun deity of the Tzotzil-speaking Chamulas of highland Chiapas, for instance, relations among the generic varieties are ranked in terms of their relative 'heat' from the ancestral source, corresponding to a "continuum" of increasing stylistic patterning using couplets (Gossen 1984:46–48). Among the Seneca of upstate New York, there is a continuum of sacred authority in speaking styles that is similar, but which corresponds to increased intonational structuring and decreased use of evidentials and hedges (Chafe 1981; Chafe 1982). Charles Briggs describes a continuum of speaking styles among the Mexicanos of New Mexico, for whom the endpoint of formality are fixed texts of hymns, prayers, and rosaries believed to have been "handed down verbatim from the generations of *los viejitos de antes* [the elders of bygone days]" (1988:327).

As an example of entextualization in Indonesia, Weyewa rituals of atonement stand out as a case in which the ultimate model of an authoritative text is not a written document, or a dialogic narrative, but a performed monologue.[5] Like the more well-known traditions of verbal art in Java and Bali, Weyewa ritual speaking accomplishes its textual authority by drawing on the special words of certain spiritual privileged forebears, under whose auspices the spokesman claims to perform (cf. Becker 1979; Keeler 1986; Zurbuchen 1987). But unlike the *wayang* shadow puppet plays, Weyewa ritual speaking employs a rhetorical form that assimilates, encompasses and dominates other voices, obliterating dialogic contingencies and alternative points of view (Bakhtin 1981:342ff; Bakhtin 1986:163; Jakubinskij 1979).[6] In Java and Bali, comparably monologic discourse is preserved in written form.[7]

The Weyewa entextualization process culminates in a narrative form known as the 'path of the ancestors'—an authoritative style that exemplifies in a singular and consistent fashion the history of the 'word' of a powerful forebear. In these climactic performances, a man sings or chants in the center of the village, each verse punctuated by an antiphonal chorus. Speaking in the voice of the ancestors, the performer enacts a text that is held to be among the most 'sacred' (*erri*), closely guarded, and authentic in Weyewa culture. Many of the generic features of the Weyewa performances (called 'blessing songs' or 'chants') exhibit similarities to the (no longer performed) spatialized narratives preserved in the written Javanese poem *Negarakertagama* (Geertz 1983a:129ff; Pigeaud 1967–1970) or the inscribed Balinese dynastic genealogies (Worsley 1972). When government officials on Sumba explain why Weyewa traditions are an example of wasteful pagan irreligiosity, many mention their unwritten, oral character. Clearly something about the oral *performance* of these texts has a unique power and significance.

The Weyewa ritual process of objectifying, extracting, and manipulating the 'word' raises important questions about the relation of text, power, and performance.[8] If the *authority* of Weyewa ritual speech derives from the use of textual structures by which the performer creates the conviction he is not speaking on his own, but on behalf of some distant person or spirit with a legitimate claim on the audience, the *power* of such a text derives from the ability to transform events, relations, and objects. By talking about power in Weyewa ritual discourse, I am not referring to an object or thing some people wield, but to an analytical notion generally concerned with manipulation and control, which is present in various situations in different ways, and which constantly changes in dynamic response to the behavior of the audience and other extra-textual factors.

In most everyday speaking events, acts of interruption, command, sharp questioning, topic control, and silencing of others through ridicule constitute direct expressions of communicative control over others. In ritual events, however, such acts of naked power—directive practices in Fowler's terms (1985)—are themselves fixed, ritualized, and scripted, at least to a greater degree than in non-ritual events. Nonetheless, the ritual spokesman also exercises what might be called "constitutive" (or "definitional") power over the situation by appropriating for himself and his supporters the rights to speak on behalf of the ancestors, thereby denying access to others who might also wish to be in that position. Thus to paraphrase Bauman's definition of performance, the assumption of responsibility for a display of communicative competence to an audience becomes the *appropriation* of responsibility (Bauman 1984). By tightening social control over privileged meanings, the Weyewa ritualists are able to exploit a form of "symbolic capital" (Bourdieu 1977:171ff) with which they transform and define obligations, structure participation in rituals, channel exchanges of ideas, cloth, cattle and land, and legitimate hierarchical relations among actors and institutional arrangements. One of the most powerful aspects of this control is epistemological: the ability to define a totalized image of social "reality" in ritual contexts—'that which is true' (a hinna takka)—that outlives particular instances of its articulation, and which encompasses and subordinates other images.

This process of creating textual authority is rooted in a denial of the "contextualized" character of discourse. But what is context? Within linguistic anthropology, there has been a gradual shift away from a notion of context as a static independent variable surrounding language (as in "context-dependent"), or as generalized situation types (e.g., "instructional context," "regulative contexts," "imaginative contexts"; see Bernstein 1971). Instead, many scholars have been drawn to a dynamic, actor-oriented, interpretive notion of context as a "frame" (Goffman 1974; see also Bauman 1984; Briggs 1988; Frake 1977; Gumperz 1982; Ochs 1988). In this view, the context is "the difference that makes a difference" for the participants in the interactional process, a resource by which they make sense of the activity in which they are engaged.[9] Shifts in context are signaled by "keyings" or "cues" (Goffman 1974:40–82; Gumperz 1982:130–152).

These cues or keyings are resources not just for comprehension but for the construction of textual authority as well. In Weyewa, the more "indexical" the cue, the more localized, emphemeral, and limited the framed discourse is likely to be. On the other hand, the more "iconic" or "conventional" the verbal keying, the more the framed discourse is likely to be ritually authoritative, ancestral, and textualized. Thus when ritual speakers signal a new topic with keyings such as "well, now . . ." or "and then you said . . .", these are relatively indexical in the Peircean sense of a verbal sign that indicates its meaning by temporal and spatial contiguity with the immediate circumstances of utterance (e.g., the referents of "now" and "you" are only clear in their actual situation of occurrence). Such cues also suggest a relatively informal, dialogic, and almost conversational mode of presentation. In contrast, if a speaker signals a shift toward seriousness in the topic of discourse with a couplet such as "He arrives by the fire, he approaches the hearth" in which neither "he" nor "fire," nor "hearth" necessarily refers to an actual object in the event, the interpretation is based on relatively arbitrary conventions and rules. The heavy use of such cues signals, among other things, a higher degree of formality and textual authority. While all speech is in some sense "contextualized," I will speak of "contextualization" as the sociocultural patterns by which actors link discourse indexically to its immediate circumstances of utterance. "Entextualization," on the other hand, will refer to the ways by which the inter-textual, cohesive, and authoritative aspects of a performance are foregrounded (Briggs 1988; cf. Silverstein 1988).[10]

Plan of the Book

This book examines Weyewa entextualization practices ethnographically. The story begins in Chapter Two with an orientation to the history and structure of social authority in the Weyewa community viewed as a series of negotiations and exchanges between forces construed as "inside" and "outside." In Chapter Three I examine how calamity ensues when the exchange relations between humans and spiritual agents are disrupted due to the failure and neglect of the 'word.' In Chapter Four, the verbal resources for recovering this alienated 'word' are examined—discourse markers, parallelism, poetic formulae, and other devices. Through statistical comparisons of sample 100-word texts, I show that the "continuum of style" in the entextualization process is reflected in frequencies of couplets, personal pronouns, demonstrative pronouns, and locutives.

In Chapter Five, these resources are put in motion as the process of atonement begins. Transcriptions of ritual speech performances show that as a Weyewa diviner attempts to discover the broken 'word,' he employs a dialogic rhetorical strategy emphasizing segmentation, differentiation, and contrast by which he sorts out principal causes and narrows down the number of relevant 'voices' to arrive at a single 'path' that explains how the victims arrived at their present predicament. The all-night 'rites of placation' (*zaizo*) which follow the divination are analyzed in Chapter Six. In these a singer, accompanied by a drum and gong, engages in a ritual speech dialogue with orators about how to establish a coordinated musical performance that re-affirms commitment to fulfilling the 'word' of the ancestors. In discussing it, they accomplish it. Chapter Seven describes the procedures by which the promises are actually fulfilled, with elaborate feasting, complex exchanges, and narrative monologues describing and evoking the sacred charter: the 'words of the ancestors.' Chapter Eight concludes with a consideration of such notions as inscription and intertextuality as cultural performances. The Epilogue examines some recent transformations in Weyewa society, along with the attempts to break apart the connection of these performances with power and authority, and to cordon off these performance genres into the realm of "art" or "folklore." I examine the generic features of some recent Indonesian language legal documents that have increasingly come to occupy a position of discursive authority.

Much of Weyewa ceremonial life has been devoted to a systematic and ritualized remembering of the 'words' of the ancestors. And herein lies much of the tale of this book. Between the 'word' of promise and its fulfillment, the gift and its countergift, the trunk and its tip, awaits a story of practical, sometimes cunning, manipulation of linguistic and symbolic structures. While the interval leaves room for strategy, status seeking, and glory, it also can result in forgetting, carelessness, and neglect of one's responsibilities. Such human creativity and weakness can be linked to the tendency to follow individual desires, blaze new trails, wander off from an original source, and create independent obligations (i.e., speak new 'words'). These proclivities carry the risk of ignoring the importance of returning to original sources and renewing one's word of honor and collective unity. Calamity results when descendants thus 'forget' to fulfill their promises, or those of their forebears.

By placing speaking at the center of the study, this book draws on a developing genre of anthropological writing known as the "ethnography of speaking" (Hymes 1974; Sherzer 1983), particularly in its ambition to enter the world of the Weyewa through their speech. I do not, however, attempt here a complete description of all Weyewa speech resources, linguistic structures, or institutional structures of authority. Readers looking for a comprehensive description of Weyewa kinship and social structure will be disappointed. In this study I focus on a particular style of speaking, and indeed, a subset within that style: the genres of ritual speech used in the context of ceremonies of misfortune. But since misfortune, as the bearer of novelty and change, is the enemy of tradition and stability, the process of restoring the ancestral 'word' as an authoritative "text" over the course of these rituals is not just a matter of linguistic or poetic significance: the verbal process is itself an ideological trope standing for the renewal of their traditional identity and a profound sense of what it means to be Weyewa.

Notes

1. Drs. Umbu Djima, "Keputusan: Musyawarah Adat Terbatas Pertama, Kabupaten Daerah Tingkat II, Sumba Barat, 17 Desember 1987" [Resolution of the First Meeting on Customary Law in the Regency of West Sumba, December 17, 1987], p. 1: "All forms of traditional ceremonies that are intentional and uproarious (*hura-hura*) including *woleka* [rites of fulfillment], feasting, slaughtering [are prohibited for five years pending review]." This decision is "based on the fact that the people of West Sumba, as they step forward in progress, find psychological obstacles that hold them back, including ceremonies that are excessive and uneconomical, and that usually damage the environment." In Keputusan No. 245, 1987, Dec. 31, 1987, by the Regent Umbu Djima, all civil employees and apparatuses of the government on the local level are expressly "forbidden" (*dilarang*) from participation in the above mentioned ritual events.

2. This phrase comes from the title of Janet Hoskins's Ph.D. dissertation (1983) on the neighboring Kodi people of West Sumba.

3. By "semiotic communion" here I do not mean that Weyewa believe ritual speech performances to be exact copies of the 'words of the ancestors.' To make such a claim for one's speech would be an arrogant usurpation of ancestral authority. I discuss this matter in somewhat greater detail in Chapter Seven on Rites of Fulfillment.

4. This phrase is borrowed from Bauman (1987b). I am indebted to Judith Irvine for many insightful comments on this section.

5. The *wayang* shadow puppet performances of Java and Bali strive for authority by "speaking the past," as Becker puts it, but remain playfully dialogic. Likewise, while the *sijobang* sung narrative performances of West Sumatra claim to represent exploits of Nan Tungga Magek Jabang and other characters that "really happened," these adventures are rendered in dialogic form (Phillips 1981).

6. By *monologue*, I am referring primarily to the *ideational* not the *participatory* structure of discourse, although these two concepts are interrelated. Thus while Weyewa divination is a monologic in participatory structure (there is only one speaking participant) it is ideationally dialogic, in that it involves the construction of a lively conversation

between distinct speaking personalities. Urban (1986) makes a comparable distinction between "semantic dialogues" and "pragmatic dialogues."

7. Pigeaud speculates that the famous Javanese political poem, *Negarakertagama* (1976–1970:IV:552) was performed orally at times of political succession.

8. This approach to verbal performance as a process of *entextualization* is part of a growing movement within linguistic anthropology concerned with examining the particulars of situated linguistic interaction in a way that engages larger issues in sociocultural theories of power and practice. Critics of conversation analysis and ethnography of speaking have complained, respectively, that it is trivial (Coser 1975), or "rather specialized" (Levinson 1983:279, 375) in its concern with self-contained performances and exotic styles of speech. Hymes (1974:65) has called for "a kind of explanation that will speaking with human history and praxis. To do this is not only to see languages as part of systems of speaking but also to see systems of speaking from the standpoint of of the central question of the nature of the sociocultural order." For some recent attempts to bridge the gap between linguistic analysis and political economy see Bauman (1987), Bowen (1989), Briggs (1988), Friedrich (1989), Gumperz (1982), Halliday (1978), Hill (1985), Irvine (1989), Ochs (1988), Urban (1986).

9. By "difference that makes a difference" I am extending some of the ideas of Silverstein (1976) and Mertz (1985), who view "context" as the motivation for differentiating kinds of signs and aspects of signs.

10. Thus where Gumperz (1982) speaks of "contextualization cues," I would distinguish between "contextualization cues" and "textualization cues."

2

The History of Land, Power, and Authority in the Weyewa Highlands

When the state recently intervened to control ritual speaking events, many We-yewa leaders expressed dismay. They were not, however, shocked or taken by surprise by the very idea. Ritual and verbal practices for Weyewa do not exist in a walled-off, specialized arena of activity separate and distinct from the "real" processes of power and authority. Indeed, pre-Indonesian structures of institu-tional authority in the Weyewa highlands have a long and complex history of articulation with verbal practices, a history which unfolds through a pattern marked by confrontations, negotiations and exchanges between categories of so-cial and religious life represented as "inside" and "outside."

The Land of the Weyewa

Among Weyewa, an important source of authority is a special relationship to certain founding acts, many of which pertain to the occupation and utilization of the land (cf. Lukes 1979:642).[1] The narratives of these foundational events have figured as rhetorical and political resources in the organization of relations with the indigenous inhabitants, the Dutch, the Japanese, and now with the Indonesians.

As the setting and referent for many of these founding acts, the Sumbanese landscape presents a remarkably stark and even harsh appearance. Like other islands in the hot and dry "outer arc" of the Indonesian archipelago extending eastward from Java (Figure 1), Sumba is affected climatically by its proximity to the continent of Australia; it characteristically experiences dramatic oscillations between long dry seasons from March to October and brief but intense monsoon rains during the months from November to February. Although it is a relatively large (11,000 km²) member of a little crescent of islands known as the Lesser Sundas (now called Nusa Tenggara) the overall population density on its savan-nah-like landscape is among the lowest in the region (approximately 37/km²). On Sumba the effects of this seasonal round are strikingly evident in the badly eroded lime and chalk soils and parched savannah grasslands of the northern and eastern coasts that greet visitors to the ports of Waingapu and Waikalowo (Wit-kamp 1912:744).[2] As one moves inland and upland on the island itself (Figure 2) from the harsh northern coast, where the only harbors are located, to the grassy hills and

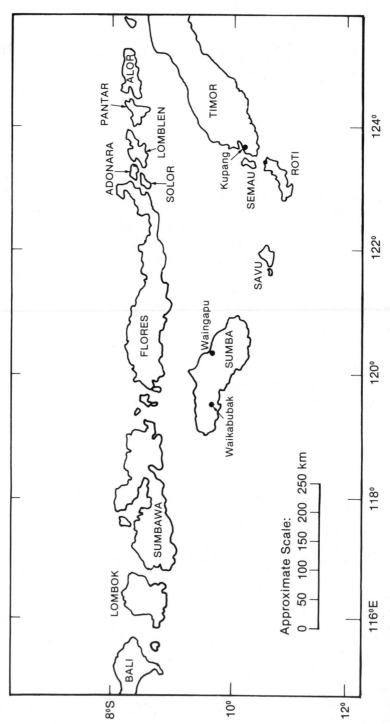

Figure 1: Map of Eastern Indonesia.

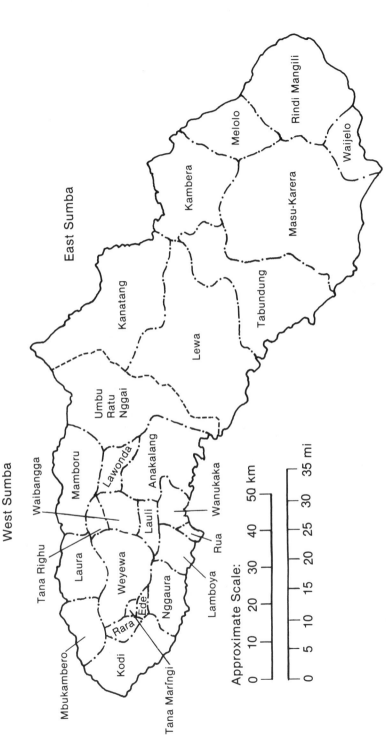

Figure 2: Ethnolinguistic map of Sumba. The lines indicating divisions between groups are approximate.

forests in the southern interior, the geology and ecology of Sumba gradually supports higher and higher densities of plants, animals, and people. The climate becomes more humid, rainfall heavier, the soil deeper, less porous, and richer in clay and basalt deposits (Metzner 1977:5,10; Pfeiffer and Meiser 1968:890). Subsistence cultivation of corn, rice, and root crops is no longer restricted to river valleys for irrigation, and rainfed garden plots here and there are terraced into the hillsides. Nonetheless, rainfall is highly unpredictable, wells are few and far between, and most, though not all, of the rivers are underground and inaccessible as irrigation sources.[3]

On the fertile and gently sloping northern face of the Yawila volcano—the highest point in the West Sumba regency (Laufer and Kraëff 1957:16)—live the Weyewa, an ethnic and linguistic group numbering some 85,000.[4] While there are several accounts circulating about how Weyewa came to inhabit this territory, most versions mention a journey originating in islands to the west of Sumba, a crossing over a 'stone bridge' (*lende watu*) from *ndima* (= Bima), and then an arrival into an interior domain. The point of embarkation varies depending on the version: some say it all began at a village called Tanggeba in central Weyewa, others say it happened on the Yawila mountain, and yet others claim this status for the great sacred gushing spring now known as *lele wulla, mata rawu* (cf. also Kapita 1976b:320ff.; Kruyt 1922:471;[5] Wielenga 1912:329). All accounts mention a hostile encounter upon arrival, followed by bargaining and exchange with either autochthonous spirits of the earth (*mori tana* 'lords of the earth'), or aboriginal inhabitants, usually labeled Lombo (see Ono 1976), or both.

According to one such tale,

> There was an ancestral figure named Yanda Mette. He went out hunting wild boars one day. As soon as he made a kill, he began roasting it. Then he noticed an earth spirit [*mori tana*]. Yanda Mette gave him some meat. After the spirit tried the meat, and found it tasty, he asked, "How did you make it so delicious?" he asked. "I roasted it with fire," Yanda Mette replied.
>
> So Yanda Mette showed him how to make a fire with a fire drill. The earth spirit asked, "Can I take the drill home?" "But then I'll never get it back!" cried Yanda Mette. "No," said the earth spirit, "I promise I'll give it back." "All right, then, make a space for me on this land, and I'll give you the drill." "All right, then" said the earth spirit, who got up to leave. And Yanda Mette called after him, "You must remember to extinguish the fire from the baseboard before you store the drill for the night."
>
> So the earth spirit used the drill, but forgot to extinguish the fire from the baseboard of the drill, and when he stowed it in the eaves of his house for the night, his roof caught fire and his house burned down. And he was very angry. When he saw Yanda Mette the next day, he said, "My house burned down because of your fire drill." "Did you remember to extinguish

the fire from the baseboard of the drill?" "No, I did not. But from now on, I will make a tax on the land, a tax on the rivers. When you cultivate plants, you must pay me first. When someone falls from a tree and dies, you must retrieve the soul from me. When someone is bitten by a wild boar, you must retrieve the soul from me. Each time you must provide me with an offering [*marata*]."

The text illustrates a tendency in Weyewa discourse about the past to express the founding acts of their history as a 'path' or 'journey' (in this case, a hunting expedition) across their landscape, marked by confrontations, negotiation, and exchange between forces of the inside and outside, or in some situations, 'trunk' and 'tip.' Various moments in their history, such as the settlement of their territory, warfare, and the slave trade are assimilated to the oppositional structure of this model. So too are key features of their social structure—fortified villages, the "raja" system of leadership, agricultural practices, and land pressure. As Weyewa ceremonial spokesmen struggle—in their rites of misfortune—to recover and re-inscribe the 'path' or history of obligations to the ancestors, they draw on these images of history and social structure as resources in building authoritative texts.

Path of the Lineage (Kabizu)

The theme of powerful "outsiders" who confront, negotiate, and exchange with the "insiders" is one that is reproduced in the narratives of lineage history as well.[6] In several of these, the ancestors of the lineage Mángutana (lit. 'Owns the Land') are said to be surprised by a figure named Yonggara Dendara. After some trickery, Yonggara Dendara provides the Mángutana folk with meat in exchange for rice seed and fertile land in irrigated fields. Yonggara Dendara's offspring separate into two groups when a younger brother (Patti Ki'i) engages in a feasting competition with his older brother (Patti Matto) and the latter commits a moral outrage, losing the battle. The elder brother moves away, thereby permitting the younger (= newcomer, outsider) to live on the ancestral land and become its new inhabitant.

The expelled elder brother founds a 'house' (*umma*) that becomes the basis for the agnatic 'lineage' (*kabizu*) known as Baliloko 'across the river,' while the younger brother (originally an outsider) founds a house that becomes the source of the raja's lineage called Lewata. These three agnatic lineages, Lewata, Baliloko, and Mángutana, are sometimes referred to collectively as 'the three cooking stones that holds up a [single] black pot' (*tullura katouda, wirro mbolo mette*). While in the past, Weyewa say, these major lineages were exogamous and possessed their own land, cattle, heirlooms, and *erri* 'sacred prohibitions' (e.g, dietary and ritual restrictions), each has become so large, dispersed, and internally differentiated that restrictions on marriage and corporate ownership apply only to co-descendants of lineage 'great houses' (*umma kalada*) in one of more than a dozen subsequently founded 'ancestral villages' (*wanno kalada*) in the eastern Weyewa region.

It is as members of such houses that Weyewa inherit the *li'i* 'words' and obligations of their ancestors. Ancestors are the prototypical insiders, represented in botanical terms as the ancient, immoveable 'trunk' (*pu'u*) of such discourse. The descendants who inherit the house are associated with latter-day, dispersed 'tips' (*lawi*). Most Weyewa do not actually inhabit such ancient dwellings (even if the structure is still standing). However, if they claim descent from its founder, they are responsible for the maintenance of the building and for the identification and fulfillment of the founder's 'words' of obligation, as well as for any debts, rights, and duties that go along with them. The acceptance of such custodial responsibilities is not a matter of inheriting a formal, named office; rather it typically involves a self-selected, ambitious individual whose wealth and oratorical abilities permit him to speak on behalf of others in the descent group. This person invariably describes these speech events as humble acts of contrition designed to forestall ancestral wrath and misfortune, but the others who allow and even facilitate these events tend to regard them as prestige-seeking self-glorification through feasting.

When the ancestral figure Patti Matto moved across the river and established his own 'house,' his male offspring began to take wives from the offspring of Patti Ki'i and vice versa. From the perspective of the lineage as 'trunk' or 'source' of authority, marriage is a means of fulfilling promises to the ancestors to produce new members to carry on the 'word.' Among Weyewa, a boy and his family acquire or 'take a wife' (*dekke minne*) for him by traveling to the residence of the girl. In order to obtain this precious, life-giving 'rice seed' (*winni pare*, i.e., someone who will yield fruit for the ancestors), they carry out an elaborate and prolonged three-stage series of ritualized encounters, negotiations, and ceremonial exchanges before bringing her home. A bride is initially an outsider. Once her brideprice of cattle, jewelry, and weaponry is fully paid, she is gradually incorporated into her adoptive lineage as she gets older and produces children. When she dies, she and her husband are addressed in the same breath as an ancestral spirit pair. Unlike young girls who 'move away' (*ndikki*) when they marry, young boys are like tips (*lawi*) or tendrils (*lolo*) attached to a stable, central 'trunk' (*pu'u*).

The Slave Trade and Internal Warfare

Beginning in the nineteenth century, much of the historical reporting by both Dutch writers and the Sumbanese themselves was concerned with the slave trade, when powerful outsiders began to penetrate the interior of the island in search of booty. An important consequence of this confrontation and exchange was the reinforcement of the "inside" in physical, symbolic, and political terms.

For safety, Weyewa lived in large fortified villages, protected against outsiders with cacti and stone walls. In political terms, the ultimate "insiders" of these villages were powerful "rajas," whose authority derived less from their subjects' acceptance of certain beliefs than from coercive imposition of will.[7] Poorer, weaker Weyewa, concerned to maintain their own physical safety as well as their ritual duties to the 'word' of their ancestral spirits, were forced into exchanges with more powerful, wealthy men who were capable of protecting them and their families against outsider slave raiders as well as from harmful spirits.

Rodney Needham (1983), in a survey of Dutch historical writings on the slave trade, reviews evidence indicating that for most of the eighteenth and nineteenth centuries and part of the early twentieth century, all of West Sumba was terrorized by roving bands of Endenese slave traders from the neighboring island of Flores. They frequently raided the interior of the island, plundering, burning down villages, and capturing people, selling their captives to rajas in the coastal areas of Sumba. Needham cites a report from this period that "everywhere on Sumba one finds the remains of settlements that have been laid waste and the inhabitants of which have been murdered or taken away as slaves" (Hangelbrock 1910:30, cited in Needham 1983:39).

From oral accounts I have collected, it also appears that headhunting, sometimes portrayed as an indigenous ceremony with deep structural connections to ritual, belief, and myth (Downs 1955; Kruyt 1922; VanWouden 1968), was intimately related to the historical practice of slave trading (see also Hoskins 1989). Raids were conducted on other villages either in retaliation or for the purpose of obtaining women and young children to sell to Arab and Florinese traders. Being less valuable as slaves, men were often killed in battle and their heads displayed as trophies in the village center (Kuipers 1982; Wijngaarden 1893). This symbolism of headhunting, maintained in some Weyewa villages to this day, powerfully evokes images of the sanctity of the ancestral village center in relation to a dangerous and threatening outside world.

In 1855, the Dutchman D. J. van den Dungen Gronovius provided a chilling survey of the state to which Sumba had been reduced (Needham 1983:26). The northwest coast of Sumba had been effectively de-populated by slave raids; "the scarcity of the population of Sumba on the north coast is caused by nothing other than the repeated and incessant trading in slaves, which has lasted for years and up until the present day has not come to an end" (Gronovius 1855:297–298, cited in Needham 1983:26; but see Needham 1987:38)[8]. One writer cited by Needham described the abandoned villages of Sumba as a "melancholy scene of neglected gravestones, fruit trees in the midst of wild grassland, abandoned ricefields, and charred houseposts" (1983:40).

When the Dutch officially abolished slavery in the Dutch East Indies in 1860, things only got worse for people in the interior of Sumba such as the Weyewa. While the Dutch were strong at sea, where they shelled and sank a fleet of Endenese slave vessels, they were weak on land. Circumventing the government's armed naval patrols, the Endenese traders set up headquarters in western Sumba, where they "turned to regular incursions into the interior; they sold the slaves they had captured there overland to central and eastern Sumba" (Needham 1983:32–33). On into the twentieth century, conditions on Sumba were described as "wild and disorderly," with "continual wars, small and great, between the tribes" (Wielenga in Meijering et al. 1927:24).

Despite (and perhaps because of) this insecurity, Weyewa during this period were depicted as a "notorious" people who fiercely protected their autonomy. D. K. Wielenga described how "even the Endenese, who are not easily frightened, do not like to risk their lives in this inland area. Once with the help of forty armed Endenese, the folk of Laora staged an invasion [of Weyewa], and had to return ignominiously without any booty" (1912:328; see also Couvreur 1917:214).[9] He remarked that Weyewa was the only place in Sumba where women also got involved in conflict; in one confrontation, women threw water laced with hot peppers on their adversaries (Wielenga 1912:328).

The Fortified Village

According to various oral and written accounts, it appears that, at least partly in response to such external threats, most Weyewa during this period preferred to conduct their negotiations with outsiders from the vantage point of large, fortified hilltop villages organized around megalithic ancestral sarcophagi, under the protection of powerful "rajas." According to Kapita,

> During this period, all of Sumba was unsafe; villages that were formerly dispersed had to be brought together into a "*paraingu*" located on top of a hill, fortified by stones and sharp and thick [cactus] thorns. If a person went out of the village, he had to go with a group equipped with weapons, to the point that even to go and fetch water one had to be accompanied by an armed group. (1976a:28)

Such descriptions, as well as similar accounts by the Dutch missionary Wielenga (1911–1912; 1916–1918), vividly highlight the emotional and symbolic significance of external threats for the organization of the village. For most Sumbanese, villages were not just places to live; they were sources of religious, physical, emotional, and political security.

Part of the status of any village as a refuge comes from its position in relation to other villages. There were (and are now) three main ranks of Weyewa 'villages' (*wanno*), in descending order of status and genealogical proximity to the origin village: 'ancestral villages' (*wanno kalada*), 'corral villages' (*wanno nggollu*), and 'garden villages' (*wanno oma dana*). When asked to name his or her village, a Weyewa might reply with any one of these three, depending on the context. Ancestral villages (Plate 1) represent the apical nodes in a kin-based and, deriva-

Plate 1: An ancestral village. Ancestral villages typically consist of high peaked thatch roofed houses organized around megalithic ancestral sarcophagi.

tively, botanical discourse about the classification of collective life. They are spoken of as the 'source' and 'trunk.' They generally consist of a cluster of between five and twenty 'ancestral houses' (*umma kalada*) representing the headquarters of various exogamous lineage and sub-lineage segments, which together make up a single agnatic lineage. At present, there are several Weyewa ancestral villages that have fallen into disuse and have no houses at all, only the rock fences and *welli umma* 'house foundations.' As the location for maintaining ancestral relics, sacred narratives, and the favor of ancient ancestors, they are usually located on the top of a hill, hidden by trees, and fortified by now-deteriorating walls of limestone and sparse hedges of cacti.

Within a given fortified ancestral village, specialized ritual roles are attached to particular lineage houses.[10] Each is characterized by the symbolism of interiority or marginality. An example from a formerly fortified village illustrates this internal division of labor. In Beindello, there are the following named houses:

umma tillu	'center house'
umma mandeta	'tall house'
umma nggau mata	'grey eyes house'
umma kere tana	'rear house'

umma Umbu Ndendo   'Umbu Ndendo's house'
umma watara   'corn house'
umma puttika   'chisel house'
umma Pirra Dawa   'Pirra Dawa's house'

Of these houses, the first five are umma rato 'priestly houses,' distinguished by carved house poles, decorated pole disks, and elaborate carving on the box over-hanging the hearth, and by the wealth of the owner. Most of the names have a story behind them, explaining the significance of the house's location and pe-culiarities of their history. But when I inquired as to how these houses were related to one another, the discussion often turned to what role each played in ritual events. Umma tillu 'center house,' I was told, is the inna ama 'mother-father' and source of the 'voice,' which implies a position of authority. No major ritual may begin without members of this house being present. Umma mandeta is the 'child of speech, child of talk' (ana panewe ana kandauke) whose respon-sibility it is to relay information and act as spokesman by extending formal invi-tations to the other houses. Umma watara 'corn house' is the place where corn and rice harvests designated for woleka celebrations are kept. Umma puttika 'chisel house' is the one responsible for ritual protocol at village-wide feasts and celebrations, ensuring that proper ritual procedure is observed. A number of other houses have even more specialized roles. For example, in rituals to which members of other clans are invited, umma nggau mata 'grey eyes house' is re-sponsible for conveying word to them. This house also is the only one qualified to act as protocol officer when umma tillu stages a large ritual event. Umma kere tana 'rear house' is responsible for sacrificing to the village altar on behalf of umma tillu. Umma Pirra Dawa 'Pirra Dawa's house' takes care of ancestral relics jointly owned by the village.

While there is general agreement among Weyewa that there are important differences in status among these houses, precisely who possesses the highest in any given context is often a matter of debate. In general, houses situated on the highest land and near to the center of the village are likely to be the most pres-tigious, but neglect of the house and poverty of the descendants of that house may cause some ambiguity. There is less dispute, however, about who is low status. Most people I spoke with in the villages of Lewata, Beindello, and Bon-dokandelu could point to the remains of specialized temple houses called ru-mata. These houses, I was told, were the corporate property of, and maintained by, the entire village. Agriculturally inactive hereditary slave 'priests'—addressed as rato—with their families formerly resided in these dangerously holy houses. For seven years, these inhabitants (usually war captives and their descendants) were "fattened." If they ever needed food or other provisions, they needed merely to beat a gong or build a large fire and nearby clan members would come to their aid. After this period, the temple had to be re-built and one of the slaves sacri-ficed for the occasion. I was also told that these temple-building ceremonies were the occasion of a release of sexual prohibitions, and for one night, men and women slept with whomever they chose. After the entry of the Dutch in the early 1900s, this practice was supposed to have been discontinued, although one old man told me he witnessed the last human sacrifice in 1930.

The secondary and tertiary villages,—the derivative 'corral villages' and 'garden villages'—were generally more exposed and vulnerable to attack. Defined by relations of marriage and descent to the 'source' village, the most temporary and vulnerable hamlets are 'garden villages' (*wanno oma dana*), which are distinguished as settlements having a small garden altar (*kambo*). These altars represent spirits brought down from the ancestral village. Hamlets of this kind generally consist of one or more affinally related households that left a 'corral village' to start a new village, but that have not yet performed the lengthy ritual procedures needed to make it a 'corral village' in its own right.

The symbolism of such ceremonies clearly define the village as a space marked off from potentially harmful external forces. To do this, the local autochthonous spirits (*wandi tana*) must be moved from the land on which the village rests through a process of exchange. This is carried out in a ceremony called *kamboka wanno* 'to pop the village' in which a pile of green bamboo is burned until its internodes explode with loud pops. The stated purpose of creating this noise is to drive dangerous spirits to the edge of the settlement, where they will be provided with an altar and receive offerings of 'hot' and 'cold' food and 'payments' (*marata*). Establishment of village space also requires building a stone plaza (*kambatu*) and wall (*kangali*) against outside intruders. Finally, in order for it to qualify truly as a 'corral village,' one of the inhabitants of the village must be buried in a tombstone there, and a 'celebration feast' (*woleka*) must be held.

The symbolic and ritual organization of the villages reflects this concern with security in the maintenance of a complex and overlapping set of relations between inside and outside, cool and hot, safe and dangerous, controlled and uncontrolled. In most Weyewa ancestral villages (Figure 3), the houses are arranged in a circle or oval pattern facing the stone plaza in the center of which is sunk an earthen 'courtyard' (*natara*). This courtyard itself is a kind of controlled, superior spiritual space (cf. Forth 1981:50). It is kept clean of debris and vegetation, and 'cool' (*maríngi*) through periodic sacrifices. Next to it are the 'village altar' (*marapu wanno*) and the 'skull tree' (*katoda*), which are sacred objects associated with the holiest spirits of the village. In many villages, encircling this courtyard one finds a ring of stone ancestral sarcophagi, which are in turn ringed by the houses. The houses of high status lineage segments are located closer to the *natara*, while lower status lineage houses are located closer to the outer stone wall, *kangali*, that encircles the village. The gates in this wall are the sites for ritual greetings of guests and outsiders, and are the location for altars devoted to protector spirits, whose task is to 'guard the gates at night, to watch the doors in the day.'

THE VILLAGE OF BEINDELLO

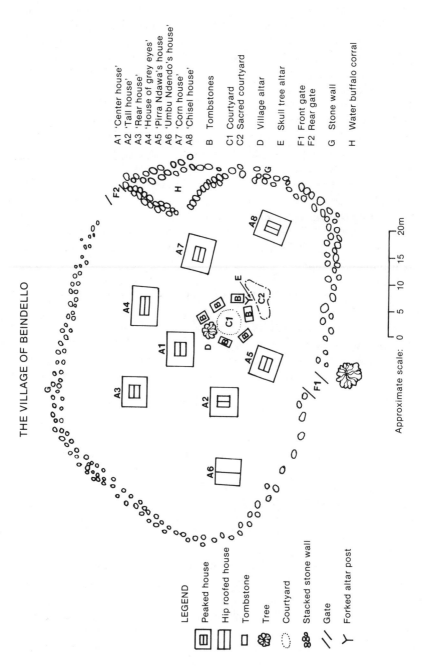

LEGEND

▣	Peaked house
▥	Hip roofed house
▢	Tombstone
❀	Tree
⬭	Courtyard
∞	Stacked stone wall
//	Gate
Y	Forked altar post

A1 'Center house'
A2 'Tall house'
A3 'Rear house'
A4 'House of grey eyes'
A5 'Pirra Ndawa's house
A6 'Umbu Ndendo's house'
A7 'Corn house'
A8 'Chisel house'

B Tombstones

C1 Courtyard
C2 Sacred courtyard

D Village altar

E Skull tree altar

F1 Front gate
F2 Rear gate

G Stone wall

H Water buffalo corral

Approximate scale: 0   5   10   15   20m

Figure 3: Plan of a Weyewa 'ancestral village.' (*wanno kalada*).

During the eighteenth and nineteenth centuries, according to Umbu Hina Kapita (1976a:28), all over Sumba people of few means or low birth were particularly vulnerable outside the village:

> Low status people [*orang kecil*] had to seek protection from powerful nobles [*marómba*], and even though they were under the protection of a *marómba*, they still [wished to] keep their own clan identity. If they did not [seek protection], they would be easily captured and sold to another place, and become a slave, and thus lose their clan name. (Kapita 1976a:28)

For Weyewa, to lose one's clan name is to lose one's identity as a person in several key respects. One's name, one's personal spirits, soul, personality, peer group, to say nothing of one's means of livelihood, come from affiliation with an agnatic lineage. Even today, descendants of people who were bought or captured and brought away from their ancestral homeland, and who thus can not demonstrate their proximity to the ancestral 'source' through material resources or kin or marriage connections, are known as either 'slaves' (*ata paangu*) or 'witches' (*ata ndaina*). As recent or marginal additions to the clan, they are seen as being far from the ancestral 'source.' Unable to intermarry with persons of noble or ordinary birth, many of them have formed their own, derivative lineages.

Weyewa "Rajas"

In many ways, the 'rajas' (*tokko*) of Weyewa in the nineteenth and early twentieth centuries were symbols of the village and lineage. Spoken of as the 'leafy white banyan tree, the shady yellow banyan' that protects the village, these men used personal charisma, coercion, and family connections to gain control over the symbols of clan identity as well: gongs, cloth, and temple headquarters, even cattle and rice fields. The familiar botanical symbolism of "trunk and tip" as an expression of hierarchy fit these men well; they were often referred to by themselves and others as 'the trunk of the tree, the source of the water.' Ritually and politically, they were associated with the inside, the source and the center of Weyewa social life.

Their central authority was legitimated partly by a charismatic personal style of fierceness and competitiveness used as a means to attract cattle, pigs and other goods for large scale feasting and displays of wealth. For Weyewa, high status is not solely determined by hereditary factors as it is in Eastern Sumba (Forth 1981:221–227). Indeed, the phrase *pa-tadi-na teba* 'competitive slaughter,' used by Louis Onvlee to describe the practice of establishing one's status through potlatch-like feasts, is a Weyewa expression (Onvlee 1980:203). Another characteristic of these rajas was their oratorical ability. Verbal fluency was essential to creating an impression of competence, ferocity, and ability to protect, if not from slave raiders, then from malign spirits. Wielenga described his encounter with Oemboe Pati, the Weyewa raja in 1909:

> Then Oemboe Pati stood up and laid open the floodgates of his eloquence. He has no equal in all of Sumba. With unbelievable speed his words came out of his mouth, tumbling and splashing, one following the sound of the other. His countenance was taut and his carriage erect. Now and then making a single broad gesture with his right hand, he stood there talking, getting all excited, so that one thinks: with lashing words he flogs his enemies. In fact, it was a "word of welcome." To the ear of the uncomprehending, he spoke friendly words like a rabble-rousing braggart. Oemboe Pati cultivates his renown and makes an impression on the "easterner" as one who is "powerful" [geweldigen]. (Wielenga 1912:330)

In return for the protection of these powerful and rich men, poor people had to pledge their labor, their military support, and even their offspring. In the past, and to a certain degree even today, people without land, cattle, or kin for protection and support were dependent on powerful men for food, wives, and shelter. For these services, the "rajas" exacted a heavy price. Samuel Roos, an early observer of life on the eastern part of the island, vividly describes this oppression: "The greediness of the Radjas and their habit of constantly demanding is actually the Soembanese' greatest burden; for it makes him never certain of his belongings" (Roos 1872:87). The raja even claimed the right to appropriate one's kin: "If the Radja demands someone's daughter as an attendant (which is not much different from a slave) for one of his princesses, then the father gives her; if he refuses, then he has insulted the prince, and his life and everything in his house is no longer secure" (Roos 1872:87).

It would be wrong to portray the authority of these men as based entirely on imposition and coercion. There was a kind of quid pro quo, a reciprocity between the leaders and their subjects. For instance, these powerful men were responsible for the proper performance of ritual duties for the whole village. When a 'word' of obligation to the ancestors was left unfulfilled, it was the responsibility of the raja to carry out the appropriate ceremonies. Poorer people, even today, view their contributions to the house-building, stone-dragging, and feasting projects of powerful spokesmen and charismatic ritualists as a kind of investment against future calamity. If one is owed a favor by a rich, powerful and competent person, as one man put it, "it is like insurance against hard times"—since one can eventually draw on these men as supporters in times of trouble.

The Dutch Intervention

When troops of the Netherlands East Indies 'mounted' Sumba (na penne dawa) in force in 1906 with forty "native" soldiers and two Dutch officers, confrontations were marked by relatively little negotiation and mostly one-sided exchange. The Dutch demanded tribute, labor, and respect for their laws and their authority. Aside from a few notable exceptions, they got what they wanted (but see Hoskins 1987). An important result of this encounter, however, was that it caused Weyewa to begin a major re-negotiation of their relationships to the symbols of the inside—rajas and fortified villages.

When Van Heutz became governor general in Batavia (now Jakarta), the Dutch launched a campaign against what they saw as the unchecked tyranny of the rajas in order to bring *pax Neerlandica* to the "tormented" island and an end to the internal slave trade (Wielenga 1911:7). The going was not easy, for this six-year-long "pacification" campaign encountered some significant setbacks as two Dutch lieutenants with forty East Indies soldiers scoured the island for the last vestiges of opposition. The Dutch force was tested by the "notorious" Weyewa in 1906, when one Dutch lieutenant was severely wounded in Wai Dindi (Wielenga 1911:328). They were tested again in 1912, when they recruited local assistance in building a road across the length of the island, and a Lieutenant Berendsen was nearly slain and his entire troop of native soldiers were killed during a nighttime raid on their barracks (Kapita 1976b:49).

One after another, the powerful, defiant rajas were tracked down, captured, and sent off to exile. New rajas, more sympathetic to the Dutch, were appointed. They were given scepters and powers of tax collection and arbitration. But this does not mean that all sources of tension had been resolved. Far from it. Although the interisland and internal slave trades were drastically curtailed, it was not until 1933 that the military detachment on Sumba was replaced by civil police.

While Dutch intervention was effective at undermining the authority of the old rajas, the Dutch were less successful at implementing a replacement plan of "self governance." When the assistant Resident A. J. L. Couvreur arrived on Sumba from Kupang shortly after 1912, he sought to justify his choices of rajas in Sumba using a model of secular-power-as-nobility ('tip') / sacred-authority-as-priest ('trunk') scheme (Couvreur 1917). Weyewa social structure, however, with its complex and shifting tri- and quadri-partite schemes of clan division and continual jockeying for control among widely distributed factions, never conformed neatly to this dualistic model. There was then, and is today, little consensus as to the meaning of the terms that Couvreur glossed as 'noble' and 'priest' (see Kapita 1976b; Waitz 1933).

According to a number of colonial and oral sources, the clan Mángutana 'possesses the land' was seen by early Dutch administrators as a kind of ritual office, and the story of the Lewata/Baliloko conflict was used to justify placing a descendant from that former clan in a position of jural authority. According to Couvreur (1917:214), the *ratoe mangoe tana* is the representative of the original owners of the land, and has alienation rights over unoccupied land. "He has supernatural power," but the *marómba* (noble) kept this might in check by threat of death. In oral histories collected from Dutch-trained Weyewa who were present at the time of the division of authority, the images that emerge to describe the relation between these groups strongly recall accounts of Aryans conquering Dravidians, complete with allusions to differences in skin color (see also Kapita 1976a:260ff.). Lewata, as the younger, usurping party, became the *mori ata* 'lord of the people,' while Baliloko, according to some Weyewa, possessed the title *mori we'e* 'lord of the water' and was thus responsible for the distribution of irrigation water at Waikelo. There was then, as now, very little agreement about such clan-based divisions of ritual and political authority.

Despite the best efforts of the Dutch administrators to separate ritual from political functions on genealogical grounds, the two remained inextricably intertwined. The term *rato* (glossed by the Dutch as 'priest') was never owned by any one lineage. It was (and still is) used in two senses: (1) as an honorific for someone who has sponsored a large number of ritual events, particularly rites of fulfillment; (2) for the resident or caretaker of one of the sacred houses in an ancestral village. While the individuals who bore the title *rato* in this latter sense are charged with the day-to-day ritual duties of maintaining a sacred house, they do not necessarily play an important role in the large scale performances carried out in ancestral villages. Indeed, they may or may not possess any talent for ritual speaking.

Ritual Community in the Garden

When the Dutch undermined the authority of the powerful rajas, they set in motion a stream of migration out of the confines of the walled hilltop villages toward the open fields and the marketplaces. Preferring autonomy and the risks of attack to a life of debt and subservience to the rajas, more and more of Weyewa's rapidly expanding population moved out to the western interior to bring ever-increasing amounts of the relatively fertile and well-watered highlands under cultivation. While the ancestral villages were gradually depopulated during this period as places for year-round residence, their significance remained as the most prestigious site for climactic rituals of feasting and fulfillment.

As the figures in Table 1 suggest, most Weyewa now live in garden settlements of one kind or another.

Unlike the ancestral villages, which are associated with hierarchy, corporate identity, and agnatic descent, as well as power and prestige, the garden villages are sites of inter-group cooperation and sharing, informality, and impermanence. In songs, tales, and popular expressions, one goes 'down' or 'descends' to the garden for the season, and one returns with one's harvest at the end of the season by 'ascending' or "rising" to the ancestral village. This oscillating yearly dispersal also draws on botanical imagery of 'spreading out,' like the vines of a cucumber or creeping plant, like 'tips' from a 'trunk.' In this sense, the yearly

Table 1: Type of Residence in Kalimbundaramane

Village type	N	Percent
Ancestral village	24	04
Corral village	116	20
Garden village	97	17
Unincorporated garden settlement	336	59
Total	573	100

Table 2: Population of Weyewa 1916–1983

Year	Population	Density (total km^2 = 606.9)
1916[a]	13,139	21.65
1933[b]	25,520	42.02
1946[c]	30,068	49.54
1961[d]	49,101	80.90
1977[e]	67,462	111.16
1983[f]	70,012	115.36

[a] From Prins (1916:21). He labels it "Waidjewa-Tana Maringi." The figures are perhaps a bit low because "exact registration of women and children is extremely difficult." People feared (correctly) that mentioning their wives and children would raise their taxes (1916:23).

[b] From E. W. F. J. Waitz, "Bestuursmemorie van de Onderafdeeling West Soemba," April 11, 1933. He includes Lewata, Tanamaringi, Waimangoera, Baliloko, Palla, Rara/ede, Taurara, and part of Tanariwu in his calculations. He originally typed 18,123, and then penned in "should be 25,520."

[c] From Hoekstra (1948:132).

[d] Manuscript files of the Statistical Bureau, Waikabubak, Sumba Barat, NTT, Indonesia.

[e] Census Department, Waikabubak, 1977. Cited in Metzner 1977.

[f] Manuscript files of the Statistical Bureau, Waikabubak, 1984.

micro-process of dispersal and re-grouping bears a similarity to the long-term macro-process of movement away from the central villages out to the garden and periodic ceremonial re-aggregation.

The general trend has been large scale movement away from the ancestral 'sources.' The centralizing force of the *wanno kalada* and the "rajas" who controlled them was eroded not only by the Dutch challenge but by demographic and ecological changes. One of the most obvious is rapid population growth, as can be seen in Table 2.

As the Weyewa population grew and more and more land was brought under cultivation, available pastureland decreased. Ever since this movement out to the gardens began, older Weyewa say, it has become increasingly difficult to maintain large herds of cattle without extensive fencing and protection against

rustlers (Metzner 1977). During this century, the average size of herds in Weyewa shows a decline, as does the per capita number of cattle.[11]

The movement out to the 'gardens' was and is today constructed as a confrontation and exchange with the wild spirits of the forests, fields, and streams.
Each year as they 'descend' to their fields to clear, burn, plant, fence, weed, and
harvest their gardens,[12] Weyewa carry out a prescribed set of ritual activities to
ensure a proper balance in the complex relations between the ancestors' spirits
and the source villages, on the one hand, and the undeveloped jungle, the gardens, the water sources, and autochthonous nature spirits on the other. The
overlapping imagery of the various levels of symbolism makes it clear that most
of the preharvest agricultural activities are viewed as a movement into the wild
and somewhat threatening forest out from a source village. For instance, an altar
must be placed at the garden's 'head' in the direction of the village. Further, no
songs may be sung while planting swidden fields, since this will attract the attention of harmful 'spirits of the land' (*ndewa tana*).

If the growing season is concerned with maintaining proper relations between the village and forest, harvest is accompanied by ceremonies designed
to ensure harmony between the human and ancestral realms. The ancestral
shoulder-slung betel pouch (*kaweda*) is brought down from the source village of
the gardeners to the makeshift hut next to the field. Various ritual offerings are
provided at named prescribed stages, including: 'descend to the fields,' 'sharpen
the ancestral knife,' 'carry the ancestral betel pouch,' 'carry the ancestral rice
basket,' 'present the rice to the ancestors,' and 'bring the rice to the village.'
Furthermore, the male owner of the rice field customarily gives his married sister
a few kilos of rice from the top of every basket, so that the rice 'multiplies and
thrives.'

Prior to Dutch intervention, Weyewa say almost everyone had at least a
small plot of continuously irrigated wet rice fields located near the fortified villages. These fields are now overcrowded. When farmers move away from this
'center,' they are not only moving away from a constant and reliable source of
irrigation and fertile topsoil but from sources of labor support. Living near their
swidden fields, pioneer farmers must contend with thin topsoil (especially vulnerable to flash floods), and must depend on an unpredictable monsoon. Out in
the 'forest' as they call it, they must also be especially vigilant against pests of the
forest such as monkeys, rats, and wild pigs, which tend to avoid the highly popu-
lated wet-rice complexes, but which can destroy an entire swidden rice field in
an evening.

If floods and pestilence are threats in the rainy winter months, during the
parched and essentially rainless months from May to September fire is a constant
danger. Weyewa live in large, high-peaked, but chimneyless and windowless
bamboo houses with grass thatched roofs. Cool during the day and warm at
night, grass roofs have many advantages, including comfort and convenience.
The roofs last for six to seven years (longer than their recent competitor—

corrugated tin), and are easily repaired with readily available materials. However, Weyewa garden settlements are generally unprotected by stone barriers and fences, and a brush fire can swiftly level a hamlet. Water sources are few and far between and it is almost impossible to extinguish such blazes once they have begun. When a house is devastated by fire, it is a matter with grave and far-reaching economic and symbolic significance.

The Weyewa face a further set of threats from each other. As Weyewa farmers move onto new, unoccupied land that was ambiguous in ownership status, land disputes have become increasingly common. Even in 1938, the Dutch controlleur G. H. Riekerk complained of "complicated intrigues" and "the mentality of the average [West] Sumbanese who is a born lawyer" (1938). Some Sumbanese prefer to settle their affairs through violence. Since these pioneer settlers are often far from other hamlets, they are exposed and vulnerable to sudden attack. Although police statistics show that the danger posed by these hazards appears to be declining in recent years, the fear of 'thieves' (*ata kedu*) and 'robbers' (*ata karebbo*) still motivates much village discourse.

Whether or not Weyewa are in some "objective" sense more susceptible to sudden misfortune than other populations need not concern us here. For Weyewa, a departure for the gardens is viewed as journey 'out' from an ancestral 'source,' and it is still customary for most families to ask for spiritual 'permission' from the ancestral village spirit before embarking on such a pioneering venture. When a misfortune does occur, it is often interpreted as resulting from neglect of the ritual center.

Preoccupations of Independence

When the 8,000 Japanese troops arrived on Sumba in 1942, forcibly inducting Sumbanese into service to work on airstrips for a planned Australian invasion, they were widely described as slave raiders, even headhunters (*penyamun*). Unlike previous assaults on the island, these attackers penetrated far deeper into the symbolic and social interior of Weyewa life and left very deep scars. While the Dutch forces were tiny and demanded relatively little from the Sumbanese, the Japanese troops were numerous, desperately in need of labor, food, and shelter, and in a wartime negotiating posture.

The Japanese invasion turned up the volume on the rhetoric of liberation and independence from feudal (*feodal*) institutions and left the Dutch-supported status hierarchy profoundly shaken. Nonetheless it is clear that Weyewa today still perceive and describe their society in hierarchical terms, as consisting of privileged insiders and marginal outsiders. There is indeed probably no matter of greater delicacy and sensitivity than the issue of rank; but it is rarely if ever openly discussed and tends to be dealt with indirectly. This situation contrasts

Table 3: Status Differences in Kalimbundaramane

Status	N	Percent
Marómba 'noble'	125	22
Orang biasa 'ordinary people'	379	67
Ata paangu 'slaves/low status'	54	09
Rato 'priest'	15	02
Total	573	100

sharply with the practice of open acknowledgment of rank in address and reference in East Sumba (Forth 1981:218). Still, my three Weyewa assistants found
it convenient to sort a census list of 573 households from the east Weyewa *desa*
Kalimbundaramane into four piles according to status (see Table 3). The number
and content of the categories were of their own choosing. *Marómba* 'noble' was
defined on the basis of both wealth and ancestry. Some relatively poor people
were still included in this category, for instance, if they had held offices in the
Dutch government in the past, or were related to the former rajas of Weyewa.
Rato roughly glossed here as 'priest,' refers either to individuals who occupied
an 'ancestral house,' or had distinguished themselves through ritual activity. In
most cases, these individuals are a special grouping within the *marómba* class.
Ata paangu, glossed here as 'slave,' was used by them to refer to a general low
status category that included both 'witches' (*ata ndaina*) and descendants of former war captives. Among these, however, was a relatively wealthy man who
owned a motorcycle and a truck. 'Commoners' were a residual, unmarked category labeled with the Indonesian phrase *orang biasa* 'ordinary people.'

Marriage alliance remains an important means of establishing one's rank.
Here again, certain key features of the marriage relationship reflect a continuing
and constant concern with the maintenance of proper relations between outsiders and insiders. For instance, a typical tension that arises from the standpoint
of a member of an agnatic lineage is between making an expensive and risky
marital alliance with a distant but prestigious clan and making a more stable and
inexpensive alliance with a more closely related but less prestigious clan. While
the first option can mean years of dependency, even servitude, and constant
tensions over repaying debts, the second can mean possibly violating rules of
incest—a confusion of the inside and outside (Forth 1981; Kuipers 1988). As
can be seen from Table 4, by far the majority of Weyewa opt for alliances with
someone of the same rank.

The practice of assigning formal leadership on the basis of rank came under
attack in the 1960s, although it is arguably still a major determinant in political
appointments in West Sumba (Mitchell 1970). Before its formal abolition in
1962, the institution of raja was further threatened in the late 1950s and early
1960s when the PKI (Indonesian Communist party), criticizing the legacy of
elitist feudalism left by the Dutch, urged landless Weyewa farmers to open up

Table 4: Percentage of Household Heads in
Kalimbundaramane Who Married a Woman
of the Same Rank

Marital status	N	Percent
Married same rank	391	68
Married higher rank	11	02
Married lower rank	16	03
Respondents not sure	155	27
Total	573	100

gardens in sacred fields and move into previously prohibited territories owned by the rajas. While these practices were later condemned, as late as the 1980s, as part of a plan to stimulate agricultural development and private ownership of land by smallholders, the Indonesian Department of Agriculture and Department of Justice in Waikabubak have on a number of occasions attempted to settle land disputes by simply giving the title to the one who works the land; thus many titles have been given to farmers working plots traditionally owned by nobility.

Currently, the Weyewa region is divided into eastern and western districts (*kecamatan*), which each have twice-weekly markets, local elections, a small civil administration office headed by an appointed official, and a police barracks. These two districts are subdivided into a total of twenty-eight *desa*[13], or 'villages,' each of which is headed by an elected *kepala desa* 'village headman' who is responsible for maintaining roads, building schools, administering a yearly grant from the central government, and generally promoting the political agenda of the modern Indonesian state. While many of these men are from high status backgrounds, high birth appears to be less important than wealth, community influence, and a general political orientation that accords with that of the Indonesian state. One of the most important roles of these men is in hearing litigation and witnessing important negotiations and feasts (see the Epilogue). As witnesses, they ensure that the slaughter tax is paid, that meat is divided properly among the guests, and that the agreements reached in negotiations are honored. Should a case develop into a major dispute, the *kepala desa* must try to settle it or recommend that it be brought to the regency court in Waikabubak. Although there are several Protestant ministers (*pandita*) and Catholic priests (*pater*) who have some influence in the community, their power in legal, political, and economic matters is subject to the laws of the Indonesian governmental system.

While the government encourages Weyewa to look to Jakarta as the 'source' of political legitimacy, to many this seems very far away. Most Weyewa do indeed pay some tax, participate in elections, and do road work when asked. But the majority still follow the advice of older lineage leaders who settle their disputes, structure their exchanges, and negotiate the allocation resources and ritual responsibilities to the 'word.' Although many important economic transactions take place in the public markets, these remain symbolically peripheral and slightly disreputable places by Weyewa standards. A deal or exchange transacted in an ancestral village is more likely to be prestigious and binding on the participants, Weyewa leaders say. Correspondingly, legal disputes settled in a government office carry less 'weight' than ones enacted in more traditional settings, but this may be changing. Many conservative Weyewa say that much violence in Weyewa could be avoided if litigation was carried on in central, ancient villages with the ancestors listening: "then liars would be afraid to speak!" they cry.

When speaking about the current tensions with the Indonesian government and its programs, Weyewa assimilate these conflicts implicitly to a debate between the inside and outside: they see the issue as one of contrast between an ancient, 'original' (*mema*), and ancestral "inside" and a recent, 'foreign' (*dawa*), and modern "outside" (Onvlee 1973:114ff.). An important forum for identifying, discussing, and resolving points of tension between the old and new is rituals of misfortune. In these, calamity is viewed as a violation of relations between the outside and the inside due to neglect of the 'word' of the ancestors. The relation between innovation and tradition, outside and inside, and new and old are important themes in the dynamics of Weyewa conceptions of misfortune and the spirit world to be dicussed in the next chapter.

Notes

1. The authority over belief and action that the Weyewa associate with the history of their land can be usefully compared with the Roman notion of founding acts linked with *auctoritas*. Steven Lukes has written that

> *auctoritas* for the Romans and throughout the Middle Ages signified the possession by some of some special status or quality or claim that added a compelling ground for trust or obedience, and this could derive from some special relation to some founding act or past beginning or to a sacred being, or some special access to a knowledge of some set of truths (Lukes 1979:642).

2. One of the first Dutch controlleurs on the island, Roskott, is reported to have said,

> The impression that this land, its people, and the social condition in which they live, made on me was not favorable. The land is infertile and dry, and not capable of being cultivated; although there is a considerable number of small rivers, brooks, and springs, but they flow mostly through such narrow cleavages and small valleys and between such high banks that the water is not usable for agriculture. And while it is true that here and there one encounters fertile pieces of land, these are on the whole insignificant (reported in Wielenga 1912:6).

3. Although many observers have been impressed with the relative harshness of the Sumbanese landscape when approaching it from the coastal regions (see Roskott's remarks in Wielenga 1912:6), a feel for the contrastive character of the landscape can be conveyed by this early Dutch observer's remarks upon visiting the Weyewa area. He describes it in almost idyllic terms:

The plains are overgrown with short grasses, and have the feel of a Dutch pastureland. The grazing water buffalo insure that the grasses do not get too high. Several ponds provide a handy bathing opportunity for these beasts, and a swimming place for large geese. . . . The hilltops, overgrown with pinang and coconut palms form a dark rim. Here is one of the nicest spots on Sumba (Wielenga 1912:308).

He remarks, however, on the lack of streams and rivers. The tiny brooks that do exist appear above ground for a short distance and then vanish without a trace underground, leaving barely enough water to wash one's hands (1912:308).

4. *Sumba Barat Dalam Angka 1987* (Waikabubak, Sumba Barat: Kantor Statistik, 1987), p. 18.

5. Kruyt mentions that

in Wajewa I heard the following story: In the old days the Sumbanese were friends with the *ana dawa kaka* 'the white foreigners,' and with *ata ndima* 'the Bimanese.' They came over a stone bridge, which once stretched from Cape Sasar to the other side. The two above-mentioned groups once came over to visit the Sumbanese for a harvest feast, and as the custom is, engaged in a 'calf kicking' contest. The foreigners won this one, and many of the Sumbanese had their legs broken. But when things progressed to boxing, however, the Sumbanese got the best of their guests, and blood streamed down the latter's faces. The end was that the Sumbanese and their guests shouted insults at one another, and the foreigners departed. Some time later, the Sumbanese found a large eel. A horseman went over to the other side so they could partake of it also, but he was so long in returning that the Sumbanese went ahead and ate it. When the invited guests finally showed up, the eel was gone. The Bimanese were extremely angry and staged a violent riot. In the end they made peace, and agreed to have a meal together. When the Sumbanese gave the Bimanese meat to eat, they gave them meat they were not accustomed to (perhaps the Bimanese were already Moslems, and the meat served was pork). They became angry once again and went back to their land. They told their hosts: 'You'll get yours!' This came in the form of a large small pox epidemic, which took many lives (Kruyt 1922:471).

6. The Dutch missionary Wielenga observed during a brief visit to the Weyewa region in 1909 that although Weyewa claimed to have belonged originally to a single group, they were composed of different factions who, due to various disputes, hardly spoke to one another anymore and constantly "fight it out amongst one another" (1912:328).

7. The term "raja" here is a Malay word which many Sumbanese appear to have used as a term to denote any powerful individual with coercive powers. Particularly in the late nineteenth and early twentieth century, it did not necessarily imply legitimation by Dutch colonial authority.

8. This is probably an exaggeration; as mentioned above, the drought-prone and chalky soils of the northern coast can support only a very sparse population under the best of conditions. Nonetheless, even settlements in the fertile areas of the coast seem to have been depopulated by the fear and reality of slave raids.

9. Couvreur (1917) remarks that the Endenese found that "West Sumba was too big for them [to conquer]. As one Endenese explained, who was forced to withdraw with a bloody head, 'their bodies are very stout.'"

10. By calling these 'lineage houses' I do not mean to imply that lineages are coterminous with them. In fact, I was told there are six major lineages associated with Beindello. The lineages of the village are listed below, and their houses, if they exist, are listed alongside them.

Kabizu 'lineage'	*Umma 'house'*
We'embyaka	None
Umbu Ndendo	Umma Umbu Ndendo
Wini Lele Moto	None
Wini Langgara	Umma mandeta
	Umma nggau mata
	Umma tillu
	Umma puttika
	Umma watara
Wini Moto Rei	Umma kere tana
	Umma Pirra Dawa
Bondo Lona	None

11. The number of horses per capita, for instance, has declined from 1.24 in 1946 (Hoekstra 1948:132) to 0.05 in 1986 (*Kecamatan Wewewa Timur Dalam Angka 1986.* Elopada: Kantor Statistik, Kecamatan Wewewa Timur, Sumba Barat. p. 37).

12. The first stage of swidden cultivation is 'opening the forest' (*wukke kandawu*) or 'clearing the jungle' (*poka ala*), which must be accompanied by 'exchange offering' (*tau marata*) to the 'lord of the forest' (*mori kandawu*). The various stages of gardening are outlined below (indentation marks sub-stages):

poka ala, tura tana	clear the forest, open the land
mawoma kandawu	clear the undergrowth
ponggo wazu	cut down trees
toda wazu	pollard the trees
katokko wazu	cut the logs
pewela pazinggo	dry out the slash
tau-ngge api kandawu pazazi	burn the cleared forest
muttu loubira	initial burn
mangopa	collect (the unburnt slash)
muttu mirita	final burn
pa-ndende katowa oma	erect the head of the garden
tondaka pare	plant rice
rawi-na kalena	make the hole
pina kalena	seed the hole
zowa-na kalena	close the hole
pa-ndende lenango	erect a guard platform
rawi-na nggollu wangora	build a wild boar fence
manairo	weed the garden
rawi kareka oma	build a harvest hut
makeni	harvest
ropo pare	cut the rice
manamo pare	thresh the rice
kunggara wulli	break off the rice stalks
kombakana pare	pick off the stalks
mawopa pare	winnow the rice
pauta pare	collect the rice into baskets

13. In Weyewa, *desa* is an imported term, designating a somewhat arbitrarily de-limited geographical area (from 9 to 50 km²) consisting of anywhere from two thousand

to four thousand souls. The term does not have the social significance that it does on Java, where the label originated. A more accurate gloss in the Weyewa case would be 'ward,' which foregrounds the administrative rather than social or economic significance of the term, but I bow here to what has become a convention of translation from Indonesian to English.

3

Spiritual Authority in the Context of Calamity: Agents, Action, and Exchange

One closely guarded myth illustrates how the failure to heed the 'voice' or 'word' represents a challenge to ancestral authority, for which the punishment is misfortune. In the story, the wise and ancient Ndangi Lawo lived a long life amidst plenty by following the 'word' or teachings of the Mother and Father Creator. Like all people back then, he would never die, because every time he would get old, he would shed his skin like a snake, be 'renewed,' and become young again. The Sun and Moon, however, would never set, and as a result, the earth would get very hot. So a young man named Mbora Pyaku went to the Creator to request that the Sun and Moon be permitted to set from time to time to cool things off.[1] The creator agreed to let the Sun and Moon "live and die and live again," as Mbora Pyaku requested, but in exchange, "when humans die, they will die forever." As soon as Mbora Pyaku thus changed the 'word' of the ancestors, Ndangi Lawo died, and people first began to cry and weep. Children began to be born, and people began to reckon time, counting the 'months and years' until they died, and they began making promises to sacrifice animals to the ancestors in order to prolong their lives. But since these 'words' of promise to the ancestors are often left unfulfilled, and 'spotted' with imperfection, misfortunes continue to the present day.

Much of the myth elaborates a tenet of Weyewa common sense—obvious to all but the most insubordinate children—that calamity is the inevitable result when one fails to honor the 'sacred' (*erri*) obligations embodied in the words of one's elders. Weyewa myths, rituals, and childrearing practices relentlessly drive home the point that children are extremely dependent on their parents. To be cut off from communication with them, or with their spirits, is to experience not only a profound sense of isolation and abandonment but exposure to terrifying forces, suffering and pestilence. For Weyewa, this is an experience of individuality that is likened to being on the margins of the social world—in the garden, on the road, dangerously vulnerable to the harmful wild spirits of the earth, forests, and fields.

Such disagreeable imbalances between inside and outside come about through neglect of one's 'word' of obligation to at least three main categories of spirit, each of which corresponds to a location in the house: (1) the 'following spirits' of the hearth area, associated with the spirits of the wife's former lineage; (2) 'house spirits' in the vestibule, associated with the agnatic lineage;

(3) 'threshold spirits' in the doorway, which are linked with the wild, individualized, and marginal forces of the gardens, fields, rivers, lightning, and animals. 'Witches' comprise yet a fourth kind of spiritual force associated with the margins of social space, but they never engage in negotiations or exchange.

The Isolated Individual and the Experience of Misfortune

For Weyewa, adherence to spiritual authority presupposes the non-exercise of private, individual judgement in the production and exchange of communicative acts (cf. Lukes 1979). In most contexts, to act and speak authoritatively is to perform under the auspices of someone else—usually one's forebears—as a delegated voice, bound by a 'sacred' (*erri*) commitment to the source. Deviance and insubordination are then construed as individually authored acts, as lonely, solitary performances which are therefore vulnerable and susceptible to criticism, misunderstanding, and supernatural assault. Breaking a promise is construed as an individualistic departure from a collective agreement.

It is impossible to appreciate the feelings of isolation that result from breaking a promise without understanding the profound sense of dependence Weyewa profess to feel toward their ancestors. In both formal and everyday contexts, Weyewa often describe the major patterns in the seasons and the life cycle as thoroughly controlled by the spirits of their forebears. These spirits, and the various minor deities under their guidance, are said to control the germination, growth, and abundance of crops, the flow of water and rain, the fertility of livestock, and the health and well-being of the community. Favorable outcomes of risky transactions such as marriage alliances, legal disputes, and forest clearings also require ancestral backing. In one of their many vivid images of this relationship, Weyewa liken these deities to the cord that a woman holds to brace herself as she squats in the throes of labor. While these spirits carry the potential for harm, they can also be a mainstay in times of crisis.

Ancestral spirits do not freely provide such goods and services, but require their descendants to reciprocate. Weyewa must pray to them with their request and describe the compensation offered. Typically, they simply request an end to misfortune, express their wish for well being and prosperity, and offer a small animal sacrifice as immediate compensation for future service. A more specific but quite common sort of deal involves designating a buffalo or pig to a particular spirit as a reward for some desired outcome. For example, a pest-free rice crop or recovery of a family member from a serious illness, if delivered, would then be paid for by a sacrifice. Depending on the request, the reward may also be a celebrative feast or house temple built in the spirit's honor. Thus, according to Weyewa religious ideology, the routine patterns of everyday existence—the production and growth of one's crops, health and well-being, the flow of water—come about through negotiation and agreement with ancestral spirits.

Failure to strike a deal beforehand is to leave oneself dangerously open to misfortune. When that 'word' is violated, neglected, or broken, then malevolent spirits cause 'misfortune,' or *podda*. The word *podda* refers not only to an extraordinarily disastrous event (e.g., crop failure, pestilence, sudden illness or death, devastating fire), but also to the *experiences* associated with that event. *Podda* also may be glossed as 'feeling' or 'sensation,' and refers to the experience of tastes, odors, emotions, heat, pressure, movement, and several other kinds of perceptions. All are disturbing to one's consciousness, and contain an element of surprise; for example, 'when he ate the mango, he tasted its sourness' (*ne ba na-nga'a uppo, na-podda-ngge mawillura-na*). As an intransitive verb, *podda* refers to the passive experience of misfortune, not to the object or cause of that experience. For instance, a common verb phrase used to describe someone's misfortune is *na podda*, which might be literally glossed 'he feels.' As a noun, 'misfortune' (*podda*) is something one is 'struck' with: 'he was struck with misfortune' (*na wenna podda*).

In ritual contexts, these experiences are associated with many images, but recurrent themes include characterizations of misfortune as personal, isolating, disorienting, violating, sudden, extraordinary and 'hot.' The personal character of misfortune, for instance, is vividly depicted in terms which suggest the event is directly aimed at the victim:

wolota mawenna	the blowgun strikes exactly
reketa manindo	the dart hits its mark

Judging from the verbal imagery of misfortune as well as from the testimony of victims, one of the most intolerable feelings following catastrophe is the sense of being singled out and personally attacked by the event. Examples of similar perceptions abound in the anthropological literature (e.g., Evans-Pritchard 1937; Middleton, ed. 1967), as well in some cases closer to home: William James, who happened to be in the vicinity of the San Francisco earthquake in 1906, felt that this event was somehow a personal blow. "First, I personified the earthquake as a permanent individual entity. . . . It came . . . direct to *me*." [2] When Kai Erickson interviewed survivors of the Buffalo Creek flood in New York State, he discovered that they "tend[ed] to regard the attacking force as something directed against them individually, an enemy whose motive is personal malice" (1977:163). Like disaster victims in many parts of the world, Weyewa want to know, not just "why me," but "why me in particular" and not someone else.

Misfortune is something that happens *to* people, violently. It is not self-generated. The couplet

pobba wali pu'u	struck from the trunk
para wali lawi	thrashed from the tip

implies that the relations between trunk and tip are shaken by an active force outside the victim. When Mbulu Renda accidentally struck his toenail while chopping wood, I asked him if this was a misfortune (*podda*). He replied, "Ah no. This is just something I did to myself. My knife is old and the handle slipped." On the other hand, when his son fell out of a tree and had to be tended in bed for a week, he regarded this as caused by an angry spirit, and he staged a divination to investigate. A certain amount of clumsiness is only to be expected, but when a mishap is so serious that it affects the conduct of one's life in a serious way, it suggests that some other agency may be involved.

Like orphans abandoned by their parents, disaster victims sometimes complain to the spirits that they were isolated and rejected. When one man's father died suddenly, he cried:

rudduka pandoku-ngga	I was set down wrongly
bondala pa-ndénga-ngga	I was just placed aside

A particularly common and vivid image of the resulting vulnerability and exposure is that of the fields, roads and streams "outside" the village:

balango maredda	misfortune in the field
podda lara dana	touched while on the road

Many ritual speech couplets represent misfortune as an experience of bodily disorientation. After seeing his ancestral house collapse due to age, one man employed the following lines:

lelapa mawo koba mata	dizzy spirit of the face
kandándaka odo kámbu ndara	trembling breast of the horse
kandándaka karoka	trembling ribs
mbiduka kazaza	limp body

One of the most common images of misfortune is that of loss of composure while out walking. The following couplet describes illness, fire, death, crop failures—in short, calamities of all kinds:

windarara witi	obstacle to the foot
tunnurara deinda	trip and fall flat

Misfortune can also be represented as a hidden obstacle in a field or marginal space:

kazoba tana rara	pothole in the red earth
katura riti kangga	a sharp stick booby trap

Falling or being startled can cause the loss of one's personal spirit, thus leaving one vulnerable to be entered by dangerous spirits of the outside. If one loses this spirit, it must be summoned through a divination and *zaizo* ceremony. If it occurs while one is a guest at someone's house, the host may be obligated to stage a healing ritual for his guest. Examples of calamities that can necessitate a rite of misfortune include:

warraka pu'u ndeta	fall from a tree
warraka ndara ndeta	fall from a horse
muttu-ngge ingi	burn one's waistcloth
warraka natara dana	fall in the village square

One man I know called for a full scale divination and placation rite when he lost his composure because his waistcloth was singed by a flying spark from a fire during a ceremony at his neighbor's house. He demanded that his host pay for the ceremony.

Misfortune is depicted as an extraordinary, novel, and innovative event; it contrasts with ordinary, everyday, or traditional events. When one man named Kurri Mbili's father died, his house burned down, and his son became ill, all in the space of one month, he described his predicament as:

ingi eka ori	waistcloth of unusual weave
kamba eka nggai	yarn of extraordinary length
nda'iki tudda tutu	there is no measuring stick for it
nda'iki ngenda ngera	there is no prior example

Suspicions of calamity begin with the occurrence of such an unusual or "marked" condition; such events call attention to themselves, and will not be ignored. A pattern of such unexplainable events amounts to a misfortune. When Winni Tondo found a dead python one morning lying in her garden, she was alarmed. But when her nephew became unaccountably ill that same evening, she began to suspect that something was amiss, and she consulted a diviner.

Misfortunes are represented as having a sudden onset and as being unexpected. In the following couplet, the sudden unpredictability of death and affliction is likened to a disorienting meteorological event:

pa-urra tillu langita	like rain out of the blue sky
pa-loddo mara tana	like a hot day in the cool season

Mbili Lali was once a very powerful and vigorous man. Gradually, over the years, he began to experience shortness of breath, dizziness, and slight deafness. When I asked him if this was a 'misfortune,' he replied, "No. This is my 'bridge' [to old age]." On the other hand, his son-in-law's sudden and unexpected fainting while in the garden provoked a lengthy inquiry.

Misfortune is linked with violations of intimate, domestic space. It comes from outside and threatens the integrity of the house:

wendora kareka	open up the house
tullara kambowo	push aside the thatch

or

zuzura kandyaka	kindling bursts into flame
tettera karangga	demolish the rafters

When the brothers living together in the village of Pu'u Nu'u suddenly got into a major dispute that escalated to the point that one of them threatened to leave, it was regarded as shocking and a grave 'misfortune.' A divination was immediately planned to look into the background of the event and see if angry spirits were implicated. Likewise, when Mbili Tondo's house burned to the ground one evening, he feared that his house spirits had fled in fear and dismay. Such a *podda* affects the security of the domestic space. A robbery attack is also regarded as a misfortune. After a robbery, for instance, gongs may be beaten to 'raise up' (*kouka*) the spirit of the house so that it is not entered by wicked agents of misfortune.

The most notable sensory characteristic linked with misfortune is excessive 'heat.' The following couplet, for instance, refers to more than bodily illness and may apply more generally to the experience of disaster:

mbangata katowa	hot aching head
malala muttu wekki	hot feverish body

Most categories of 'illness, pain' (*karoduka*) are associated with excessive heat. Trauma (wounds, burns, broken limbs), rashes (*kara*), intestinal ailments (*kazarraka ti'a*), as well as tooth- and headaches are all considered illnesses which cause 'heat.' Mental illness is excluded from this category, as are a number of congenital and developmental disorders and several slow-moving degenerative illnesses.

The Spirit World

When things go smoothly, there is no need to question the authority of one's judgments or choices. But when calamity occurs, Weyewa feel personally singled out, an experience which compels a confrontation with motivation and intention—not only their own, but those of others. They need to know under whose auspices a particular act was carried out, and by what prior agreement. Many researchers have noticed that when misfortune strikes people, they tend to take it personally, and assume they are victims of a motivated act (Erikson 1977:163–164). "'The tendency to see ourselves as the focus of other people's actions' noted by Heider [1958:120] has as its corollary the tendency to see other people's actions as likely causes of what happens to us" (Frake 1980:70). Or in the words of Bertrand Russell, "One of the odd effects of the importance of the principle which each of us attaches to himself is that we tend to imagine our own good or evil fortune to be the purpose of other people's actions" (Russell 1950:151), to which Charles Frake has added, "this tendency seems more pronounced when bad things happen to us. A reasonable amount of good fortune is only our fair share, but even a little bit of bad luck may well be someone else's fault" (Frake 1980:71).

When discussing misfortune, Weyewa ritualists are often quite aware of alternative, "modern" explanations for calamitous events. Many are even familiar with the details of these more scientifically-based arguments and believe them. One diviner I know attended a three week course sponsored by the World Health Organization designed to teach folk healers the basics of first aid and public health. But, like the Azande (Evans-Pritchard 1937), Weyewa want to know: "Why me and not someone else; why my house and not another; why now and not another time?" If, when examining the pattern in their lives—the 'path that was traveled' (lara li pa-li-na)—they see a sense of coincidence and repetition, it may be more than strictly empirical explanations can handle (see Frake 1980:73). As Roland Barthes has observed, "Repetition always commits us to imagining an unknown cause. . . . Chance is supposed to vary events; if it repeats them, it does so in order to signify something through them" (Barthes 1972:191). If an event occurs once, it may be only chance; if there seem to be several portentous signs, then it is time to consider other explanations.

Weyewa ritualists do not normally reduce the responsibility for malevolence to a simple act of individual authorship or to an act of naked aggression on the part of some thoroughly evil agency. Despite the imagery of individuality associated with misfortune, Weyewa are usually less interested in finding a single agent who caused the calamity than in exploring the ruptured relationships among specific actors who participated in the event. Thus when Lende Kenda's horse threw him after seeing a snake, he did not explain his broken arm in terms of the angry earth spirit that caused the snake to be there, nor in terms of his father's failure to sacrifice to that spirit many years back, but in terms of the disrupted lines of communication between father and son, human and spirit world, such that the 'word' of agreement between these parties was neglected. As the diviner put in a subsequent divination,

nda'iki li'i pana'u   there were no words of instruction
nda'iki li'i pananggo   there was no voice of command

Although Lende Kenda's father had made a deal with the earth spirit in the past, he never fulfilled it; when his father died, the responsibility for his father's li'i 'word' rightfully belonged to his son. As a good member of the family, Lende Kenda is required to make good on his father's debts. This does not mean, however, that the son is solely responsible for the calamity that befell him. Nor is the father responsible for having died before fulfilling his agreement. He did not *plan* to die without fulfilling it; one does not plan one's own death. Rather, the problem derives from the accumulation of several individualistic (and thus deviant) relationships toward the 'word' itself, the agreement to exchange with the spirit world. Identifying, re-affirming, and fulfilling this promise is the goal of Weyewa rituals of atonement.

There are three main categories of spirit with whom one may enter into exchange, and who correspond to different positions in the house. Since most significant interactions with one's parents and family members occur inside the house, its hearths, pillars, and vestibules are regarded by Weyewa as appropriate sites from which to carry on communication and exchanges with those who have died. Spirits of the married women's lineage are sometimes found in the central hearth region or kitchen portion of the house. Spirits of the man's agnatic lineage are located in vestibules and on the pillars of the house. The minor deities of the forests, fields, and streams subordinate to those of the ancestral spirits possess altars located near the doors and entryways, corresponding to their marginal position in the family spiritual life.

The words of exchange with these spirits are binding because they are *erri*, which in this context may be translated 'sacred authority.' Although the concept is often used in negative contexts, in the sense of 'taboo,' or 'prohibition,' it also possesses positive and creative connotations. Spirits, places, and words are said to be *erri* 'sacred.' When one makes a promise with ancestral spirits, the spirits of one's in-laws, or spirits of the earth, Weyewa say they *rawi-na erri*, literally, 'make [it] sacred.' A symbol of such sacred agreements is often a sheaf of grass bound in a hoop and hung in a conspicuous location: from the eaves of a house, on a fencepost, or from an altar. Thus *erri* is associated with a binding commitment requiring the non-exercise of individual, private judgement. Failure to submit to the authority of the words spoken at the time of its creation results in supernatural retribution.

Marapu Loka 'Spirit of the Mother's Brother'

An important source of calamity among the Weyewa is the penetration of the *marapu loka* 'the spirit of the mother's brother' into a domestic scene as a result of unpaid debts and unresolved tensions. This does not necessarily refer to the spirit of the actual 'mother's brother' of the male head of the household. Instead, it refers to an ancestral spirit from the agnatic lineage into which a man's wife was originally born. Ideally, a man takes his 'mother's brother's daughter' (*angu leba*) as a wife, but even when he selects a spouse from another permissible category of relation, the wife's father may also sometimes be spoken of as *loka* or *pa-loka*. More commonly, in such circumstances, the spirit is referred to with the label *marapu pa-deku* 'following spirit,' which means a spirit who follows the woman from her natal village to the village of her husband's lineage.

PLAN OF THE WEYEWA HOUSE

A Fire (api)
B Cooking stones (tulura)
C Hearth (rabuka)
D Vestibule (mbali tonga)
E Chamber (koro)
F Pallet (tandingo)
G Spirit platform (kere ndoka)
H Pantry (kere pandalu)
I Divination post (pari'i urrata)
J Head post (pari'i toddu)
K Foot post (pari'i tènda)
L Pantry post (pari'i kere pandalu)
M Water jar (pandalu)
N Entryway (kawùnga papenne)
O Altar shelf (leki)
P Front corner (bali mata)
Q Veranda (bangga)
R Raised platform (ponnu koro)
S Pantry door (binna kere pandalu)

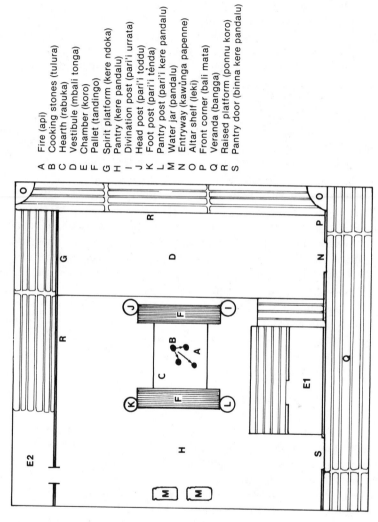

Figure 4: Floor plan of a Weyewa house.

This spirit contrasts with other spirits by not having an altar—indeed not really having a proper place in the house at all. While it is sometimes identified with a place near the hearth, there is no designated location from which to address this spirit.[3] Whenever it is identified in the house it spells danger, an unsettled presence in the house, one that threatens the order of the domestic space. Its very existence represents a violation of relations between the inside and the outside in the house.

Ideally, a woman foresakes her parents' lineage when she moves to her husband's house in this system of agnatic descent and virilocal residence. In the ideology of the Weyewa lineage (*kabizu*), marriage represents a gradual incorporation of a female outsider into the clan, accomplished through a series of unequal exchanges between parties represented as *wera* 'wife givers' and *lazawa* 'wife-takers.' These begin when the boy's family 'knocks on the door' (*tunda binna*) of the girl's house by bringing a knife and horse in exchange, for which they are reciprocated with a pig and a cloth. If negotiations proceed, and the 'rice seed' (*winni pare*, i.e., bride-to-be) is available, then several weeks or months later the boy's party approaches the girl's house again, accompanied by payments of knives and several head of cattle. They negotiate with the *wera* 'wife-givers' over how much brideprice (*welli*) should be paid. It is usually a minimum of ten head of cattle plus gold *mamuli* pendants. They also negotiate the complementary countergift, usually at least one large pig and small basket of handwoven men's waistcloths and women's sarongs. Once the amounts are agreed to (the groom's payment may be as high as several hundred head of cattle), then a pig is sacrificed and the ancestors of the girl's family are informed of the 'word' (*li'i*) of agreement between the families. The betrothal arrangement is symbolized with the phrase 'bind the porches together, erect the prohibition on the eaves' (*kette-na katonga, weri-na kawendo*). The final stage occurs when the 'promise' is partially fulfilled, the boy's family delivers a large (mutually agreed upon) portion of cattle, jewelry, and knives, and the girl 'moves' (*pandikki*) to her husband's house. The rest of the marriage payments—which may amount to several animals—are exchanged over the course of a lifetime as ritual needs arise.

Upon arriving, the girl begins a gradual process of incorporation into the lineage. When she enters the house, she is greeted with a sprinkling of coconut milk, a ceremonial washing also given to newborn children. Although she and her husband initially sleep in the room near the front of the house (see letter E1, Figure 4), they eventually move to sleeping on the more central *tandingo* 'pallets' (see letter F) closer to the 'hearth' (*rabuka*) when children are born. For Weyewa, this is a privileged feminine space associated with familial intimacy.[4] The wife spends much of her day on the front porch, in the 'pantry' (*kere pandalu*, letter H), and near the left front side of the hearth. The left rear area is associated with her mother-in-law.[5] Until the wife is much older and her own children are married, she must avoid the sacred ancestral heirlooms in the attic reliquary (*umma dana*), and areas in the right side of the house (*mbali tonga*, letter D, and *kere ndoka*, letter G) associated with the spirits of the agnatic lineage.

If the 'word' of agreement with the spirits of the girl's agnatic lineage is not properly fulfilled after several years, then these spirits become restless, and may 'follow' her to her new village, causing calamity.[6] When Ninda Toro's brothers came to visit her husband's village asking for a water buffalo to bring to a funeral sacrifice, her husband refused. He argued that her brothers had not yet properly reciprocated for the cow and water buffalo he had brought to their placation rites two years ago. Although they had offered him a small pig as temporary compensation, they had still not lived up to their agreement. Nonetheless, Ninda Toro was greatly upset by her husband's refusal and took it as a personal attack on her family. Shortly afterwards, the buffalo her brothers had asked for was stolen, and Ninda herself fell ill and nearly died. A divination determined that a 'following spirit' was at work in the hearth area of the house causing these difficulties. A water buffalo was procured to offer to the spirits of Ninda Toro's agnatic lineage, a 'placation rite' (*zaizo*) was staged to enact the exchange with Ninda Toro's brothers, and the imbalance between spiritual forces of the inside and outside was rectified.

Spirits of the Ancestors

Perhaps the most common source of calamity is the wrath of the 'ancestral spirits' (*marapu*). While the term *marapu* among Weyewa may be extended to refer to spirits of all kinds, including autochthonous and personal ones, its focal meaning rests with the spirits of deceased forebears traced through the agnatic line. The degree of sacred authority (*erri*) is hierarchically associated with their level of genealogical distance from the speaker (see Hoskins 1988:32): the most ancient are the most holy. Associated as they are with the continuity, fertility, and nurturance of the agnatic lineage, ancestral *marapu* are rarely addressed as single individuals. Rather, they can be identified in discourse by their husband-and-wife paired names, a designation calling attention to their role in the procreation and generation of the clan.

Marapu in this sense may refer to spirits represented by a wide range of objects stored in the attic reliquary (*umma dana*). Ancestral sacra—gongs, pendants, knives, spears, headcloths, and certain favorite objects belonging to the deceased—may be retrieved and displayed during special feasts, particularly in moments when the 'word of the ancestors' is fulfilled and the spirits are very much part of the ceremony. In some attics, there are carved heads (*kazala tou*, lit. 'false person') that represent ancestral *marapu*. Unlike objects in other parts of eastern Indonesia, these are usually not exchange items, but are inalienable symbols of the personal identity and prestige of the ancestor who acquired them (cf. Traube 1986:76ff.). These sacra often possess couplet names that hark back to the event in which they were bestowed.

No spirits are more intimately linked with the house than ancestral spirits. For Weyewa, like many peoples in eastern Indonesia, the house is more than shelter—it is an exceedingly complex symbolic structure built according to strict principles intended to reflect the social and cosmic order (Fox, ed. 1980:10). When I asked my diviner friend Mbulu Renda why one does not place the primary altars to the ancestors in the center of the village or on the tombstones of the deceased, he replied, "We always met with our fathers and mothers in the house. They fed us in the house, they clothed us in the house, they put us to sleep in the house. So we offer them food in the house. That's how we do it." Unlike the 'following spirits' of the wife's lineage, ancestral spirits are believed to inhabit the house permanently. They possess fixed altars where they receive their food offerings and to which prayers are directed.

Unlike the 'following spirits' of the wife's lineage, which are sometimes found in the pantry (kere pandalu) on the left side of the house ("left" as one faces the house from outside), the altars of the ancestral spirits are addressed on the right side of the house, in a space called the mbali tonga 'vestibule.' A kind of inner porch,[7] the vestibule is a roughly two by six meter space defined along its length on the hearth side by the low (about one-half meter) wall divider (koro) and on the far side by a long low bench, the 'raised guest platform' (ponnu koro kulla or ketendengo) (see letter R in Figure 4). On non-ritual occasions, a large plaited mat and chickens' nesting baskets are often kept in this space.

An important focus of ritual activity in the vestibule is a small shrine located at the rear of the house in the vestibule hallway. It consists of a broad raised shelf which may be called the 'spirit platform' (kere ndoka, lit. 'buttocks of gold'). In ritual contexts it is called the 'source of the spirits' (mata marapu) and is considered the most sacred altar in the house (see letter G on Figure 4). Though occasionally used as a seat by the household head and an honored guest while eating a ritual meal, essentially this entire space enshrines the ancestors of the inhabitants of the house. The soot-blackened sacred relics stored here include an 'ancestral betel pouch' (kaleku kaweda), in which some betel ingredients and small knife and sharpener are kept. An 'ancestral basket' (kadongge kaweda) used for collecting the first fruits of harvest, holds some chicken feathers, shredded coconut, rice pannicles, a small winnowing basket, and an old sword. The 'divining spear' (numbu urrata) and musical instruments (if owned) are also kept here.

Here in the inner vestibule, these spirits may be addressed by their sacred names. Because the names are erri 'sacred,' they are not to be frivolously invoked. The performance of the names themselves is associated with a kind of binding authority, in that their enunciation commits the speaker to some kind of exchange with the spirit. Once, early in my research, I checked the accuracy of the couplet name of a certain spirit by reciting it aloud to a man claiming descent from the spirit. Instead of being pleased, he looked very uncomfortable. When I asked why, he said, "You said [the spirit's] name, but I have nothing to give it." The spirits so addressed fall into three categories: the 'ancestors,' the 'intermediaries,' and the 'creator spirit.' The ancestors are often referred to as 'the mother guest, the father guest' (*kulla inna, kulla ama*) or simply *marapu*.

Ancestral spirits are usually addressed using a teknonym referring to their children, or a couplet name. The actual names of the ancestors are often paired as husband-wife:

Ríngi Ndende	(name of male ancestor)
Dada Leba	(name of female ancestor)

Sometimes, the spirits are referred to by their teknonyms:

inna Lende	mother of Lende
ama Lende	father of Lende

Sometimes, a more laudatory, lengthy praise name is used, as in this case when a man offered a chicken to his ancestral spirits in exchange for a successful harvest:

yemmi	you
a pa-ana-na pare	who gave birth to rice
a pa-zuzu-na lelu	who suckled the cotton
a lili-na kaleku	who carried a betel pouch
ndari rewa	decorated with beads,
a nakka-na keto	who holds a knife
ullu omma	with a gold handle
kulla Inna	spirit of the Mother
kulla Ama	spirit of the Father
yemmi	you
a temba tabbo lindaka	who keeps the plates level
a remba koba kallu	who keeps the cups suspended
tena tanggibila-ngge	[like a] ship that lists
li'i-mi	toward us is your voice,
ndara tamodela-ngge	[like a] horse kneeling toward us
lomma-mu	is your tongue
yemmi-do-na	you
a kambala pa-kayutta	are the rope we hold onto,
a kandawu pa-talira	the forest behind us

The symbol of ancestral spirits—'shoulder pouch' for the male and 'rice basket' for the female—are normally removed from the 'spirit platform' and brought down to the fields once a year. The sacra themselves are usually placed temporarily in the makeshift 'garden huts' (*kareka keni*). The more permanent altars ('shadow' [*mawo*] and 'head of the garden' [*katowa oma*]) are established in the fields and remain year round as locations where ancestral spirits may be addressed. When the harvest is brought back to the home village, the sacra are returned to their original location. Very important, apical ancestors may only be addressed in an 'ancestral village' (*wanno kalada*). Since they are symbols of the unity of the entire lineage, it is disrespectful to invoke their names in a 'garden village' (*wanno oma dana*), or engage them in an exchange which only affects a small number of lineage members. Such figures are only addressed 'using a ladder' (*wai-na nauta*); that is, indirectly through other ancestral spirits as intermediaries. The following mythic hero of the lineage of Beindello was offered several water buffalo and indeed an entire new lineage house indirectly through lower-level ancestral spirits:

ka ya-na na'i	and so you offer it to him:
Umbu Tindo Rato Pana	Umbu Tindo Lord of the bow
a pana mata lodo	who shot the sun
Umbu Tokko Wai Lapale	Umbu Tokko by the water
a pana mata wulla	who shot the moon

The ancestral spirits expect that feasts and animal sacrifices will be staged in their honor and out of gratitude for bountiful harvests. Neglect, ignorance, and unkept promises are a major source of misfortune. When Lende Tondo reaped his largest rice harvests ever in 1984, in his enthusiasm he tried to take ten of his sacks of grain directly to the Chinese stores in the regency capital of Waikabubak to exchange for cash. As he waited for a covered pickup truck (*bemo*) to haul away his rice, he was hit by a motorcycle, and his face was severely disfigured. Subsequent divination revealed several broken promises, including one to his ancestors to the effect that, if he received a bountiful, pest-free harvest, he would haul the rice back to his ancestral village and stage a large feast. When he failed to do so, he was struck with misfortune.

Misfortune may also be visited on agnatic descendants of a man who long ago neglected a promise to his ancestors. When Lende Kamia's son drowned shortly after Lende had put away a bumper rice harvest, he discovered that his grandfather had never been properly buried. The old man had been temporarily laid to rest near a stream, and the presence of his restless spirit was bothering the local water spirits there. These water deities were agitated and took away the life of his son. He resolved to fulfill the 'promise' to bury his grandfather properly and bury his son in the same sarcophagus.

Like the most ancient ancestral spirits, the 'creator spirit' is too holy to be addressed directly. One does not enter into direct exchanges with it. Mediator spirits convey one's words to the Creator. One of these is the 'child of speech':

ana pulu	child of speech
ana kandauke	child of talk
a ndikita pa-la'o	who goes back and forth

a noneka pa-mai	who shuttles in between
a pa-toma-na mbarra Inna	who sends it to the Mother
a pa-dukki-na mbarra Ama	who conveys it to the Father
pulu pa-kanikita-ngge	[who] speaks with precision
ngiki pa-kawolera-ngge	[who] examines thoroughly

The other intermediary is the 'spirit of the house post':

lambe a mbelleka	the wide house post collar
pari'i a kalada	the great house post

While these intermediaries may be addressed in 'branch villages,' the most 'sacred' (*erri*) deity of the entire Weyewa spirit world can only be mentioned in the 'ancestral village.' This deity lives in 'heaven':

loda manda elu	field of tranquility
pada zuma zawa	meadow of bounty

This dual gendered deity may not be addressed directly. As a 'creator spirit,' it may be referred to as

mori	Lord
Inna a mawolo	the Mother who makes
Ama a marawi	the Father who creates
Inna ndukka inna	the Mother of mothers
Ama ndukka ama	the Father of fathers
Inna ndukka biza	the most holy Mother
Ama ndukka mandi	the most sacred Father
nda pa-zuma ngara	whose name is not spoken
nda pa-tekki tamo	whose name is not uttered
a pa-makke mata	who makes us shy
a kamomo wiwi	who strikes us dumb
a rawi-na kabani kabola	who makes handsome youth
a wolo-na minne kabola	who creates pretty women
a angata wolla limma	who separated our fingers
a kanga wolla wa'i	who separated our toes

The sacred authority of the Creator Spirit derives from association with the fundamental act of procreation. From this spirit, human beings were entrusted the responsibility for orderly procreation and sexuality; incest is regarded as among the most heinous and disruptive of crimes. Creator spirits are particularly angered by it, since it violates a fundamental promise (*li'i*) humans must keep to the Creator—to be pure in their procreative acts. When Winni Toro and her maternal uncle had sexual relations they kept it quiet until her son died suddenly of an intestinal ailment. In her distress, she began accusing herself of wrongdoing. A diviner was summoned, who elicited her story. A lengthy and expensive placation rite was performed, she was ceremonially bathed, and her trangression was expelled from (cast "outside") the village.

Spirits of the Threshold

As one moves away from the spiritual source of the house and toward the outside, one leaves behind the encompassing spiritual authority of the ancestral deities, and moves into a realm of more individualized spiritual responsibility and liability, symbolized by the presence of myriads of specialized deities to whom one can be personally and directly obligated. Located in the right corner door lintel (*mbali mata*, lit. 'turning the eyes'), the triangular altar (*leki*, see letter O on Figure 4) for these spirits is a place where one can leave offerings of rice, betel and areca nut which are then conveyed to the specialized spirits of the village, forest, fields, and the outside, non-domestic world generally. The sacred authority of these spirits tends to be associated with specific promises and agreements made on an individual basis in exchange for specialized services.

Illnesses with clearly defined sets of symptoms and sudden onset, are often associated with bad relations with these spirits. For instance, autochthonous spirits of the land are often blamed for such diseases as hepatitis and diarrhea. Spirits of the streams may be linked with chills and cold sensation. Rashes may be caused by spirits of animals who have characteristics that resemble the symptoms. A rash with large blotches, for instance, is sometimes said to be caused by the spirit of a snake with similar markings.

As go-betweens to more sacred deities, these spirits are directly addressed. One such mediator, who shuttles between the inside and the outside, is the 'messenger spirit.' Referred to in ritual speech as *Tawora pinda leti, Karaki pinda namu*, or more briefly as *Tawora Karaki*, this spirit is found in every house, but is said to be owned by the Mángutana clan. He has a long list of couplet names referring to his maleness and his intrepid adventures over hill and dale on behalf of other deities. An omniscient spirit sometimes likened to a net, he generally does good deeds, such as retrieving lost souls and conveying payments (*marata*) to earth spirits, but he sometimes causes stomach ailments.

Certain specific maladies may be attributed to the medicine spirit (*marapu moro*) belonging to another household. A frustrated suitor might invoke this deity to cast a spell over his lover, or to change the minds of stubborn negotiators in marriage ceremonies. Others might approach this spirit to make themselves invisible before raids (*moro makebbela*) and invulnerable to poisons (*kondu*). To survive or neutralize the effects of this spirit, a special sacrifice must be made.

A series of severe natural calamities such as fire, pestilence, flood, and death of cattle, or intense, high fever suggests that angry ancestral spirits have sent the 'hot spirits' (*marapu muttu*) on a mission of vengeance. These spirits go by a number of names, depending on the clan. Some common ones include 'the lightning spirit' (*marapu kamillaka*), 'the owl spirit' (*marapu wanne*), 'the angry spirit' (*marapu mbani*), all of which exhibit the characteristics of maleness and destructiveness:

a pa-mandauta doti	who is feared
a pa-mai-nggu engge	who commands respect
a tibbara-na watu	who crushes the stones
a debara-na ngamba	who splits the valley

Particular individuals may form personal associations with these spirits, commanding them to carry out specific acts of vengeance and retribution. Several lineages are said to possess special relationships with one or another of these special spirits, whose services may be obtained by an outsider in exchange for a cloth, a chicken, and a knife.

Residents of the village of Wone, for instance, are said to have a particularly strong relationship with the lightning spirit. When Daud Landango, a lapsed Catholic, decided to open a new garden in a piece of unused land formerly used by someone in the village of Wone, he was afraid that he would bring down the wrath of the lightning spirit. He visited Wone, and sought their protection by paying them a small fee in exchange for protection. He told me that he never had any trouble as long as he has worked that piece of land, 'not even a scratch.'

Weyewa also possess 'prohibition spirits' (*weri*). These clan-owned guardian spirits provide retribution for the violation of sacred taboos or magical warnings. Angering them can have very specific consequences. The 'snake prohibition' (*weri nippe*), for example, consisting of a piece of coconut leaf bent in a circle and hung from a stick, might be erected in the garden of its owner to ward off thieves and trespassers. Violators are smitten with a pain in the stomach resembling the consequences of a bite from the *nippe* snake. The pain will not abate until the perpetrator goes to the owner of the prohibition, confesses, and asks for special medicine. Other such magical prohibitions include the 'lightning prohibition,' the 'owl prohibition,' the 'eagle prohibition,' and the 'crocodile prohibition' (see Kapita 1976b:372–374).

Witchcraft

One other important source of misfortune among the Weyewa is witchcraft. Weyewa often say that a major reason for witches to attack is the refusal of an offer of exchange (i.e., the refusal to offer the 'word'). For example, a witch came to visit Mbulu Rewa's store one day and asked for a special deal on some coffee he wanted to sell. Mbulu refused. The following night Mbulu's store was robbed, and he attributed the attack to witchcraft. It was not that the witch himself had committed the break-in, but that Mbulu had been bewitched into falling so deeply asleep that he could not hear the intruder. Weyewa are very careful around suspected witches and often accede to their wishes so as not to make them angry.

'Witches' (*ata ndaina*) are contrasted with 'humans' (*ata pi'a*), and are said to engage in various inhuman acts such as anthropophagy, flying about at night with green flames spewing from their anuses, and turning into rats. Certain marginal, low ranking lineages are said to be the source of witchcraft. Associated with the outer peripheries of social space, these lineages and their members are said to be 'from the other side of the lake' (*bali omba*). In one myth, the ancestors of a reported 'witch clan' were said to have been found in the field and brought into the village to be used as slaves. Encounters with witches can thus be viewed as a confrontation with outsiders of low rank. Weyewa are particularly careful not to marry persons of witch rank; the slightest hint of a kin association with people of this witch category can confound the most intimate marriage alliance.

Witches are said to cause harm unconsciously while they sleep. The soul or spirit of a witch reportedly exits the person's navel at night and flies about, alighting on the house of the intended victim. Once inside he or she may change into a rat. When the Weyewa hear rats scuttling about on the rafters of their house at night as they sit around the fire, they sometimes comment that these may be witches looking for victims. If the witch has no particular grudge against the victim, he or she may take three hairs from the upper arm of the person. But often, the witch cuts open the belly of the victim, neatly eats the liver, sucks the blood, and after closing up the body, silently departs without a trace, leaving the victim weak and helpless. Weyewa try to be careful not to offend witches, because they fear such reprisals. Thus it is very difficult to get Weyewa to discuss witchcraft openly; they fear someone might hear them discussing rank, resent them and cause harm.

Witchcraft represents an intrusion of persons of low rank into one's midst. Although witches continue to be associated with the 'outside' of Weyewa society, in recent years persons of the 'witch' rank have made impressive economic progress. The first covered pickup truck (*bemo*) used as a public conveyance in the domain was in fact purchased by a person descended from a 'witch' lineage. As a result, some Weyewa feel persons of witch rank are increasingly becoming a threat, and are more and more likely to penetrate one's house at night and eat one's liver and soul.

Summary

For Weyewa, misfortune (*podda*) results when persons exercise their judgment as individuals and thus fail to recognize the authority of, or otherwise abide by, collective agreements and conventions. Weyewa victims of calamity represent the experience as an isolating, disorienting imbalance between forces of the inside and outside. When one fails to live up to marriage exchange obligations, for instance, 'following spirits' intrude from the outside into the privileged interior domain of the hearth and associated consanguineal family. 'Ancestral spirits,' associated with the inside of the house, often flee in rage when angry, leaving the house dangerously exposed to outside forces. 'Spirits of the entryway' mediate between the world of the ancestral spirits and the wild spirits of the earth, forests and streams. They are individualized and specialized spirits, and are amenable to personal, even private negotiations and exchanges. Witches are also associated with the 'outside' and are increasingly seen as posing a threat to the stability and integrity of domestic and personal space.

Notes

1. According to one version of this tale, the earth was too hot because there were two suns, and so one was shot out of the sky with an arrow by a figure named Umbu Tindo. McKinnon (1983:36–43) describes a similar myth from Tanimbar, in which Atuf, a culture hero, spears the sun into pieces, making the earth habitable.

2. Henry James, "On Some Mental Effects of the Earthquake," in *Memories and Studies* (New York: Longmans, Green, 1911), p. 212. Cited in Erikson 1977:164.

3. One man told me that he addressed the *marapu loka* spirit in the 'threshold' of the house; others disagreed with his practice.

4. The open-slat *kewi* 'smoking rack' that hangs directly above the hearth fire is sometimes compared to female genitalia; of the hearth area generally, Weyewa say, *nyawi pandou dadi ata* 'that is where people are born.'

5. There is a left-right, female-male pattern to the symbolism in the house that is expressed, among other things, by the arrangements and symbolism of the house posts and cooking stones. The three cooking stones (see letter B on Figure 4) are placed in a triangular arrangement in a slightly sunken box of sand. The two rocks furthest to the left are called 'female cooking stones' (*tullura bei*) while the one furthest to the right is known as the 'male cooking stone.'

6. A number of older Weyewa men I have spoken to say that disputes over brideprice have become worse in the past few decades. This is plausible, since as average herd size declines, the ability to fulfill promises made as long as thirty or forty years ago during periods of relative plenty correspondingly decreases. The number of horses per capita, for instance, has declined from 1.24 in 1946 (Hoekstra 1948:132) to 0.05 in 1986 (*Kecamatan Wewewa Timur Dalam Angka 1986*, p. 37).

7. The phrase *mbali tonga* may be more literally glossed as 'the floor on the other side': *mbali* 'other side,' *tonga* 'floor.'

4

'Words of the Ancestors' as a Continuum of Style

To bring order into their relationships with the spirits, Weyewa ritualists 'plant the word' (*katukku li'i*). Like some anthropologists (e.g., Bloch 1975), Weyewa ceremonial specialists like to represent these 'words' in unitary, monolithic terms. They describe them as a single 'trunk,' or an immoveable and unchangeable 'stake' fixed in the earth. However, this mode of speaking in fact varies stylistically across genres and performances. While conventional couplets are regarded as the distinctive and constitutive feature of these 'words,' this dyadic register of 'ritual speech' (*panewe tenda*) exhibits a "continuum of style" corresponding to degrees of "saturation" in the ritual frame of performance (Bauman 1984). Even in categories of ritual speaking where the parallelistic poetic form predominates, the couplets exhibit a range of structural shapes and semantic functions.

General Overview of the Weyewa Language

Weyewa see the couplets, discourse connectives, pronouns, and reported speech that appear in ritual discourse as characteristics of the 'Weyewa language' (*panewe Weyewa*). In order to understand how features of the language play a role in the construction of authoritative discourse, or the 'words of the ancestors,' it will be helpful to provide briefly a short outline of the social, structural, and stylistic attributes of the language.

Weyewa consider themselves speakers of *panewe Weyewa*. Since intensive contact with the Dutch began in the early 1900s, the Weyewa name has been subject to a variety of pronunciations and spellings: Wadjewa (Kruyt 1922; Wielenga 1912), Waidjewa (Prins 1916), Weewjewa (Hoekstra 1948), Wewewa (Renard-Clamagirand 1988; Onvlee 1973:165), Veveva (Needham 1980), Wawewa (Forth 1981:4), Waiyewa (Kapita 1976a:261), Vaijeva (Needham 1987:10). In my experience, the word Wadjewa, (sometimes spelled Wedjewa, or Waidjewa) with the "dj" pronounced as a voiced alveopalatal affricate, is an *exonym*; that is, it is not normally used by the people to whom it refers among themselves. The reduplicated term Wewewa (reportedly from *wewa* 'to search') used by Onvlee now appears in many modern and official contexts—for example, Bible translations, government documents, and district maps. Although a few have claimed that it refers to the "search" of the original ancestors for a place that was

fertile and uninhabited, there seems to be little agreement on this folk ety-
mology. As it rarely occurs in everyday speech, and never in myths or ritual
speech, I have not followed this usage. The spelling Weyewa is used here to
represent how they themselves designate their language and ethnic identity.

As a noun, *panewe* can refer to a language, dialect, or style of verbal discourse. One speaks of *panewe Weyewa* 'the Weyewa language,' *panewe Kodi* 'the
Kodi language,' and 'our language,' as in 'he knows how to speak our language'
(*na pánde panewe dou-nda*). It can be modified in adjectival noun phrases to
differentiate non-lexically more specific varieties—for example, *panewe pa-
zallu-na* 'playful, joking speech'; *panewe kawozzoka* 'nonsense speech'; *panewe
lawolo* 'lying speech'; *panewe mboto* 'serious speech'; *panewe zili* 'evasive
speech'; *panewe do awa* 'just talking'; *panewe oma dana* 'garden speech'; *panewe
bua mane* 'young boy's speech.' As a verb, *panewe* is predicated of someone in
the act of speaking. Unlike *tekki* 'to say,' *panewe* implies responsive interaction.

For purposes of this study, Weyewa may be described as an "ethnolinguistic
group," insofar as linguistic identity is essentially coterminous with ethnic identity. According to a 1978 estimate based on a sample survey of 440 households
in one subdistrict, 29 percent claimed to be entirely monolingual in Weyewa.
Another 45 percent of those sampled could passively understand some of the
Indonesian national language (*bahasa Indonesia* or *panewe dawa*, lit. 'language
of the foreigners') which is used and positively valued as a *lingua franca* in
interethnic contexts, in government offices, in the schools, and in the (Chinese)
shops and marketplaces of Waikabubak, Weetabula, and Waingapu. The remaining 26 percent had some degree of proficiency in spoken Indonesian as well
as Weyewa. A much smaller percentage yet claimed to be literate in Indonesian
(10 percent). Today, one hears a certain amount of Indonesian-Weyewa "hetero-
glossia" in everyday colloquial Weyewa, especially among young adults who
have attended school.

Weyewa belongs to the Austronesian group of languages. Speakers claim
that it is mutually intelligible only with the Lauranese, Mbukamberan, Edenese,
Tanamaringi, Raran, and westernmost Lolinese dialects, but shares many vo-
cabulary items with the Laboyan and Kodinese languages to the south and west
respectively. It is more distantly related to eastern Sumbanese-type languages
such as Wanukaka, Anakalang, Memboro, and Kambera. Dyen believes the
most closely related non-Sumbanese language is Bima (Dyen 1978; see also
Wurm and Hattori, eds. 1983).

The structure of the Weyewa language has yet to be fully described, though
some preliminary attempts have been made (Onvlee n.d.; Onvlee 1973:166–
177). The most characteristic feature of its morphology is affixation. There
are three verbal prefixes, marking passive, causative, and what Onvlee calls
"distributive" constructions (Onvlee 1973:173). Weyewa possesses nine verbal
suffixes: a genitive (*-na*), a discourse marker (*-ngge*), a future event marker
(*-langge*), an incompletive (*-po*), a perfective (*-ba*), two modals (*-do* and *-ki*),
and two statives (*-we* and *-wa*).

The preferred ordering of the major sentence constituents is verb-initial. Possible orderings include V$_t$OS ([Transitive] Verb-Object-Subject):

Na kouka kai-ngge ne numbu na kaweda
3s pull anyway-CTV DET spear DET old [person]
'The old man pulled out the spear anyway'

and V$_i$S (Intransitive Verb-Subject):

A *mate kuwa-ba-na a touda ata*
3pp die all PST 3pp three persons
'All three people died'

Syntactically more marked word orders topicalize the subject or object by placing them first in sentence initial position, followed by a topicalizer *a-* or a pause, which is then followed by a verb or predicate construction. An example of a subject first construction is the following:

Ka-nyakka na   Ngongo Ndimmu, kabani mbani-wa
And so   that Ngongo Ndimmu, man   bold stative

'That Ngongo Ndimmu, he was a brave man'

The object may also be topicalized (Object + Transitive Verb), where the subject is not expressed as a full independent constituent.

Hidda katowa-da a-deke-wi ka a-ngíndiwi ne'e Beindello
Their trophy heads-theirs   they-took-theirs so they-brought-theirs there to Beindello
'The heads, they took them, they brought them [as trophies] to Beindello'

The phonetic inventory of Weyewa is relatively simple (see Orthographic Notes), consisting of ten vowels and seventeen consonants and semi-vowels. Like many of the languages in Sumba and eastern Indonesia, the Weyewa language possesses phonemically preglottalized and implosive bilabial and dental stops (Onvlee 1950). An interesting issue phonologically is the intervocalic doubling of consonants and the consequent allophonic variation of interconsonantal vowels, a matter with considerable orthographic implications (see Orthographic Notes). The canonical word form is CVC(C)V, although in rapid speech the final vowel is often elided.

The most salient stylistic category is 'ritual speech' (*panewe tenda*), which may be contrasted with the residual 'plain speech' (*panewe bora*). As I use it, the phrase 'ritual speech' refers to a distinctive parallelistic (or "dyadic," see Fox 1988) style of communication that is required for (and in some ways constitutive of) ceremonial occasions in which spirits are addressed. This does not mean that all the talk uttered by performers in such circumstances is 'ritual speech': indeed, some of it is rather colloquial in character and does not exhibit the distinctive couplet features. It is a "style" of verbal discourse (Ervin-Tripp 1972) in that it represents a selection among alternative styles, a measure of internal consistency and predictable co-occurrence of linguistic features, such as parallelism, frequent use of dialectal variants, and heightened rhythmicity, that set it off and "mark" it as different from other styles of speech. Weyewa 'ritual speech' may also be considered a speech "register" (Halliday 1978:35) in that it contrasts with other linguistic varieties in terms of the situations in which it is appropriately used.

After some consideration, I have decided to avoid the phrase 'ritual language,' since it is sometimes used to suggest something more abstract than 'speech' (e.g., Grainger 1974). Furthermore, the phrase 'ritual language' more appropriately applies to a speech form that is historically distinct from that used by the majority of a given linguistic community, such as Latin (of the Occidental Catholic church), Vedic Sanskrit (of the Hindus), or Pali (of Theravada Buddhists). As Hymes suggests, "Where common provenance of a stock of lexical materials is in question, one . . . [may] speak of *languages* and *dialects*" (Hymes 1974:59). Although *panewe tenda* differs markedly from colloquial speech in its phonology, syntax and semantic structure, by and large the source of these differences is not another language, but a distinctive stylistic tradition within the Weyewa repertoire of speech. The vast majority of words and grammatical processes in ritual speech are Weyewa in provenience.

Although Weyewa recognize 'ritual speech' (*panewe tenda*) as an entity distinct from 'colloquial speech' (*panewe bora*), and point to couplets as the basis for this difference, in actual practice it is inseparable from the genres with which it is expressed. There is no pure ritual speech outside of genre: all ritual speech performances have some kind of generic form, some kind of utterance type into which they fit and may be classified. To examine ritual speech as a monolithic whole is to ignore the contrastive character of a particular performance in relation to other categories of ritual speech expression.

The listing in Table 5 provides a glimpse of the diversity of Weyewa ritual speech genres. Weyewa genres may be divided into two main groups: those in which the 'ancestral spirits' participate, and those in which the audience and participants are human. The first thirteen ritual speech categories, labeled here "politico-religious genres," are all performed by men in the context of ritual events. With the possible exception of the ceremonial greeting (*pazimbala*), all are conceived as dialogic exchanges consisting of a sacrificial offering between the representatives of a patrilineal kin group and the spirits of deceased ancestors and various tutelary spirits.[1] In the "relatively dialogic" genres, the performer actually addresses the spirits, and his performance is more or less contingent on their responses. In the more "monologic" genres, the performer acts as the mouthpiece or 'voice' (*li'i*), of the ancestral spirits, and he expects only formulaic ratifications from his human audience. Since to varying degrees all of the "politico-religious" genres give voice to the ancestral spirits' moral and political

Table 5: Genres of Weyewa Ritual Speech

Politico-religious genres		
1. *Pazimbala*	'Ceremonial greeting'	Relatively dialogic
2. *Bara*	'Offertory prayer'	
3. *Urrata*	'Divination'	
4. *Tau-na li'i*	'Oration'	
5. *Zaizo*	'Placation song'	
6. *Ndondo*	'Celebration song'	
7. *We'e maríngi*	'Blessing song'	
8. *Pawowe*	'Headhunting song'	
9. *Payoyela*	'Ligntning song'[a]	
10. *Oka*	'Chant'	
11. *Kanúngga*	'Migration narrative'[b]	
12. *Newe marapu*	'Ancestral narrative'	
13. *Ngi'o newe*	'Narrative lament'	Relatively monologic
Personal genres		
14. *Nggeile*	'Wet rice planting song'	Relatively dialogic
15. *Padengara*	'Work song'	
16. *Pawaiyonggo*	'Dragging song'	
17. *Nggeloka*	'Wailing'	
18. *Matekula*	'Eulogy'	
19. *Lawiti*	'Harvest song'	Relatively monologic

[a] I have never witnessed actual performances of either the 'headhunting song' or the 'lightning song'; however, analysis of short samples of each song, performed for my benefit by experienced spokesmen, convinces me that these are two distinct genres. My Weyewa assistants also expressed a strong conviction that these two genres were coordinate taxonomically with the other genres listed, despite their current somewhat exotic and rare status.

[b] *kanúngga* 'migration narrative' is a general cover term for a generic narrative form which may be employed within a number of other kinds of performances, including the *we'e maríngi* 'blessing song,' *pawowe* 'headhunting song,' and *payoyela* 'lightning song.' Some *newe marapu* 'ancestral narratives'—tales about the origins of the Weyewa domain—also exhibit this narrative form. The genre *ngi'o newe* 'narrative lament' also sometimes contains these *kanúngga*-type sub-plots. The latter are part of a sung myth, and are held to be particularly sacred by some performers as an evocation of the sufferings of their ancestors.

charters for the descendants, errors in performance are regarded unfavorably, and may even be subject to fines.

The "personal genres" possess a different relation to the 'voice.' Here the voice expressed is that of an individual, sometimes that of the actual performer. It may be male or female, young or old, or even that of a spirit, animal, gong, or mythical figure in a narrative. In most cases, the song reflects the performer's personal experiences and inner states. Although some of the songs are regarded as ancient, errors in performance are not thought to result in supernatural retribution, as is the case in the politico-religious genres. The topics and settings of performances vary widely, particularly with the harvest songs, which are now performed according to less formal criteria. Even the compositional format is less restrictive; indeed, the conventional couplet structure is sometimes systematically violated for emotional effect, as in the *nggeloka* 'wailing' genres performed by women.[2]

The central genres making up the process of ritual atonement for misfortune are 'divination' (*urrata*), 'placation rites' (*zaizo*), 'chants' (*oka*), and 'blessing songs' (*we'e maringi*). Genres and events are not always the same thing. While *urrata* and *zaizo* are labels for *both* discursive genres *and* the larger events in which they occur, 'chants' and 'blessing songs' label *only* the genres *within* larger, differently named events associated with rites of fulfillment: *woleka* 'celebration feasts' and *rawi umma* 'housebuilding' respectively.

From "Context" to "Text": A Weyewa Continuum of Style

My first clues to the systematic connection between variations in linguistic forms and the ritual and ideological pattern of the rites of misfortune came in March 1979, when Petrus Malo Umbu Pati brought me his own personal ethnographic notebooks. On the lined sheets of these well thumbed but carefully protected schoolbooks (see Figure 5) he had recorded what he described with some reverence as the 'voice of the ancestors' (*li'i marapu*). Dating back as far as 1955, most of the written texts corresponded to performances of a mythical narration enacted in the final stages of rites of misfortune. He had transcribed some of them from memory, others were dictated, while yet others were derived from cassette recordings. As far as I know, he worked independently and was unaware of any other similar efforts, such as that of the Dutch trained East Sumba scholar and former government official Umbu Hina Kapita (1976a, 1976b).

As Elinor Ochs (1979) has observed, transcriptions of speech can reflect and even shape theoretical orientations toward language. Writers selectively attend to certain features of discourse and ignore others, guided powerfully by an image of what constitutes a "text." What Petrus's texts showed were preferences for lists of neat, perfect couplets. He laid them out on the page in a tidy column, not unlike verses of psalms in his Malay Bible or stanzas of songs in his Protestant hymn book (see Figure 5). The couplets themselves consisted predominantly of proper names—place names or personal names. Largely missing from these texts were what Emanuel Schegloff has called "conversational detritus" (1982:74), which Weyewa view as signs of unkempt 'garden talk'—personal pronouns, reported speech, "back channel cues," and other discourse markers which index the emergent features of discourse as conversational performance (Schiffrin 1987; see also Tedlock 1983:147).[3]

Petrus was not alone in his preferences. Some months after he showed me his notebooks, I visited a relatively isolated Weyewa village for the first time. An elementary school teacher brought me a written document taken from a tape recording of a performance of the 'voice of the ancestors' in the final stages in the ritual process of atonement. In a pattern similar to that employed by Petrus, this writer had arranged the material on the page so as to emphasize its couplet structure and minimize the discursive markers and other non-couplet materials. Similarly, in texts of the 'voice of the ancestors' (*li'i marapu*) narratives from the neighboring district of Laura published by Kapita (e.g., 1976b:267ff.), this east Sumbanese scholar includes only couplets consisting of proper names. In all cases, discourse markers, pronouns, and quotation frames are rare.

The intriguing dispreference of these writers for anything but couplets in

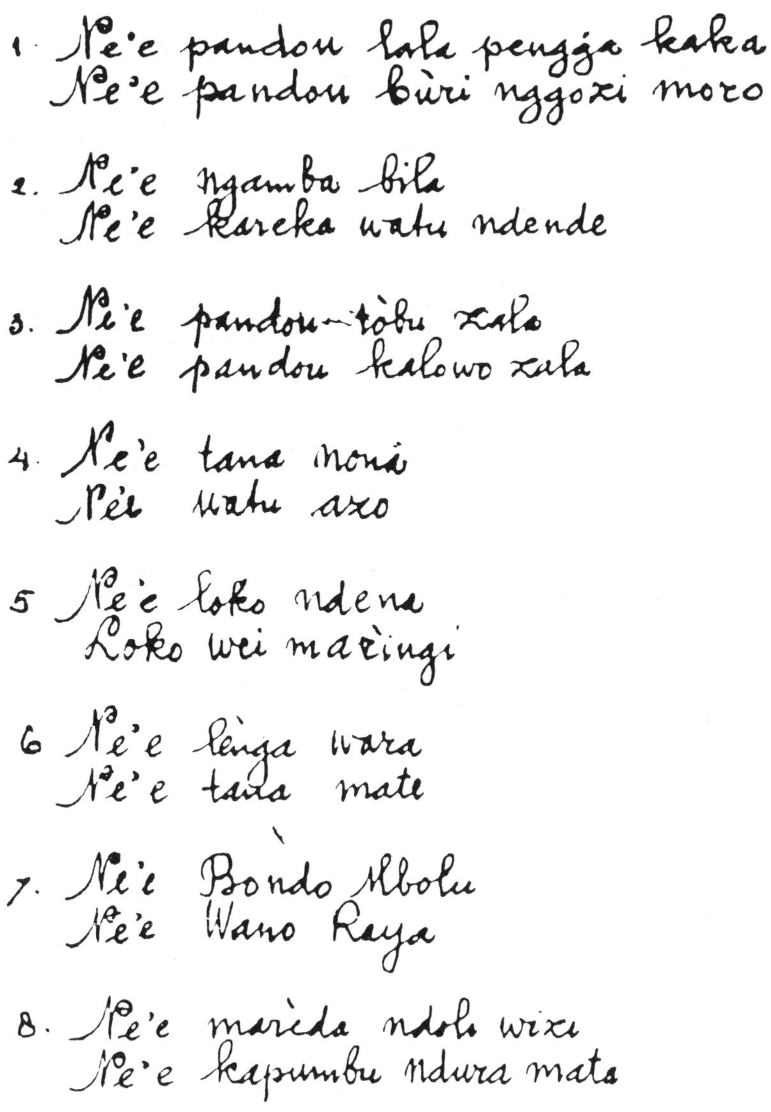

Figure 5: Petrus's transcription of a *li'i marapu* performance.

sacred 'voice of the ancestors' suggests testable hypotheses about the relation between formal and informal speech. Is there a systematic relation between formal linguistic features and authoritative discourse? In what follows, I investigate the changing role of a variety of linguistic forms across genres of ritual speech performances. The verbal process of ritual atonement for misfortune, beginning with divination, followed by *zaizo*, and culminating with rites of fulfillment (chants and blessing songs), I argue, corresponds to a "continuum of style."

What distinguishes the early stages from the final ones (among other things) is the relatively frequent use of demonstrative and personal pronouns, reported speech, and discourse markers—*indexical* linguistic forms culturally associated with novel, individualized, spontaneous, and dialogic speech. These kinds of discourse, in which verbal forms are linked to their objects of reference through contiguous relations in the situation of utterance I will refer to as "contextualized speech." In the latter phases of rituals of atonement, by contrast, the speech is rich in canonical parallelism. While all such couplets are *indexical* in that their use suggests involvement in the ritual frame of performance,[4] they are *symbolic* in the sense that they rely for their significance on an image of decontextualized, semantic meaning (Mertz 1985; Peirce 1974).[5] The meaning of such discourse points away from the particulars of the immediate performance situation, toward other texts, toward its own internal coherence relations, and toward other times, other identities, and other places (see Becker 1979). The image of authoritative couplets *par excellence* is proper names, which are poetic forms understood by Weyewa as referring to spiritually potent and superior individuals and places. These forms of speaking I describe as representing relatively "entextualized discourse."

Since "context" is crucial for establishing this continuum of Weyewa ritual speech genres, it will be useful to clarify what I intend with its usage. The notion of "context" has been so widely used in so many different senses by scholars from different backgrounds and interests that it is in danger of losing its meaning unless it is defined in each case.[6] The sense I am concerned with here is that conveyed in the verb *contextualize*, and its expanded nominal, *contextualization*. The verb form is convenient because it suggests a process, and implies an agent. Gumperz (1982) and Goffman (1981:188ff.), for instance, speak of "contextualization conventions" and "contextualization devices" as verbal strategies employed by interested actors in a social scene. Thus context is not an abstract independent variable in a hypothesis (e.g., as in the phrase "context-dependent"), but a resource in the construction of meaning.

Such an actor-oriented, agent-centered approach to contextualization requires an appreciation of the ideological significance of this process as well as its semiotic properties. Within the Weyewa ideology of language, the identification and definition of contextualized language figures in highly charged debates: it may be contrasted with convention and tradition when questioning what true "ritual speech" really is.[7] Whether or not one speaks with the "true words of the

Mother and Father" depends (among other things) on how conventional, monologic, and metaphorical one's words are. These words differ from what may be
called "contextualized" speech, associated with relatively indexical, impulsive,
novel, individualized, dialogic, and localized talk.

Demonstrative Pronouns

In the ideology of Weyewa ritual, speech that is closely tied to a local situation or event is relatively disvalued. One of the more derogatory assessments of
ritual speech is the comment that 'it is garden speech' (*panewe oma dana*); that
is, it is provincial discourse tightly knit into its local setting, with few implications for the community as a whole. As the 'tip' to an encompassing, more
permanent 'trunk,' local speech stands in this sense as *token* to the supra-local
and superior *type* of pan-Weyewa discourse considered most authoritative (cf.
Traube 1986:68).

In this light, it is worthwhile considering the use of demonstrative pronouns
(or spatial deictics) that link speech to its context of use. John Lyons has remarked that "deixis, in general, sets limits upon the possibility of decontextualization" (Lyons 1977:646). It is difficult, if not impossible, to interpret and
analyze deictic words outside the situation of utterance. It follows that speech
containing many and varied deictic words referring to the spatial location is likely
to require a considerable amount of specific information about the particular
circumstances of performance for it to make sense.

The Weyewa language possesses a relatively elaborate paradigm of spatial
deictics, or demonstratives, which are organized by such distinctions as the motion or orientation of the referent (toward the speaker/away from the speaker/
neutral), visible/invisible, animate/inanimate, and plural/singular (for a partial
description, see Onvlee 1973). The distinctions of movement can also have temporal connotations: events that move towards the speaker are usually in the future, while events that move away from the speaker are generally in the past. In
addition, Weyewa deictics optionally code the relationship of speaker to other
participants in the speech situation. For instance, there is a three-way distinction
that operates through morphological transformations of the root *ne-* : *newwe*
'here by me,' *nenna* 'there by you,' *nekke* 'there by him/her/it.' In highly contextualized speech, not only are deictics in general a frequent occurrence, but such
personal inflections are especially common. Table 6 offers a general comparison
of the frequency of demonstrative pronouns in the four most important and
distinctive genres of rites of atonement.

In general, these usages are relatively personalizing; they clearly situate the
speaker as a culturally constructed "self" in relation to what she or he is talking
about. This does not mean that the referent of the "I" in all cases indexes an
egocentric subject. Indeed, as Tanz (1980) argues, deictic terms can have a cate-

Table 6: Frequency of Demonstrative Pronouns
in Four Genres of Weyewa Ritual Speech (average
number of occurrences in sample 100-word texts)[a]

Genre	Average no.
Divination	7.33
Placation rite (*zaizo*)	3.5
Chant	3.6
Blessing song	2.9

[a] Ten 100-word samples from each genre were selected by choosing transcriptions from what my assistants and I considered "relatively typical" performances. We selected samples from every tenth page of these texts until a full ten samples were reached. While I made every effort to be systematic, I provide these statistical compilations less to make a de-contextualized and authoritative claim of representativeness than as a way of offering a suggestive dimension on the ultimately contextual meanings of ritual speech in the lives of the Weyewa.

gorizing function, labeling certain kinds of situations and events in sociocentric terms. Thus the "there by me" in Weyewa discourse may not refer to the actual sender, but to a speaker created in a reported speech frame, such as a spirit or a person who is not present. Nonetheless, such usages—particularly when they occur in a wide variety of inflections—create the impression of multiple, differentiated individual personalities participating in discursive interaction. Examples are discussed in Chapter Five on divination.

Personal Pronouns

In Weyewa ritual ideology, non-authoritative, but contextualized speech is also personal and individuated. After a long night of placation oratory, one of my assistants complained about a particular speaker: "His speech is full of 'I, I, I, I'." A frequent admonition of ritual orators is that speaking participants not behave like "puffed up cocks, like coy dogs," and instead subordinate the self and its personal interests to the collective 'word' of the ancestors. Highly contextualized speech makes specific and frequent reference to particular individuals in performance event, while ancient and ancestral speech, if it makes such references at all, mentions the names of apical ancestors, from whom a large number of the audience share common descent. While copious indications of individuals in the actual speech event are appropriate in certain circumstances, such as divination, it is negatively valued in other circumstances, such as placation rites.

Personal pronouns are an important means by which a language links speech to individuals or cultural categories of individuals. Almost all languages,

Table 7: Free-Standing Personal Pronouns in Weyewa

Pronoun	Translation
Yauwa	I, me
Wou	You [singular]
Nya	He/him, she/her, it
Hito	We/us [inclusive]
Yamme	We/us [exclusive]
Yemmi	You [plural]
Hidda	They, them

Table 8: Frequency of Free-Standing Personal Pronouns in Four Genres of Weyewa Ritual Speech (average number of occurrences in sample 100-word texts)

Genre	Average no.
Divination	5.7
Zaizo	5.5
Chant	2.1
Blessing	0.0

however, have ways of avoiding or emphasizing personal references. In Weyewa, most verbs are prefixed for subject, and more optionally for object. For emphasis, however, an additional, free-standing pronoun may be added (see Table 7). Free-standing subject pronouns usually follow the predicate, as in

ku-deku takka na bongga **yauwa**
I follow truly that dog   **I**
'I really followed that dog'

where the (boldfaced) first person singular pronoun *yauwa* serves to emphasize the role of the subject in the action described by the verb. Such pronouns may also precede indirect and direct objects.

In speech events such as divination, free standing personal pronouns are especially frequent. They differentiate participants into various roles as speakers, addressees, and third person objects of reference; they can also serve to delineate multiple and shifting points of view and distinctive voices. The personae that emerge in divination are numerous and related to one another in complex ways, and pronouns bear much of the weight of differentiating them. By contrast, in 'chants' and particularly in 'blessing songs' the language is relatively impersonal: there are few personae introduced in these narratives, and even those interrelationships are relatively clear to the audience. Thus personal pronouns are rarely emphasized and repeated. These contrasts are reflected in Table 8.

Reported Speech

An important feature of Weyewa contextualized speech is dialogue. Dialogue suggests fragmentation of discourse into distinct positions, lack of complete uniformity and unanimity, and multiple performers expressing unique, subjective perspectives in the context of interaction. While in some circumstances, images of dialogic turn-taking are positively valued, (e.g., *mbyali monno mbyali*, 'one side then another [speaks]'), as in litigation and marriage negotiations, they can also connote disorder. I recorded the comments of one sponsor of a placation rite who warned before its beginning that he did not want 'each man to speak his mind' (*tekki dou, tekki dou*) back and forth in a dialogic fashion. Indeed, a common image for a lack of unity is dialogic genres of song and riddling used in the neighboring districts of Lawonda and Wanukaka:

ndau kedeka Lawonda-kana	do not make riddles like Lawondans
ndau lawiti Wanokaka-kana	do not sing [cryptic] Wanokakan songs

As V. N. Volosinov (1973:117) has remarked, the "productive study of dialogue presupposes . . . a profound investigation of the forms used in reported speech, since these forms reflect basic and constant tendencies in the active reception of other people's speech, and it is this reception, after all, that is fundamental also for dialogue." Deborah Tannen (1986) observes that such encoding of one another's speech through quotation is a way of creating and maintaining involvement in narrative discourse rather than making an exact copy of what was said. Reported speech, she argues, is "constructed dialogue."

Attributions of speech to another source are a remarkably common contextualizing feature of certain genres of Weyewa ritual discourse. These imputations of discursive practice are accomplished largely through the use of a category of verb I have come to call a locutive.[8] After some consideration, I have rejected the label quotative which in common parlance in linguistics refers to a distinct class of uninflectable particles whose import is to collectivize speech rather than individuate it (Whorf 1956:119).[9]

Although these locutive verbs impute individualized and particularized experience to the source, this experience is not differentiated linguistically according to sensory or perceptual criteria, as is the case with the evidentials described in Wallace Chafe and Joanna Nichols (1986). The use of these "locutives" does not depend on the nature of the evidence on which a statement is based, or the modality through which the information was received. Reported speech phrases in Weyewa are not differentiated according to whether the speaker received the framed information through hearsay, or through visual, olfactory, or tactile cues.

Instead, an important dimension of choice in Weyewa locutives is inflection for speaker and hearer. While these *verba dicendi*, or "verbs of saying," are obligatorily inflected for speaker/subject, they are only optionally declined for hearer/recipient. Locutives are usually postposed to the statement that is being quoted. In most contexts, the verb can be glossed 'say' or 'will.'

a. Locutives inflected for speaker
lunggu	'I say'
lummu	'you say'
hinna	'he, she, it says'
limma	'we (excl.) say'
hinda	'we (incl.) say'
limmi	'you (pl.) say'
hidda	'they say'

b. Suffixes for hearer/recipient
-ngga	'me'	*-ma*	'us' excl.
-nggu	'you'	*-nda*	'us' incl.
-ni, -na	'him, her, it'	*-minggi*	'you all'
		-ndi	'them'

A sample inflection: *lummu-ngga* 'you say to me'

In Weyewa ritual speech, reported speech frames "contextualize" discourse by particularizing it. That is, by defining the author, one frames it as belonging to a specific party and thus not to the group as a whole. Reported speech multiplies the perspectives and points of view in discourse by clearly differentiating the sources of utterances (Bakhtin 1981). In Weyewa ritual ideology, this differentiated, individuated, and particularized speech is likened to the 'tips' of a tree in contrast to the more authoritative, monologic 'trunk,' which, in a single, unitary 'voice of the ancestors,' speaks for the entire group of descendants.

In addition to particularizing discourse, locutives have a distancing effect, as when a diviner calls attention to the exclusiveness of his own particular position by claiming shared speech with the source, excluding the hearers:

O ka ba hinna-ko	O if that is the case
ba lummu-do-wangga . . .	if that is what you say to me . . .

that is, the spirits are communicating exclusively *to him*. More commonly, locutives communicate distance by differentiating the two parties in a dialogue—for example, "that's what you say, but this is what I say." At the same time, in such cases, the speaker is by implication more closely knit to the members of the party with whom he shares discourse.

The differences in the frequency of locutives in the Weyewa genres of misfortune ritual are noted in Table 9.

Table 9: Frequency of Locutives in Four Genres of Weyewa Ritual Speech (average number of occurrences in sample 100-word texts)

Genre	Average no.
Divination	5.67
Zaizo	2.50
Chant	2.50
Blessing	0.00

Discourse Markers

As Weyewa spokesmen struggle to identify, placate, and finally satisfy the spirits, they progressively organize their discourse in ways that approximate the 'voice of the ancestors.' This monologic 'voice' is an ancestral charter narrative in which the main aspects of their way of life are established. It is held to be a model of coherence, not just of discourse but of social life in general. The ideal of how this kind of coherence should be expressed is a list of place names and personal names.

From the standpoint of ritual ideology, discourse markers can be unwelcome reminders of the non-referential, interactive, and dialogic nature of the process of narrative construction. Unlike proper names, these devices such as *nyakka* 'so that,' *ne ba hinna* 'now,' *takka* 'but' do not refer to objects or places in the past; they instead are "sequentially dependent elements which bracket units of talk" (Schiffrin 1987:31; cf. Hymes 1981:102–105, 151ff.) in the here and now. While they are relatively detachable syntactically from a sentence, they are particularly common occurrences in the initial position in an utterance. Prosodically quite variable, they are *meta-communicative*, in that they are concerned with the structure of the message and the relationship among participants rather than the referent of the message (Bateson 1972; Schiffrin 1987:328–329).[10] Among other things, they function to create discursive order in the immediate performance situation.

Although discourse markers in general help to create coherence (Schiffrin 1987), some do so by *differentiating* both participants and ideas, while others achieve this by *fusing* and *linking* them logically. The former might be viewed as a "contextualizing" strategy, insofar as it points toward the relations between language and its extra-linguistic features; while the latter might be viewed as a "entextualizing" strategy, insofar as it points toward text-internal features of the discourse. I suggest that there are preferences for particular kinds of discourse markers in certain genres (see Table 10) and that these preferences are related to the coherence requirements for particular ritual events. In divination, instead of using markers that boldly fuse meanings and create equivalences between

Table 10: Frequency of Discourse Markers in Four Genres of Weyewa Ritual Speech (average number of occurrences in sample 100-word texts)

	Average no.			
Genre	*'but'*	*'now'*	*'well'*	*'so that'*
Divination	7.1	6.3	1.0	0.7
Zaizo	2.0	1.1	5.7	1.5
Chant	0.0	0.7	0.0	8.3
Blessing	0.0	0.7	0.0	7.1

clauses, the diviner's use of the markers such as 'but,' and 'now' create coherence across (couplet) clauses by *contrasting* them (cf. the "brittle segmentation" of Ndembu divinatory symbolism; Turner 1975:232–33). This verbal strategy makes sense in an atmosphere of communicative uncertainty, with a diverse audience, and multiple points of view. In *zaizo* placation rites, on the other hand, one of the most salient discourse markers is *malla* 'well,' a marker of response. In these all-night dialogues between orators and a gong- and drum-accompanied singer, one of the main goals is to create an interactional icon of harmonious communication with angry spirits—and thereby placate them. Use of *malla* indexes this responsiveness. Finally, text comparisons show that *nyakka* 'so that' is by far the most preferred of discourse markers in rites of fulfillment: 'chants' and 'blessing songs.' These markers create coherence by linking the ideas expressed in prior couplets with upcoming couplets in terms of a cultural logic of cause and result.

In divination ceremonies, the lexicalized clause *ne ba hinna* 'now' and *takka* 'but' are especially frequent as discourse markers which place ideas in relation to one another as *contrastive*. In the following divination text, a performer's use of 'but now' calls attention to himself and to the implied contrast of what he has said before with what he is about to say. After he affirms that he has indeed completed the act of sitting properly in the place for an appropriate performance of a divination ceremonial (i.e., 'scratching the house post'; lines 3–5), he then contrasts his *completed* act with matters left *undone* (i.e., neglected ritual obligations; line 7):

newwe ba lunggu	here [by me] I say	1
ba ku-tomana	that I arrive at	
zokala kandanga	the jointed spot for stretching	
ba ku-dukki-na	that I come to	
kerita pari'i	the place for scratching the house post	5
takka ne ba hinna-we	**but now**	
ba katinna tedda kati wo'u	as you have left partially chewed fodder	

In line 6, the import of 'now' is not so much to direct the listener's attention to some absolute temporal frame of reference (e.g., in opposition to 'then') as to shift the audience's attention to the speaker's development of ideas, asking them to notice the contrast of the upcoming discourse with what preceded it. Its use calls attention to the speaker, insofar as it is up to him to provide the new and upcoming material (cf. Schiffrin 1987:228ff). The use of *takka* 'but,' as in English, likewise establishes contrast with prior discourse and calls attention to the speaker's role in supplying coherence.

In *zaizo* placation rites, a particularly frequent discourse marker is *malla*, which might be glossed as 'well.' Like its English counterpart, it begins speaking turns and displays the speaker in a particular participation status—that of the respondent (Schiffrin 1987:103). One important function of *malla* in Weyewa *zaizo* performances is ratification. The following pattern, in which an orator addresses a *zaizo* singer and has his participation ratified with *malla*, is typical:

orator: *dyoo, zaizo!*	hail, singer!	1
singer: *malla!*	well?!	
orator: *zaizo!*	singer!	
singer: *malla!*	well?!	
orator: *li'i-nda-ndi li'i* . . .	Our voice to them was the voice . . .	5

Another important function is to mark what follows as a response to a question, as opposed to a continuation of someone else's ideas in discourse. Orators in *zaizo* often precede their remarks in this way with *ka malla*. . . . 'well, then . . .'

In the following text, an orator responds to the rhetorical question of why a misfortune occurred, by replying that the ancestors Dangu Ngíndi and Mángu Mema hear and see everything (i.e., they were aware of the sins and shortcomings of their descendants and were punishing them). He precedes his answer by saying 'well' on line 2:

ba appa-ko pa-hinna dénga-na?	so why did this happen?	1
ka malla	well then	2
na katillu rénge wondo	with ears like a *wondo* bird	3
na mata eta mbali	and narrowed eyes	4
Dangu Ngíndi	Dangu Ngíndi hears	5
Mángu Mema	Mángu Mema sees	6

A discourse marker with a strikingly different set of pragmatic and textual meanings is *nyakka* 'so that.' Its textual meaning is to mark one clause as being the *result* or *outcome* of another. It suggests a logical, almost syllogistic progression of ideas, usually expressed in narrative rather than dialogic form. It is by far the most common form of discourse marker in the narrative genres characterizing the final stages of rites of atonement. Although the selection of clauses depends partly on pragmatic factors, such as audience knowledge and participation, the primary focus of meaning is on the creation of relations between units of text and the logical inevitability of their relations.

In the following text from a 'blessing song,' the singer suggests that since traditional feasting practice has become so inadequate ('no more chickens crow') in Nyuralele (place name for Weyewa), the participants are now all swarming ('like rats in a row') toward a major ritual event (i.e., the one in which they are currently engaged).

Nda pa-kuku-da-we manu-ngge	No more chickens cluck,	1
nda pa-weka-da-we wawi-ngge	no more pigs squeal,	2
Nyura lele Mayongo	here in Nyura Lele Mayongo	3
We'e Pabobaaa Yarraaaooo	here in We'e Paboba Yarra	4
[		
chorus: ooooo	ooooo!	
nyakka-na lolungo malawo-na	**so that** we proceed like rats in a row	6
nyakka-na burungo tawewe-na	**so that** we parade like pheasants	7
	in formation	

In non-ritual, non-narrative speech, its use may signal the end of the speaker's turn at talk, after which the next participant may respond to the implied conclusion. In this case, however, it connects logical statements in the development of a narrative that is simultaneously described and enacted.

Textualizing Devices in Weyewa Ritual Discourse

While demonstratives, personal pronouns, some discourse markers, and locutives tend to link speech closely to its situation of use, there are important "textualizing devices" in the Weyewa verbal repertoire, which function within their ritual performances to detach discourse from the immediate contraints of utterance and attach it to a shared, coherent, and authoritative tradition: 'the voice of the Mother, the voice of the Father.' In this section I will consider the role of dyadic parallelism and proper names in the creation of such texts.

Weyewa themselves consider couplets to be the central characteristic of authoritative texts. The fundamental principle of parallelism has two main aspects (Fox 1977b:60). The first is the general tendency of poetic language to employ repetition in the form of "recurrent returns" and "repeated figures" and sounds (Jakobson 1966:399). In this respect, parallelism is a manifestation of the linguistic and cognitive binary principle of opposition, in that repetition forces comparison, on an auditory, semantic, and grammatical level, between linguistic elements. The second more specific usage of the term has to do with parallelism as a customary poetic practice in particular cultures. It refers to the tendency of poems and other literary discourse to be composed of pairs of lines. It is considered "canonical" when it enjoys an obligatory and conventional status as a compositional principle. Such is the case in Weyewa ritual speech, which consists largely of couplets.

This parallelistic principle in speech is also elaborated into a kind of cosmic principle. As Fox puts it, "It is a linguistic convention that social wisdom and indeed significant knowledge of a ritual sort must be expressed in dual terms—in binary or dyadic form" (Fox 1980a:16). Rodney Needham goes further: "The significance of a particular is established by linking it in a contrastive association with an opposite particular" (Needham 1980:41).[11]

The presence of couplets in Weyewa ritual speech is salient for the Weyewa themselves. When describing its general shape to me, informants repeatedly used the phrase 'speech that is paired' (panewe a pa-nggobba). If one inadvertently pairs two lines of speech in non-ritual settings, it may draw laughter and the comment, "why are you speaking ritual speech?" Minimally, a couplet consists of two conventionally paired lines, in which the first is paralleled by the second in rhythm and meaning.[12] A stock example of a couplet is as follows:

kadu nda pa-toda	horn that cannot be clipped
ulle nda pa-roro	tusk that cannot be cut

a couplet that refers to an invincible, irrepressible person.

Although parallelism is indeed an impressive characteristic in Weyewa ritual speech, it is not uniform stylistically or semantically. For instance, not all ritual speech genres use couplets to the same degree. Some genres, such as blessing songs, are composed entirely of couplets, while others, such as divination, generously employ contextualizing devices to link the couplets to their immediate social circumstances. Differences in the frequency of couplets can be seen by counting the number of words that are not part of any couplet phrase in the four genres of misfortune ritual listed in Table 11.

Far from a simple pairing of one line with another, parallelism in Weyewa is poetically complex, exhibiting considerable variation in line length, line-internal and inter-lineal rhythmic patterning, semantic relations and lexical provenience. Weyewa ritual speech couplets reveal their complexity along several dimensions. Phonologically, couplets create parallelisms in a variety of ways.

Table 11: Frequency of Unpaired Words in Four Genres of Weyewa Ritual Speech (average number of occurrences per sentence in sample 100-word texts)

Genre	Average no.
Divination	4.2
Zaizo	2.0
Chant	2.0
Blessing	0.12

Some are almost entirely repetitive from one line to the next (except for the final elements in boldface):

ne'e kapu'u dadi **roro**	that was the origin of the **firesaw**
ne'e kapu'u dadi **koze**	that was the origin of **firedrill**

and some are internally repetitive lexically:

nya a **nakka**-*na pa-***nakka**	he who **holds** the **holder**
nya a **toro**-*na pa-***toro**	he who **grips** the **gripper**

or alliteratively—

ba **woli** *wale*	If one invites an answer
ba **dande**-*wi déngi*	If one solicits a request

—while still others have virtually no formal repetitions at all (except for rhythm):

ndara ndende kiku	horse with a standing tail
bongga mette lomma	dog with a black tongue

One important resource for the creation of parallelisms is the importation of words from neighboring languages (cf. Fox 1974:80ff.). While the overwhelming majority of ritual speech words are of Weyewa provenience, many couplets create strikingly different sounding synonyms by drawing on comparable lexical items from the languages of Kodi, Laura, Loli, Anakalang, and even Indonesian.

In the following examples, some aspect of the word (and its corresponding gloss) written in capital letters is of non-Weyewa orgin. The provenience is listed below the couplet in parentheses. In the following couplet not only is the word *asu* 'dog' foreign to the Weyewa language, but the phoneme *s* is relatively rare and is restricted to the eastern districts (Anakalang, Kambera)

ndoli-bai ndara	the horse is tired
ndodo-bai ASU	the DOG is exhausted

As a result of this tradition of lexical borrowing to make word pairs, certain sounds appear in Weyewa ritual speech that are absent in the everyday 'plain speech.' The phonemes /gh, j/, for example, all occur in *panewe tenda* couplets, but not normally in colloquial language.

Sometimes, this borrowing occurs to create a synonymous pair. For example, in the couplet (Laura)

ana PANEGHE	child of SPEECH
ana kandauke	child of talk

which refers to a particular deity, the Lauranese word *paneghe* 'to speak' is borrowed to form a pair synonymous pair with the word *kandauke* 'to talk.' In *paneghe*, the Laura phoneme /gh/, a voiced velar fricative, is a sound that does not occur in the everyday Weyewa inventory of sounds.

In a similar way, the voiced, alveopalatal affricate /j/ does not occur in Weyewa except in ritual speech words borrowed from any one of the neighboring languages of Anakalang, Wanukaka, Memboru, or Kodi. For example, the couplet

| *na ndikirai JARA-nggu* | my HORSE turns back |
| *na winggirai bongga-nggu* | my dog reverses directions |

which refers to a change of pace in a ritual speaking event, contains the word *jara* where the common Weyewa word with the same meaning is *ndara*.

Weyewa couplets do not borrow prefixes and suffixes from other languages as often as they borrow sounds and words. In general, affixations to the verb are Weyewa in origin and function to create a "frame" within which lexical variation takes place. When such morphological transformations occur in ritual speech, they almost always happen in the confines of a couplet; curiously, it is relatively rare to find heavily affixed verbs outside a couplet environment.

ka toma-na	as he arrives	1
teppe pa-pa-wekkara	at the welcome mat	2
ka dukki-na	as he reaches the	3
mama pa-pa-ndalara	prepared betel quid	4

In the couplet above, the boldfaced affixes highlight the parallel morphological processes occuring between lines 1 and 3, and between lines 2 and 4.

Couplets have semantic "kernel" elements to them, which become the basis of poetic expansions and elaborations. A very common couplet in *zaizo* performances is the following, which indicates that the requisite performers are present.

| *mattu mata* | the faces are complete |
| *tanga wiwi* | the lips are paired |

As far as I know, this couplet can not be further de-composed and still retain its original meaning, but it can be expanded and syntactically transformed, although its parallel structure remains intact:

nda mattu-po-ma mata	our faces are not yet complete	1
nggyanggara kaderi	in line and looking up	2
nda tanga-po-ma wiwi	our lips are not yet paired	3
ndondukana zazi	reined in and ready	4

The additional parallel lines on lines 2 and 4, 'in line and looking/reined in and ready,' cannot stand alone as a couplet by themselves; they may only be added to the relatively autonomous "kernel" couplet *mattu mata/tanga wiwi* 'faces complete/lips paired.' Male Weyewa spokesmen generally feel that longer couplets are better than shorter ones, and less repetitive ones are better than repetitive ones. One well known ritual orator often boasted to me about the length of the couplets he used in ceremonies. He felt such extended lines were preferable when performing the 'voice of the ancestors.'

Syntactic form is a resource in the entextualization process in at least two ways: (1) it figures in the creation of parallel lines of couplets; and (2) it is a way of creating supra-couplet structures. The lines of couplets are almost always parallel syntactically. A particularly common structure is Verb Phrase + Object. Although the verb is inflected for subject, the independent subject slot at the end of the string is left unfilled.

nda ku-tura tana pamba	I don't cultivate new rice fields
Neg I cultivate land pond-field	
nda ku-poka ala omba	I don't clear virgin jungle
Neg I clear jungle fresh	

Another common, but more marked, syntactic structure in a couplet line is a topicalization of the subject with the particle *a*. In the following couplet, each line consists of Subject + Particle + Verb Phrase:

nya a pobba wali pu'u	(it is) he (who) throttles from the base
nya a para wali lawi	(it is) she (who) thrashes from the tip

The creation of supra-couplet structures is particularly frequent in the latter stages of the atonement process, in 'blessing songs' and 'chants.' In general, this is accomplished by filling one of the (VOS) syntactic slots with its own couplet, thereby making it impossible to interpret the meaning of the phrase without a second couplet to complete the sentence. In the following example, the (intransitive) verb phrase is expressed in a single couplet, followed by another couplet that functions as the sentence final subject, thus creating a clear stanza-like textual structure.

Nyakka-na lolungo malawo-na	Thus they proceed like rats in a row
nyakka-na burungo tawewe-na	thus they parade like pheasants in formation
ngara ndukka ole Inna-nggu	all of our Mothers
ngara ndukka ole Ama-nggu	all of our Fathers

A similar, but less disjunctive effect can be achieved by extending a single line of a couplet to include a free-standing subject phrase, which in this case is the proper name of an ancestor:

ne ba na pa-lengge-we lawi-na	thus he orders the tip to depart
Mbyulu Nggollu Wolla	Mbyulu Nggollu Wolla
na ba na pa-kedde-we pu'u-na	thus she orders the base to rise
Winni Tenda Zapa	Winni Tenda Zapa

Semantic Conventions of Couplets

In addition to their phonological and syntactic roles, Weyewa ritual speech couplets are conventional and memorized units of meaning, with their own semantic integrity. The semantic functions of these units of meaning, however, vary significantly, from evocative metaphorical reference to denotation and "typification" with proper names.

Couplets in Weyewa ritual speech are regarded as bearing a fixed meaning that indexes the 'voice of the ancestors.' What a number of scholars seem to have focussed on, however, are the meanings of the individual word-pairs, such as the 'tail/tongue' opposition above. Leon-Portilla describes the couplet style of the pre-Columbian Mayans in the following terms:

> It consists of uniting two words which complement each other, either because they are synonyms or because they evoke a third idea, usually a metaphor. . . . Examples of this are the following: flower-and-song, which metaphorically means poetry, art and symbolism; skirt-and-blouse, which implies woman in her sexual aspect; seating and mat which suggests the idea of authority and power; face and heart which means personality (Leon-Portilla 1969:76–77; cited in Bricker 1974:368).

In Fox's analysis of Rotinese parallelism, he attempts to carry the semantic analysis of word-pairs a step further. He argues that "each dyadic set [i.e., word pair] is a unique semantic grouping" (Fox 1975:110). By charting which words pair with which and by "tracing the relations among the semantic elements," Fox believes that we can "get a glimpse of the cultural code of the Rotinese" (Fox 1975:111).

The Weyewa would appear to present an interesting contrast since they do not evaluate the meanings of the individual word-pairs apart from the context of a couplet; that is, they do not see the lexical pairs as "unique semantic groupings." Thus the pairing of horse with dog in the couplet,

ndara ndende kiku	horse with a standing tail
bongga mette lomma	dog with a black tongue

which refers to a good orator, has a different meaning altogether from that derived by juxtaposing the horse and the dog in the couplet

na ndikkirai ndara	the horse turns back
na winggirai bongga	the dog reverses directions

which refers to a change of mood, pace or subject in a particular activity. It is even sometimes the case that a given lexical pair in a couplet has no particular significance other than a rhythmic one. For instance, some word-pairs seem to contribute little to the meaning of a couplet as a whole and function merely to emphasize the rhythmic relationship between the two lines. In the couplet

na ndolibai ndara-nggu	my horse is tired
na ndodabai bongga-nggu	my dog is exhausted

which refers to the fatigue of the participants in an all-night speaking event, my informants told me that the horse/dog pair was not linked with the idea of weariness, but was placed there *ka na-ndua punni-na* 'so that it has a nice sound.'[13] The importance of rhythm in the formation of couplets is further underscored by the observation that the Weyewa words for representing the opposition of "left/right"—a key opposition that finds expression in house architecture, marriage relations, and altar symbolism—are not themselves paired as part of a couplet. This may well have to do with the discrepancy in syllable length between the two terms: the word for 'right' (*kawana*) is three syllables in length, while the term for 'left' (*wello*) is only two. Pairing the two of them would violate Weyewa norms of euphony and style.

Proper Names

Not all Weyewa ritual speech couplets *refer* to their objects in the same way. Rather than designate categories, couplets consisting of proper names appear to denote unique individuals—persons and places. Despite the apparently specific nature of these dyadic sets, they are in fact the sets most closely guarded and intimately associated with the spiritual authority of the 'voice of the ancestors.' The value attached to these proper names can be glimpsed in the following couplet for the creator spirit:

nda pa-tekki tamo	one whose name is not uttered
nda pa-zuma ngara	one whose epithet cannot be mentioned

In Weyewa ritual speech, the couplet names of places and persons are reverential titles, whose use not only indexes respect of the speaker toward the referent, but also indexes the authority of the referent itself. As mentioned in the previous chapter, one must not frivolously pronounce the name of a spirit, for in many contexts it is tantamount to inviting the deity to engage in an act of exchange.

Table 12: Frequency of Couplet Proper Names in Four Genres of Weyewa Ritual Speech (average no. of occurrences in sample 100-word texts)

Genre	Average no.
Divination	0.7
Zaizo	2.0
Chant	4.0
Blessing	3.4

While everyone in Weyewa has a binomial proper name (assigned shortly after birth by observing which of a recited list of names of agnatic ancestors evokes a sucking response in the infant), only particularly wealthy and powerful individuals have couplet names, which usually associate the individual with possessions acquired in lavish feasts. Likewise, places (e.g., villages or houses) that have couplet names (sometimes a long list of them) receive such epithets in the context of particularly significant ritual performances associated with that location. While these names do suggest uniqueness and individuality, they imply a renown that *encompasses* and transcends rather than divides. Persons and places who bear such names are spoken of as 'centers' 'cores' and 'sources.'

As Table 12 shows, couplet names are relatively infrequent in rites of atonement until one approaches the textual pole of ritual discourse. In divination, reference to unique individuals is ordinarily accomplished using personal pronouns, often free-standing ones. Specific ancestral spirits may be addressed quite directly in a vocative mode:

wo'u, Lyende!	you, Lende!
a pa-ana-na pare	who gave birth to the rice
a pa-zuzu-na lelu	who suckled the cotton

This avoidance of couplet names in divination is also true of place names. In the corpus of divination texts I have collected, places are simply denoted by either demonstrative pronouns or colloquial binomial names—for example, *Pu'u Nu'u* 'Base of the Coconut Tree.' In *zaizo* placation rites, use of couplet names for people and places is more frequent, as orators construct narrative accounts—'the path that was traveled' (*lara li pa-li-na*) of how and where particular misfortunes took place.

Couplet names of people and places are an important resource in the construction of authoritative 'words of the ancestors' in the final phases of rites of atonement. Like the writer of the Mayan classic narrative *Popol Vuh*, who Dennis Tedlock observes took "great trouble to set down . . . names and point them out as names," Weyewa ritual spokesmen carefully use proper couplet names in such a way that the "authority of the names seeps over into the events that are constructed around them as the narrative proceeds" (Tedlock 1983:274). Performers set great store by the accurate recitation and dramatic revelation of these names. Inappropriate, non-ritual usages or incorrect delivery can provoke harsh criticism by other participants and even supernatural retribution.

The use of couplet names in chants and blessing songs highlights their textual character. A couplet name is a conventional symbol of the non-uniqueness of an individual or location; it suggests a significance to a particular place or person that extends beyond the denotation of a definite object. The unique event, usually a naming ceremony in which the couplet name was bestowed, launches a historical transformative process in which an indexically, situationally established relation comes to be a *symbol*, which stands for, among other things, ancestral authority. This process of "typification" (Parmentier 1987) corresponds in many ways to the process of entextualization in rites of atonement.

ba ku-kedde mángu Inna	as I proceed with my Mother
ne'e Kambiata Lai Tangiobba	to Kambiata Lai Tanggiobba
ka-nyakka ku-kedde mángu Ama	as I proceed with my Father
ne'e Parioro Lele Nammu.	to Parioro Lele Nammu.

ka nyakka ku-tomma-ngge	and so I arrive	5
Lewata Mandiangga	at Lewata the Tall	
ba ma tullura katouda	as three upright [men]	
ka nyakka ku-dukki-ngge	and so I arrive	
Kaliaki Winno Wole	at Kaliaki Winno Wole	
ba ma wolona kambatu mbittaka	as we create a smooth village plaza	
		10

Conclusions

As the essential verbal resource by which Weyewa constitute 'words' of promise and agreement with the spirit world, Weyewa 'ritual speech' is not a homogeneous, stylistically undifferentiated phenomenon. Indeed, it exhibits considerable variation across genres. The tendency among Weyewa ritual speech genres of misfortune toward greater use of conventional couplets and decreasing frequency of demonstratives, pronouns, and locutives corresponds to statistical regularities exhibited in sample texts. But this is admittedly a rough, brute-force measure of a subtle, complex, and symbolically elaborate relationship among different forms of discourse. While it gives us a broad overview of the ways in which genres of speaking fit together within their sociocultural system, we also need to examine in detail the ways in which these regularities are played out in the context of actual events by real speakers. Subsequent chapters take on this task.

Notes

1. Even in the *pazimbala* greetings, the spirits are believed to be present and listening, even if not directly addressed. Moreover, after the performance, animals are sacrificed in their honor.

2. In Kuipers (1986) I described these women's genres as *matekula*. On subsequent research visits, I learned that there is some regional variation in the usage of this term and that what are described *matekula* in some parts of eastern Weyewa are more widely known as *nggeloka* throughout the rest of the district. I have followed the latter usage.

3. While Schegloff was referring primarily to "bits of talk and behavior produced by other than the 'main speaker'" (1982:74), the notion fits equally well to the discourse of a single speaker.

4. Even the personal genres of ritual speech, which do not occur in ritual contexts, gain their peculiar power through an intertextual association of couplet speaking with ancestral authority.

5. Cf. here Roland Barthes's remark: "The kind of discourse that pretends to exist only posterior to events assumes a semiotics in which there are only two terms: the sign and its referent" (Barthes 1967:74).

6. Bernstein (1971) uses context to mean generalized situation types (e.g., "instructional context," "regulative contexts," "imaginative contexts," etc.); Roman Jakobson spoke of context as the "referent" of an utterance (1980:81); Hymes speaks of a "setting or context" (1974:13,23). For others, context refers to the non-linguistic *and* linguistic knowledge of the speaker (e.g., Lyons 1977:574) and/or speaker and audience (Ochs 1979) that is used in interpreting and using speech. Silverstein (1976) and Mertz (1985) develop a particularly sophisticated notion of context as the motivation for differentiating kinds of signs and aspects of signs.

7. Thus, in the Weyewa case, Gumperz's phrase "contextualization convention" would be oxymoronic.

8. I am indebted to Harold Conklin, Webb Keane, and David Konstan for discussions on the use of this term.

9. An example of an uninflectable quotative of this kind is the Hopi *y'aw* "'so' in the sense of 'according to the story'" (Whorf 1956:119).

10. Schiffrin calls attention to Bateson's useful distinction between *meta-linguistic*—discourse whose subject is language *per se*—and *meta-communicative*, which is communication implicitly or explicitly concerned with the codification of the message and the relationships between interlocutors (Schiffrin 1987:303).

11. Actually, Needham overstates his case here. The significance of "particular" need not be established by its semantic "opposite," but occasionally by its synonym, such as in the following couplet referring to a speech partner:

a nggoba-na panewe	the counterpart in speech
a papa-na kandauke	the partner in talk

12. This definition of couplet is in contrast to the usage of Gossen (1984:408–411) in which a "couplet" may or may not involve syntactic parallelism.

13. Still, the detachability of the horse/dog pair for rhythmic purposes does suggest a certain poetic autonomy and conventional stability, even though not a fixed semantic one. Noting these regularities, Fox has called for the compilation and comparison of lists of word-pairs from different regions in eastern Indonesia (Fox 1988:25). He cautions, however, that "these lists would illuminate not so much a common literary tradition as a common metaphorical inheritance" (Fox 1988:25).

5

Sorting out the 'Word': Divination as Dialogic Performance

The striking variety that characterizes Weyewa ritual speaking is more than an ethnographic and linguistic issue: from the standpoint of ceremonial performers, it represents an obstacle to be overcome in the process of restoring spiritual and social order. Divination constitutes the first formal stage in carrying out this task. Cognate with the Indonesian word for 'letter' (*surat*), the Weyewa term *urrata* 'divination' stands for a verbal performance in which specialist speakers attempt to inscribe and thus "fix" the uncontrolled, disorderly communication between humans and the spirit world so that the source of misfortune can be identified and the true 'word' of promise to the ancestors can be re-affirmed and fulfilled. By using a rhetorical strategy emphasizing segmentation, differentiation, and contrast, Weyewa diviners attempt to sort out the principal causes, narrow down the number of relevant 'voices,' and arrive at a single 'path' that explains how the victims arrived at their present predicament.

While divination has been depicted in the ethnographic literature as an effort to control the supernatural through primitive technology, in Weyewa, divination is more appropriately viewed in communicative terms as a dialogue. Weyewa explicitly describe the event as a means of organizing communicative relations, structuring access to valued ideas, and regulating exchanges of the 'word' between humans and the spirit world. The emotional power of the image of dialogue can be appreciated when we understand that for most Weyewa, 'divination' is not a happy event. This first formal step toward atoning for misfortune is clouded by the dreadful emptiness of feeling cut off from communication with the ancestral spirits and by feelings of guilt and responsibility. For the victims, the stony silence of the spirits is likened to a parent abandoning its child—one of the most terrifying experiences a child can have and a major preoccupation of Weyewa myths and folktales. Many deeply affecting narratives recount the pathetic and tragic efforts of orphans who desperately seek to re-establish communicative exchange.

Reconstituting the dialogue with the ancestral 'Mother and Father' is a central theme of divination. This systematic procedure begins when a specialist diviner conducts an interview with the victim and the victim's family. The client acknowledges fault by admitting neglect of ritual obligations to the spirits. This act of contrition is described as the assumption of responsibility for traditional duties and their authentic performance: to 'remember the right horn, and remember the old song.' Then, using simple technical media (a spear or three short ropes), the diviner engages the spirits in a verbal dialogue to determine which spirit is angry, the reason for the wrath, and what might be done about it. He asks that the spirits 'receive my questions, reply to my arguments'—that is, re-establish lines of communication. He proposes segments of a narrative re-construction of the 'path that was traveled' by the victim leading to his or her downfall and asks the spirits for confirmation. The event does not normally include attempts at treatment such as drugs, trances, or massage.

Divination is spoken and not sung, and more oriented toward establishing and contrasting referential meanings than toward exhibiting features of delivery. In general, the language of divination is highly "contextualized" and concerned with creating coherence among several distinct and contrasting points of view by employing quotations, deictic expressions, and discursive markers. This ten-dency toward a rhetoric of differentiation and contrast is expressed through the animal augury that inevitably accompanies every divination performance. By inspecting eggs and the entrails of sacrificed chickens, pigs, and buffalo, Weyewa attempt to sort out the responses of the ancestors to their questions.

Even as the dialogue is re-established, however, the drive for a more en-compassing narrative, monologic representation begins. This is adumbrated in the diviner's preoccupation with reconstructing the 'true' narrative 'path' of mis-fortune and the allusions to the "textual" character of the augury. These "inter-nal dialogues" between context and text, dialogue and narrative, 'tip' and 'trunk,' develop even more fully over the course of the ritual process of atonement con-sidered in subsequent chapters.

Techniques of Weyewa Divination

In the first description of Sumbanese 'divination' through western eyes, a shipwrecked sailor viewed Sumbanese divination technology with more than a little skepticism. In this 1836 report, based on the experiences of a man who apparently lived in Laboya (a neighboring region to Weyewa) for several months, the author focused entirely on the diviner's procedure for manipulating the physical objects of his craft. According to one Weyewa method, the diviner seats himself on a mat in the house and shoves the tip of a spear into the low wall at the base of a sacred house post. Holding his left hand fast on the end of the shaft, he stretches his right hand along its length toward the wall. If his thumb touches the post, this is a yes, and otherwise, the response is no. The writer marvels that "it is indeed extraordinary, that without any priestly trickery, such a belief, so palpably false, should have apparently persisted for so many centuries" (Kruse-man 1836:78). Since the diviner could easily influence the response by adjusting the position of his left hand on the spear, the sailor was not impressed (cf. also Kruyt 1922:480).

Unable to understand the verbal content of the performance, the sailor could not appreciate the dialogic character of the event. Since the visual context

Plate 2: 'Fathoming the spear' divination. Holding his left hand fast on the spearshaft, the diviner stretches towards the wall with his right hand. If he touches the wall, this is a positive sign from the ancestral spirits.

is only part of the performance, and indeed a subordinate part of it, what was being produced was not simply a set of unintegrated, yes-no responses. In fact, the diviner's main task is to create coherence from the chaotic circumstances following a misfortune by balancing, contrasting, and evaluating distinct perspectives and points of view in a way that makes sense both to the spirits and to the human audience. It is a delicate task of social criticism at the same time, as it must adhere to aesthetic norms of verbal performance.

Weyewa actually possess two main forms of *urrata* divination: *ropa kapudda* 'spear divination' (lit. 'fathoming the shaft') and *mowala* 'rope divination' (see Plates 2 and 3). In my experience among Weyewa, *ropa kapudda* is more common, but according to Kruyt (1922:481) rope and a kind of lontar-palm divination are commonly practiced in the eastern parts of the island. Although the rhetorical procedures are nearly identical, a number of diviners to whom I spoke expressed some reservations about the validity of rope divination. Rato Kaduku, for instance, said, "It is easier lie with the *mowala* cords. If you use a spear, you cannot lie. If your hand does not reach, you cannot force it." Despite such misgivings about certain methods, all of them insisted that the method chosen is a matter of personal preference on the part of the diviner.

Although 'rope divination' (*mowala*) apparently occurs in other parts of Indonesia and Sumba (see Kruyt 1901; Kruyt 1922:480 ff.), Weyewa myths repre-

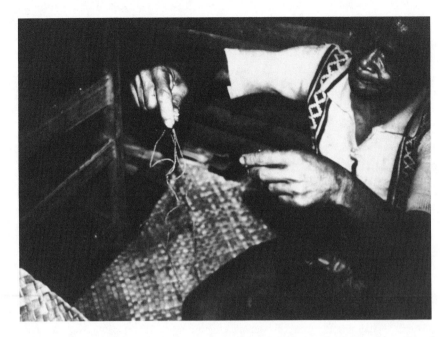

Plate 3: Rope divination. The diviner has just unraveled the tips of the ropes from around his right hand. The tips fall away, indicating a negative response to his question.

sent it as of autochthonous origin.[1] In Weyewa practice, this divination method employs three approximately 40 cm long barkstring cords, each of which is folded in half and wrapped around the index and third finger of the right hand. Thus wrapped, it is difficult to distinguish which of the six exposed rope ends are part of the same cord. The diviner selects two of these, joins each with another cord tip, and then lifts them in the air, leaving the remaining two. If the two strands that are ignored actually are opposite ends of one and the same cord, it will drop to the floor. This is a negative response, while if the cords all remain suspended in either hand, the answer to the posed question is yes (*tama nggollu dana* 'it enters the livestock pen [below the floor]').

Focus on the Neglected 'Word'

When describing their process of conducting divinations, diviners emphasize both the importance of examining the neglect of 'words' of promise to the spirit world and the utter helplessness of clients to accomplish that task. When he first enters the house of a sick person to perform a divination, the diviner Kaduku usually proceeds systematically. He told me:

There are questions one asks, there are questions raised: "How have you been living? What is lacking? Regarding how you have lived, if there have been 'words,' tell me." There are some people who don't know at all how they have been living or why! They just don't know how to think about their own lives! Thus the diviner pays attention; he pays attention to what they say, and it comes out little by little what led up to the illness.

Like a woman sorting out (*pende*) dirt and chaff from the grain in her winnowing basket, the diviner selects certain topics to focus on and rejects others, pointing them toward the issue of the neglected 'word.'

While the divination rituals I attended exhibited considerable variation, all of them turned up ritual neglect as the main reason for misfortune. Sponsors are usually men, acting in their capacity as the ones responsible for the ritual obligations of the household. The victims are both men and women, young and old, and may sometimes even be animals. The seriousness of the calamities varies widely, from singed waistcloths to repeated deaths in the family. The cause for the divination is often expressed in terms of problematic responsibilities to the spirit world. While, in most cases, the victim is assumed to have been neglectful of ritual duties, in some cases, the divination is conducted simply to make sure that there has been no neglect—for example, preceding a major undertaking such as a housebuilding, tombstone-dragging or large-scale feast. To give a sense of the range of causes and explanations, I present in Table 13 data from thirteen cases of divination involving misfortune that I have personally witnessed.

Urrata at Ryandaka, July 1979

In July of 1979, I witnessed an emotionally charged divination event, in which the diviner pleaded with the spirits to re-open communication with the contrite victim of calamity. It occurred in a small isolated garden hamlet, perched on the edge of a broad irrigated plain of wet rice fields. As my assistants and I picked our way slowly down the rocky and steep path to the grass-roofed dwelling, I learned from my friends that the event was prompted by the repeated illness of the victim, Malo Dunga, his wife's death, the failure of his crops, and the death of his horse and water buffalo. The cause of these thunderstrokes of misfortune, he believed, was that he had converted to Christianity and neglected his ritual duties.

As we arrived at the house, we did not pause on the veranda for the customary chew of betel and areca nut, but were invited immediately to climb up inside, indicating that the performance was about to begin. We sat down next to the diviner, Mbani Mata, on woven mats unfurled in the vestibule (*mbali tonga*), and watched as he slit the throat of a chicken and prayed over it, asking the blessing of Malo Dunga's ancestral spirits. Mbani Mata, like other diviners, had had no formal training in the task, joined no secret cult, and fell into no

Table 13: Clients, Causes, and Explanations in Divination

Sponsor (sex/age/status)[a]	Calamity	Explanation
Male, 50 yrs. old, wealthy	Death of wife, mother, nephew	Broken promises to spirits to hold feast, to consecrate harvest
Male, 50 yrs. old, wealthy	Sudden death of nephew	Neglected promise to rebuild house
Male, 37 yrs. old, wealthy	Acutely ill son	Incest in the family
Male, 45 yrs. old, poor	Death of buffalo	Strained relations with wife's ancestors
Male, 70 yrs. old, average	Serious injury to son	Complex history of neglect towards ancestors; failure to rebuild house; bungled harvest ritual
Male, 51 yrs. old, average	Fever	Conversion to Christianity resulted in neglect of ritual duties.
Male, 70 yrs. old, average	Drowning of child, crippling injury of sponsor	Spirits angered over dilapidated altars
Male, 48 yrs. old, wealthy	Singed waistcloth; loss of personal composure	Strained relations with brother over ritual duties
Male, 70 yrs. old, average	Bitter feud between sons	Mutual neglect of ritual duties
Male, 60 yrs. old, wealthy	Death of daughter	Failure to fulfill father's promise to stage a feast
Male, 80 yrs. old, average	Acute illness of daughter-in-law	Son's adultery
Male, 70 yrs. old, poor	Death of wife	Failure to properly bury father
Male, 43 yrs. old, wealthy	Collapse of house	Neglect of ritual duties

[a] Ages are approximate, since only Weyewa born since World War Two are likely to know their age with any precision. By "status," I simply mean whether the sponsor is considered 'wealthy' (*ata pote*), 'average' (orang biasa [Ind.]), or 'poor' (*ata milla*). The 'wealthy' category roughly corresponds to the noble and priestly categories described in Chapter Two, while the 'poor' category overlaps with the 'slave' status.

trances. What is required is an ability to speak in ritual couplets, some familiarity with the case (Weyewa very rarely call on a complete outsider), a concern for ritual details, and a sympathetic demeanor. One must also be a male. I have heard that sometimes women practice divination in their own homes in desperate situations, but apparently they never do so for payment. Diviners tend to be forty or older, since the older a person is, I was told, the more likely he will be to be familiar, through long experience, with the history of a particular family or lineage who calls on his service.

For his pains, Mbani Mata could expect to receive *mata api* (literally, 'eye of the fire'). This consists usually of a set of three gifts, often a length of cloth, a chicken, and a knife. Diviners may also be paid in cash, which in 1984 amounted to between 2000 and 3000 rupiahs (US$2–3.00). The diviner's payment also varies in relation to the scale of the event. If a pig or water buffalo is slaughtered at the event, the diviner may also receive a substantial slice of the meat. I was sometimes told that the diviner is supposed to receive the right foreleg and the head of any large animal slaughtered, but in practice this seems rare. If, as is usual, only a few chickens are slaughtered, his portion will be correspondingly less. The personal and kinship relations between diviner and client also are a factor determining the pay; the greater the intimacy, the lower the payment. When I asked one wealthy man why he gave his close kinsman, a famous diviner, a small chunk of meat as payment, he replied: "Why should I give him a large payment? Tomorrow he will come by my house and borrow my horse, eat my rice, drink my coffee, and sit on my mats. We always help each other."

In the ward of Kalimbundaramane, where I worked, out of a population of 4,295, there were at least nine men whom I know practiced divination for pay. While most diviners work part-time, there are two men I know who devote their full-time energies to the task, one of whom was the diviner attending Malo Dunga. In both cases, the man's wife and children tend the gardens, while the man's contribution to his household economy consists of his earnings of meat and trade items, such as cloth and knives.

The Pre-divination Discussion

After Mbani Mata finished his prayer offering, several elder male agnatic relatives of Malo Dunga, and one or two elder women, then began a discussion concerning the events leading up to the misfortune—'the path that was traveled' (*lara li pa-li-na*). Typically, these discussions are informal and preliminary, with an "off-stage" character. They consist of voluntary admissions of wrong-doing, and some suggestions as to what might have led up to the misfortune.

After about an hour, Mbani Mata, the diviner, seemed to feel that he had enough information to begin the divination performance. He got out three small ropes (*kalere mowala*) from his waistband, and began the performance by tossing a handful of husked rice towards the corners of the house in an offering to the deceased parents of the victim, Koni (female) and Mbili (male).

The *Urrata*

[Diviner tossed a handful of husked rice behind him and in front of him]

nenati yaza	there's some rice
terre-ngge neti-ngge	take it there

wo'u Kyoni	you, Koni	
·*wo'u Mbili*	you, Mbili	
peina	why	5
ka ku-woti-nggu panewe	do I bring my speech	
wo'u wotto-nggu Kyoni?	to you my sister Koni?	
peina	why	
ka ku-aila-na kandauka	do I haul my talk	
wo'u Mbili lazawa-nggu?	to you, my brother-in-law Mbili?	10

At this point, after a brief pause, Mbani Mata cued the narrative framework of the divination with the generic, formulaic orientation *kedde-na* 'in the beginning.' The story unfolded as he described how, after Mbili paid Koni's brideprice (with 'bits of metal') and took her home to Bondongaingo, he had a dispute with his own family (the 'rope broke off/the bird flew the cage,' lines 20–21). As a result of this altercation, he took Koni back to Lewata, her origin village, because he also had kinfolk there (lines 28–30). As the diviner told it, Mbili then moved on to the village of Nggollu Wini with his wife, but left his young son, Malo Dunga, behind in Lewata, orphaned there with his in-laws (lines 38–40). As a result, Malo Dunga, enraged at being abandoned, had "nothing to say" to his parents (line 42).

Kedde-na na wa'i-ba-ngge	In the beginning, there were	
kandipuka kamba tana, olumu	some bits of iron, y'know [for]	
kabani Umbu Tirrika	the boys of Umbu Tirrika clan	
nyakka wo'u nyango . . .	so you now . . .	
ka atti-kai-ba-ndi	and so also	15
kamba wawi	cloths and pigs were sent	
nyakka	so that	
ne'e-nggu Bondongaingo	you were there in Bondongaingo	
ba ka dukki-we manna-na	and then some time ago	
na-mbiata ndara	the horse's rope broke off	20
na-lera keila	the bird flew the cage	
wo'u Mbili	for you Mbili	
li mbali mata wo'u Mbili	you went out the front door Mbili	
li kere pandalu wo'u Kyoni.	you went out the back door, Koni.	
Eee	Awww	25
wotto-nggu	my sister	
nyakka	so	
ole dadi, wo'u	you came as a kinsman	
nyakka	so	
ngindi-wa Lewata	he took her to Lewata	30
nyakka	so	
ole dadi wo'u	you came as a kinsman	
ka ngindi-wu Nggollu Wini	then you went to Nggollu Wini	
nyakka	so	
na karammi-we pandou-mu.	your place was in order	35

Ba ka hinna-wa
   ka nda'i-ki nati ana mane-mu
   pa-leto belli
   pa-tumba belli
    ba lakawa ki'i-wa
na dukki-we ne ba hinna ne'e
   "ndai-ki pa-tekki-nggu"

Even so
   your son was not there with you
   just tossed off
   just dumped off
    when he was still a little child   40
and so now
   "I have nothing to say"
           [says Malo Dunga]

After a pause, the diviner continued discussing Malo Dunga's plight as victim of misfortune. He told how Malo Dunga, presumably an adult by this time in the story, came down with a fever while living in the Lewata-owned garden village of Lyallara, and afterwards discovered that his wife had died. As a result of these calamities, Malo Dunga "fled" to Christianity (lines 50–52), running away from his ancestors. Though he was peaceful, his crops failed ("nothing grew"; line 60). He began to wonder if his ancestral spirits were angry (line 64) and finally he "returned" to them (line 77).

Hulu wa'i, wangge wa'i
   na mbangata katowa
   malala muttu wekki
    ne'ena tana Lyallara

Way back then
   his head was fevered
   his body was hot   45
    when he was in Lyallara

mbangata katowa
malala muttu wekki
"haa peinggo?" hinna
   na-nggaupa zeda
   na minne-na.
Na-mate, na-kendu poddu dana.

a fevered head
a hot body
"why are you doing this?" he said
   and he discovered the death   50
   there, of his wife.
She died, and he fled to Christianity.

Dukki nemme
   nggobba-na deku-ngge
   na nduwa-we
   na-mandaka-wa.
Na-mandaka-wa,
   nda na-dadi mbarra limma
   nda na-dadi mbarra wa'i
   nda na-timbu-ki-we
    mbarra limma
   nda na-timbu-ki-we
    mbarra wa'i-na

When he got there
   as things turned out
   it was fine   55
   he was at peace.
While he was peaceful,
   his hands gave birth to nothing
   his legs gave birth to nothing
   nothing grew   60
   through the effort of his hands
   nothing grew
   through the effort of his legs

"Ka pei-mu-ngga-ngge?"
   ka hidda-ba
   kulla Inna
   kulla Ama
"oro-do-na-ndi
   li'i ba nda-ku li-we"

"What have you done to me?"
   so said   65
   the spirits of the Mother
   the spirits of the Father
"because
   the voice which I did not follow"

pa-tekki Inna
pa-tekki Ama
nyakka
   "*nda na-timbu-we*
   mbarra limma
   mbarra wa'i"
hinna.
Na-wali.
Na-wali neti.

the words of the Mother   70
the words of the Father
so
   "nothing grew
   through the efforts of his hands
   through the efforts of his legs"   75
he said.
He returned.
He returned here.

The diviner, speaking on Malo Dunga's behalf, said that he promised to bow down before his now-deceased parents, hugging them and embracing them at the waist. He raised this topic (line 89), so that like a small child he might be dragged back home by the waist and buttocks, and like a horse, he might be reined. After all this contrition, he wondered, why won't the spirits accept his pleadings, and answer his arguments?

"'*Ka ku-doupa kemba-na Inna-nggu*'
   lunggu-wa-ngga
'*ka ku-wapu-we kombu-na Ama-nggu*'

   lunggu-wa-ngga"
hinna.

"Then I will hug my Mother by the waist"
   I said to myself   80
'then I will embrace my Father by the
   waist'
   I said to myself"
he said.

"*Pei-mu-ngga*"
   hidda-ba-na
      kulla Inna-nggu
   hidda-ba-na
      kulla Ama-nggu.

"What are you doing to me?"
   said   85
      the spirits of my Mother
   said
      the spirits of my Father.

Nyakka ku-boti-nggu panewe
nyakka ku-aila-nggu kandauka
"*ngga'i ka*
   ba wa'i-ko-ngge
      pa-beti lénga la'a
         ngga'ika wazi kere kambu
ngga'i ka
   ba atti-ko-ngge
      a lénga mai
         ngga'i ka ndabi zazi ndara"
hinna pa-tekki-na-nggu
ana mane-mu
wo'u Mbili!

So I brought up this topic of speech
so I raised this matter of talk with you   90
"so that
   if there was
      something that was tossed too far
         let it be dragged back on its butt
so that   95
   if there was
      something that went off too far
         let the reins of the horse jerk it back"
these are the words to you
by your male child   100
oh Mbili!

"*Ka 'peina*
   ndau zima li'i pa-tuwa?

   ndau wale wata?
   ne ba hinna!'

"So 'why
   won't you receive the voice of
                  pleadings?
   won't you respond to arguments?
   right now!"   105

lummu-ndi	you say that to those
zora-urra	spirits:
Lyali	Lali
a pa-ana-nggu pare	who gave birth to the rice
a pa-zuzu-nggu lelu	who suckled the cotton 110
hinna pa-tekki-na-nggu	such were his words to you
nati ana kabinne-nggu	my nephew
monno	and
hinna pa-tekki-na-nggu	so were his words to you
ana mane-nggu.	my male child. 115

The diviner then suggested that, in light of the fact that the contrite Malo Dunga has now remembered his customary duties, the ancestor should ask himself why he shouldn't resume dialogue with him once again. If the ancestral spirit does agree to say that, then he should signify this in the configuration of cords. When the ropes fell away, signifying a "no" answer, the diviner angrily asked why. After all, the diviner protested, Malo Dunga has suffered a calamity (line 140), his crops failed (line 145), and he is now contrite (line 147).

Nya-do ka ba hinna-ko-ngge	So, if that is the case
"na-lolo-ko-wa	"if he remembers how to sing
lawiti mangga muri	the old song
ana-nggu	my son
na ape-ko-wa	if he recalls 120
kadu ndou kawana	the horn on the right side
wolla-nggu	my offspring
a ka nda ku-zima tuwa	why shouldn't I receive his pleadings
a ka nda ku-wale wata?"	why shouldn't I respond to his
	arguments?"
lummundi, Mbili!	you say that to them, Mbili! 125
zandekka "lunggu" lummu!	just once, "I say that" you say!
Bau zima-do tuwa	If you receive his pleadings
bau wale-do wata	if you respond to his arguments
tama nggollu dana!	fall into the corral!
ba ndau zima-do tuwa	if you don't receive his pleadings 130
ba ndau wale-do wata	if you don't respond to his arguments
lángo tanda	then let the sign be
kawukku-na zai-zai-mo!	the binding coming apart!

[Diviner joins the tips of the cords and unravels them; the ends fall apart]

"Indaki"!	"No!"
appa ka nyakka hinna-do-ngga?	why did he say that to me? 135
ka "nda ku-wale wata!?"	Why say "I don't respond to the
	arguments?"
ka "indaki!?"	why "no!?"
ba lunggu mema-do-ngge	I say this indeed
ba lenga	because

na dadi-we balango maredda
na dadi-we podda lara dana
nyakka nda na-dadi-we
  mbarra limma
nyakka nda na-dadi-we
  mbarra wa'i
na lolo-do lawiti mangga muri
na ape-do kadu ndou kawana

there occurred a calamity in the fields 140
there occurred a mishap in the road
so that nothing grew
  from his hands
so that nothing grew
  from his legs   145
he remembers the old song
he recalls the horn on the right side

Since Malo Dunga had offered blessings upon Mbili, the ancestor, the diviner tried again to urge the spirit, Mbili, to reciprocate by saying that he accepts Malo Dunga with a happy heart. The diviner quoted Malo Dunga as urging Mbili to signify his agreement by letting the cords 'fall into the corral' (line 157). This time, Mbili agreed.

"'ku-malangi-wu ne ba hinna'
  ba hinna-ngga ana mane-nggu
  ka ku-dimba ndua koko

  ku-dimba ndua ate"
ne pa-tekki-mu
  lummu-do Mbili!
  lummu-do Koni!

"'I bless you now'
if that is what he says to me
  let me receive him with a happy
    throat   150
  I accept him with happy heart"
those are your words
  you say that, Mbili!
  you say that, Koni!

Hinna-do-ngge Malo Dunga
  "zandekka 'lunggu' lummu"

So says Malo Dunga   155
  "Right now 'I say' you say that"

Tama nggollu dana!
Keketa . . .
Huuuu, nyado!

Fall into the corral!
Lift it up . . .
Yeahhhhh, OK!

The diviner continued to question the ancestors for about an hour: Are you angry about a botched harvest ritual last year? Was the death of a water buffalo linked to this? Was there a feasting obligation engendered by one of his forefathers that has not yet been fulfilled? Was a 'following spirit' from Malo Dunga's mother's village bothering him? Was this because Malo Dunga's father had failed fully to pay her brideprice? Will you, Mbani Mata asked, show us a definite sign of approval or rejection in the liver of the pig about to be slaughtered?

After Mbani Mata had obtained affirmative answers to these questions, and no one in the immediate audience proposed any others (as occasionally happens), then he requested permission to end the divination and looked for a sign of approval. Once he got it, he took a short rest and then prepared to offer the chickens and pigs to the ancestors as sacrifices. With a serious and contrite demeanor, Malo Dunga began to discuss informally with his family members how many cattle it would require to fulfill these neglected, but nonetheless binding, words of promise.

The Structure of the Text

Unaccompanied by drums, gongs, or other performers, the diviner must create coherence on his own through a variety of pragmatic and rhetorical devices. Although the rhetorical pattern of his speech is initially narrative, this discursive form is represented as something accomplished interactively. He does this by constructing discrete narrative chunks and presenting them for inclusion in, or rejection from, the overall story. This strategy of segmentation, differentiation, or sorting the true 'voice' of the spirits from the false results in the gradual accomplishment of a narrative form: 'the path that was traveled' that leads up to the present misfortune.

Narrative Structure

After the initial offering of rice, the diviner begins with a relatively unvoiced narrative. Each portion of the story is segmented, not by changes in speaking voices, but by narrative framing and orientation devices. For instance, in line 11, he signals the narrative, reportorial frame by using the keying phrase 'in the beginning':

Kedde-na na wa'i-ba-ngge	In the beginning, there was	11
kandipuka kamba tana, olumu	some bits of iron, y'know [for]	
kabani Umbu Tirrika	the boys of Umbu Tirrika clan	

A few lines later, on line 19, the end of the previous frame and the onset of the next frame is signalled by another formulaic phrase, 'and then some time ago':

ba ka dukki-we manna-na	and then some time ago	
na-mbiata ndara	the horse's rope broke off	20
na-lera keila	the bird flew the cage	

Other coherence strategies in organizing the narrative include 'way back then' (line 43), and 'when he got there' (line 53). When dialogue does emerge as reported speech in this early part of the performance (e.g., line 42 below), it is contained within the overall narrative frame of the story, and does not reflect a change in the responsibility for the structure of the discourse.

pa-tumba belli	just dumped off	
ba lakawa ki'i-wa	when he was still a little child	40
na dukki-we ne ba hinna ne'e	and so now	
"ndai-ki pa-tekki-nggu"	"I have nothing to say"	
	[says Malo Dunga]	

Divination as Dialogic Interaction

Despite the palpable fact that only one individual is speaking, and although many of the initial groups of lines are narrative in form, the responsibility for the structure and content of the discourse shifts from that of the diviner alone to include that of the spirit world as well. As this occurs, the pragmatic form dominating the latter half of the text is one of dialogic interaction. The diviner appears to oscillate at times between representing the discourse as authoritative tale on the one hand and emergent dialogue on the other, but the image of dialogue, I would argue, becomes the overriding one. This can be seen in the expressed aims of the diviner, the framing devices that he uses, the use of reported speech, and the ideological meanings of dialogue as an icon of social divisions.

Even from the beginning, the presentation of narrative is framed not as an authoritative monologue, but as a turn at talk. On line 5 of the divination text at Ryandaka, for instance, the diviner justifies the narrative that is to follow as a very long speaking turn, as "speaking" that can be "carried" or "hauled" back and forth between interlocutors.

peina	why	5
ka ku-woti-nggu panewe	do I bring my speech	
wo'u wotto-nggu Kyoni	to you my sister, Koni?	
peina	why	
ka ku-aila-na kandauka	do I haul my talk	
wo'u Mbili lazawa-nggu?	to you, my brother in-law Mbili?	10

Similarly, in another performance I recorded, the narrative act of "telling the path" of the ancestral Mother and Father presupposes an interlocutor, a "partner in talk."

ne bau papa-na panewe	when you are an interlocutor in speech,
ku-tekki-ko lara Inna	I can tell the path of the Mother
ne bau nggobba-na kandauke	when you are a partner in talk
ba ku-tekki lara Ama	I can tell the path of the Father

Beginning with line 64 in the text above, the voice of the ancestral spirits begins to emerge.

"ka pei-mu-ngga-ngge?"	"what have you done to me?"	
ka hidda-ba	so said	65
kulla Inna	the spirits of the Mother	
kulla Ama	the spirits of the Father	

As the tale proceeds, this voice increases in frequency and importance. It eventually becomes clear that the diviner sees the establishment and indeed enactment of dialogue with this voice as one of the goals to be achieved in the ritual.

On line 123, for instance, the diviner urges Mbili, an ancestral spirit, to ask himself why he shouldn't re-open dialogue with his son. He not only describes the act of re-opening dialogue, but asks Mbili to confirm that he wishes to instantiate it:

"a ka nda ku-zima tuwa	"why shouldn't I receive his pleadings
a ka nda ku-wale wata"	why shouldn't I respond to his
	arguments?"
lummundi, Mbili!	you say that to them, Mbili! 125
zandekka "lunggu" lummu	just once, "I say that" you say!

This is indeed a very common expressed goal of divinatory discourse: the accomplishment of dialogic interaction.

After the initial narrative orientation, locutive verbs come to play an increasingly salient role in the differentiation of speaking participants, some of whom are quoting each other. On line 148 of the text from Ryandaka, for instance, the diviner quotes the spirits, who in turn quote Malo Dunga's contrite statement 'I bless you now,' to which they respond by saying "I accept him." After having constructed this dialogue, he urges the spirits to accept the authorship of that statement, resulting in a quote within a quote:

"'ku-malangi-wu ne ba hinna'	"'I bless you now'
ba hinna-ngga ana mane-nggu	if that is what he says to me
ka ku-dimba ndua koko	let me receive him with a happy
	throat 150
ku-dimba ndua ate"	I accept him with happy heart"
ne pa-tekki-mu	those are your words
lummu-do Mbili	you say that, Mbili!
lummu-do Koni	you say that, Koni!

The Ideological Significance of Dialogue

While on the level of participatory structure, divination is clearly a monologue (there is only one individual producing utterances), Weyewa diviners seem preoccupied with establishing that, on an ideational level, their discourse is dialogic, involving a change of speaker and listener roles, turn-taking, and contingent responses. For them, the dialogic form is itself an ideologically charged sign vehicle which suggests differentiation, segmentation, change, and instability in social relations. In ritual contexts, it is associated with potential challenges to social stability, such as misfortune, or initial interactions with potentially threatening or disruptive outsiders, such as angry spirits, slave traders, marriage partners, or foreigners. Dialogue as a genre is temporary, and occurs at transitional points in human social relations. Its unstable, emergent character suggests movement toward a new relationship.

In comparison to monologic forms of ritual discourse among Weyewa, dialogue does not occur in situations that emphasize solidarity, but rather in those
that stress difference and individuality. Examples of other ritual speech dialogues
beside *urrata* are marriage negotiations, ceremonial greetings (*pazimbala*), placation rites (*zaizo*), and celebration feasts (*woleka*). In each of these, the emphasis is on the resolution or settling of differences among various parties to the
event—between the bride-taking and bride-giving parties, between humans and
the spirit world, or among the living descendants of the ancestors.

Insofar as dialogue implies particularity, individuation and differentiation
among the participants as insiders and outsiders, it is something to be overcome
in the search for order, stability, and calm. Divination is but a phase in a quest
for resolution. But dialogue is better than no communication at all. Talking to
oneself is an image of utter desolation among Weyewa, a sign of total despair or
even insanity. Thus the diviner begins by depicting himself as engaged in conversation, actively participating in talk with ancestors:

a papa-na panewe	interlocutor in speech
a nggobba-na kandauka	partner in talk

He depicts the discourse they are involved as a dialogic interplay, with contingent
responses:

nyakka na-mbale li'i panewe	thus he responds to the 'word' of the speech
nyakka na-nonga li'i kandauka	thus he puts forward the 'voice' of his talk

But while a client may take some solace from this depiction of the 'word' (*li'i*) of
divination as part of a participatory dialogue, it is still far from the voice of
ancestral authority that is the key to atonement.

Segmentation and Contrast in Divinatory Discourse

Consistent with this theme of individuation and segmentation of distinct
perspectives in discourse, the markers used in divination tend to create coherence through contrast and differentiation. In the following text taken from a
divination performance by Mbulu Renda in the village of Kolo Lara in 1984,
the diviner describes the victim's near death and subsequent act of contrition (by
reciting myths praising ancestral fecundity, e.g., one titled "crocodile thigh/cu-
cumber breast"), which are then *contrasted* with the discourse marker 'but' to
the following clause, which explains that no spirit was causing those misfortunes,
exacting retribution, or pushing her to repent:

nya mate tippa mate	she died, almost died
dukki-we ne loddo ne'e	arriving up to this day today

ba na-toma-na	when she reached the
kenga ana woza	thigh of the crocodile child
ba na-dukki-na	when she arrived at
zuzu wai karere	the breasts of the cucumber
takka	**but**
nda'i-ki a	there was no
ndara rai rekka	horse playing tit-for-tat
nda'i-ki a	there was no
bongga rai zudda	dog being pushy

The use of 'but' as a discourse marker which creates coherence through contrast is a common occurrence in divination texts (see Chapter Four) and is consistent with the theme of 'tip'-like differentiation and individuation that characterizes the initial stages of following misfortune. Unlike other discourse markers such as 'so that' and 'thus,' which function to link clauses and fuse meanings, 'but' functions disjunctively, segmenting and breaking apart the significance of the discourse and indexing the role of the speaker in supplying the coherence.

The use of 'now' functions in a similar way. Beginning with line 102 in the divination text from Ryandaka, for instance, the diviner urges the spirits to resume dialogue with Malo Dunga. By using the discourse marker 'right now' he implicitly *contrasts* the *accepting* behavior described in the couplets with their *rejecting* behavior in the past. The use of 'now' not only indexes discourse time, but "leaks over" into the current time frame, helping to create a sense of the immediate, emergent character of the discourse in which he is engaged.

"ka 'peina	"so 'why	
ndau zima li'i pa-tuwa?	won't you receive the voice of	
	pleadings?	
ndau wale wata?	won't you respond to arguments?	
ne ba hinna!"	**right now!"**	105
lummu-ndi	you say that to those	
zora-urra:	spirits:	

The Uses of Sensation and Demonstrative Speech

The process of restoring and recovering the lost meanings of the 'word' following misfortune is also a sensory one. When misfortune strikes, it is said to be so overwhelming that what results is described as a kind of sensory loss, a dulling of the mind, protecting it from what it can not bear to comprehend. When the full impact of sudden misfortune is first 'felt' (*podda*), ironically Weyewa say they feel nothing. It numbs the senses into shock. "When I walked over the hill and saw my house burning and my children and wife outside screaming, I could not see, and I could not hear," one man told me. His words echoed those of a couplet expressing the anesthetization of the senses caused by painful experience:

| *mata nda eta* | eyes do not see |
| *tillu nda renge* | ears do not hear |

This "psychic numbing" in the context of calamity results in a kind of denial by Weyewa. This kind of behavior,—a kind of perceptual insensitivity—is negatively valued and must be overcome. Of a rude and graceless person Weyewa say, *nda na podda-ki paríngi* 'he does not feel the wind,' he has a thick skin and cannot feel.

In response to this intolerable condition, the diviner's task is to expose what has been denied to the senses. Like the misfortune itself, the diviner in his struggle to identify the problem becomes 'hot':

| *nya a wengo-we kuru* | he whose chest chafes |
| *nya a rara-ngge mata* | he whose eyes are red [inflamed]. |

The process of coping with calamity in subsequent ceremonies is thus regarded as ritual 'cooling.'

The diviner's speech does not soar off into discourse about ancient history, or the abstract symbolism of cosmic origins. Rather he portrays his quest as a process of "exposing" what has been "hidden" from the senses. The "exposure" produced by divinatory discourse is likened to natural events:

| *na-wunnga-ta lelu* | the cotton boll has opened |
| *ngawu-ta binu* | the cocoon has opened |

and

| *lebaka-na koba zimma* | the clam's shell is opened |
| *wallera-na wanno wowi* | the home of the sand crab is revealed |

The diviner's method is to 'scratch the soil, and dig the earth' to lay bare the 'tracks and spoors' of the ancestors. Only by discovering their 'path' and tracking it to its 'source' can he tell the sorry tale of human neglect, missed opportunities, and outright dishonesty that leads to calamity.

Deixis

The diviner represents one aspect of his task as that of making available to the senses what previously was not. One way in which language draws on the immediate sensory experience of the participants is through deixis. *Deixis* is a term deriving from the Greek word for pointing or indicating. It is a label used by linguists to refer to a class of words such as the English *here* and *there*, *this* and *that* (Buehler 1982 [1934]), personal pronouns, and temporal adverbs such as *now* and *then*. Simply put, these are words whose interpretation depends on access (perceptual or indirect) to the situation in which the utterance is produced (Fillmore 1982:35; Hanks 1984; Levinson 1983:54ff.; Lyons 1977). When a Weyewa diviner says, *newwe ne'e-minggi teppe ndeta* 'here on this mat by me,' unless we can see where the speaker and the mat are, we have a hard time understanding exactly what he is saying. Typically, unless we are in a position to observe or otherwise experience the relation between what is said and what is referred to, we cannot make sense of the utterance: we cannot simply use a conventional interpretation of what is intended by 'here,' we must experience it.

Such appeals to direct experience play an important role in divination. The Weyewa system of spatial deictics permits the audience a demonstration of the spirits' location vis a vis the speaker. Rather than using prepositional phrases, such as 'nearby' (*mbarra*) or 'next to' (*tiddi-na*), which draw on conventional understandings of spatial relations and do not imply anything about the speaker's location, the speaker often *demonstrates* with deixis the relationship between what he is saying and what he is referring to. For instance, after each question the diviner poses to the spirits, he tosses some rice, saying *nenna yasa* 'there, that rice [by you].' The word *nenna* 'there by you' implies that the speaker is in an experiential relationship with an interlocutor (albeit one is unseen). The very first lines of the divination from Ryandaka illustrate this:

nenati yaza	there's some rice
terre-ngge neti-ngge	take it **there**
wo'u Kyoni	**you** Koni
wo'u Mbili	**you** Mbili

As in English, the boldfaced deictic words in the Weyewa text cannot be properly understood outside the immediate context of utterance. The diviner's discourse does not simply explain, it *demonstrates* experientially the relationships in question.

Weyewa spatial deictic particles[2] are a paradigmatic subset, inflected for person, as in 'here by me,' 'here, there by you,' and 'here, there by [him, her, it].' Rather than adopting a single perspective, such as 'here by me,' as one might expect in a monologue, one finds in divination a wide range of person inflections, not only 'by me' but also 'by you' and 'by him.' That deictics of this kind are frequent in divination speeches is readily apparent from even a superficial examination of a transcription. A statistical comparison offers further confirmation (see Table 6, Chapter Four).

Evaluation: Augury as Response

As the diviner looks for clues to the misfortune, an important turn in his dialogue with the spirits may appear in the entrails of the chickens and pigs slaughtered after the performance. These signs are sometimes compared to 'letters' from the spirits: "this is *our* book" one man told me as he inspected a chicken duodenum (cf. Hoskins n.d.).

Although the configuration of blemishes is interpreted in terms of an internally coherent code-like set of structural relations, each sign within the augury system takes on its meaning in relation to the spoken dialogue with the spirits that precedes it. Weyewa augury is a response to a dialogic turn that went before it. On occasion, however, it is also a prediction about the success of future events. If the entrails are free of blemishes, or the blemishes appear on a part of the entrails that can be seen to be consistent with the diviner's interpretation, then this is a positive sign, a blessing or a nod of approval for what went before. Once, after inspecting a chicken duodenum following his divination performance, a diviner turned to me with a big grin and a "thumbs-up" sign, saying the Indonesian word *setuju*! '[the spirit] agrees!'

The primary Weyewa methods of augury—divination of pig and chicken entrails and egg yolks—exhibit a lateral and radial symbolism. Anomalies in these anatomical structures are interpreted as disturbances in the relations between 'sources' and 'tips,' 'villages' and 'fields,' on the one hand, and between 'close kin' and 'distant kin' on the other. Thus the procedures for interpreting such omens may be seen as broadly consistent with the general Weyewa conception of calamity as imbalance in relations between the inside and outside.[3]

Largely a casual operation, augury is not restricted to specialists. I have never heard of anyone who was called in for this purpose alone, or who was asked to do it for a fee. After an animal is slaughtered and disemboweled, but prior to cooking, the chicken or pig entrails or egg contents are always passed around for examination by anyone with an interest. There do not appear to be any restrictions on the time of day, place, or participants in this kind of behavior, but someone inevitably performs an examination. Those with an interest are more frequently male than female, and more often older than younger. In general, at least one adult male in every household has some competence in this kind of divination.

Sometimes small animals are slaughtered for the sole purpose of consulting their entrails. Because this practice is obviously expensive, it is usually performed only with chickens or eggs. It is also only done in cases of acute illness of humans or cattle, or of great anxiety preceding or following some large undertaking such as litigation, a raid, marriage negotiations, or a long trip. The animal's parts may still be eaten afterwards, however.

Chicken Augury

The dichotomous structures in Weyewa expressions about misfortune are particularly explicit in the 'interpretation of chicken omens' (*eta aye manu*). Augury associated with domestic fowl (*manu*) focuses on the analysis of the configuration of the duodenal loop (*aye*) and the adjoining parallel pancreatic lobes (*lende aye*) located in the large intestine (see Figure 6). After the throat of the chicken is slit and its blood collected in a plate and watched for portentous signs,[4] the feathers are singed off in the fire. Its abdominal cavity is opened, and the duodenal loop is pulled out and exposed for viewing. Weyewa say that the whitish-colored tubes of the loop should be parallel and without kinks, constrictions, or blemishes. The right and left sides are associated with fixed meanings. These meanings may be represented in Table 14.

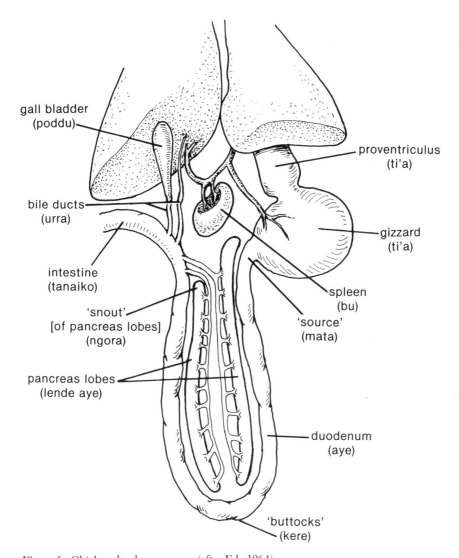

gall bladder
(poddu)

bile ducts
(urra)

intestine
(tanaiko)

'snout'
[of pancreas lobes]
(ngora)

pancreas lobes
(lende aye)

proventriculus
(ti'a)

gizzard
(ti'a)

spleen
(bu)

'source'
(mata)

duodenum
(aye)

'buttocks'
(kere)

Figure 6: Chicken duodenum omen (after Ede 1964).

Table 14: Chicken Duodenum Categories

Left side	Right side
tanggu ata pi'a	*tanggu marapu*
'the human side'	'the spirit side'
'tip' or 'buttocks'	'source'

In general, while the specific parts of the entrails are labeled in metaphorical terms, their significance is always interpreted in terms of an ongoing dialogue with the spirit world. Between the two lobes of the loop and pancreatic lobes there should be a long narrow empty space, which is referred to as the *loko* 'river.' If the 'river' is long and unobstructed, this is a sign of long life, but more generally prolongation, depending on the dialogic context. If the river is short, whatever is being discussed will happen quickly (e.g., the sick person will die). Since the pancreatic lobes should be roughly parallel, if one of them branches off and connects to the other side, this is interpreted as *pa-kadanga ritta-na* 'joining like *ritta* tree [fruits]' and can be a sign of over-intimate contact between two things normally kept apart; e.g., it can be a sign of incest, depending, again on the context. If the pancreatic lobes on the 'spirit side' are longer than those on the left side, then misfortune will occur (again), but if they are even, then a proper balance has been established by the ritual events preceding it.

The upper right side of the duodenal loop is called the *mata aye* 'the source of the [duodenal] loop.' The 'buttocks' (*kere aye*) are at the tip of the loop, while the 'beak of the chicken' (*ngora manu*) is at the tip of the pancreatic lobe on the left side. Distance between the inside 'source' and the outside, peripheral 'beaks' and 'buttocks,' is usually interpreted in temporal terms: if long, then the time between initiation of an event and its completion will be long, otherwise not. If the loop is red and rashed on the right side near the 'source,' this means that some ancestral spirit is angry; if it is red and rashed or constricted near the 'buttocks,' or tip, then one of the wild, forest spirits such as 'spirit of lightning' is angry. Notches, twists, blemishes in one side or another, in the 'source' or the 'buttocks' are all cause for comment. In my experience, however, 54 out of the 71 *aye manu* auguries that I witnessed over one eight-month period were considered 'good' (*ndua*).

Pig Liver Omens

Pig liver omens (*ate wawi*) involve the interpretation of the condition, size, and unusual features of the various lobes and other structures of the pig liver (see

Figure 7). Here the inside/outside symbolism appears clearly, with house 'mats' (*teppe*) and house 'eaves' (*kawendo*) to the left, the 'village' (*wanno*) and its symbol, the 'banyan tree' (*maliti*) in the middle, and 'fields' to the right.

Chicken duodenum symbolism, mostly lateral in character, does not map directly onto pig liver symbolism, which is somewhat more radial in orientation, but there are some broad similarities. In both, signs pertaining to human and domestic concerns are found on the left, and signs pertaining to forest and jungle spirits are on the right. In the pig liver, however, there is a clear center, or 'source,' represented by the 'village' and 'banyan tree,' associated with ancestral spirits and the stability of the village polity.

The *ate pawulla* 'lifted lobe' (literally 'liver lobe that can be lifted up and down'; see letter A in Figure 7) is usually the first one to be inspected, and also reflects this radial character quite clearly. The parts of this lobe closest to where it is attached to the rest of the liver,—i.e., its center—represent the 'client' or 'sponsor' of the ceremony (*mori pu'u*), and generally are the location for signs concerning people closely related to the sponsor of the ritual event. As one progresses out, away from the center toward its edges, one moves toward signs concerning people more distantly-related extended family (*ole katonga dana*) and 'affines' (*loloka*). If this lobe has a blemish or hole in it, or is otherwise flawed, the sponsor of the event or someone close to him in one of these other categories will soon suffer great misfortune:

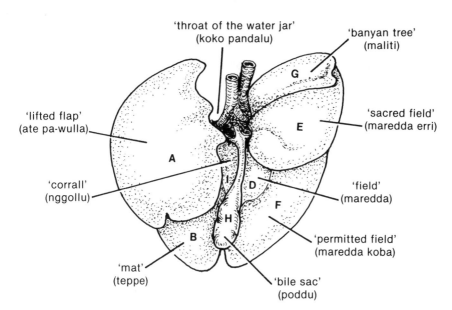

Figure 7: Pig liver omen (after Popesko 1970).

tukku ate   pierce one's heart
teba ngawu   stab one's spirit

was the couplet used by one specialist to describe the feeling of misfortune brought on by such an omen.

On the lower edge of this lobe are found the *wiwi* 'lips,' the length of which is associated with the performance of the ritual spokesman. If long, then what he has said thus far has been competent; if short, then another opinion might be considered. If the bottom edge of this lobe leading into the lesser omentum is notched, this is called 'a broken road' (*mbata lara*); this is a particularly bad sign to have appear at the beginning of protracted ritual proceedings such as the grand final stages of a marriage negotiation, and is occasionally the cause for abandoning further talks. It can also mean that the ritual spokesman, in his interpretation of misfortune, has been lying or is hiding something. The outer edge of this lobe toward the top is the *kawendo* 'eaves.' If this is 'blemished' (*parate*), this pertains to someone on the periphery of the social circles discussed in the preceding dialogue.

The *ate pawulla* lobe rests upon another liver lobe called the *teppe* 'mat' (see letter B). The relative size, length, and orientation of these two parts are sometimes seen as signs of the relationship between the in-laws in marriage. If they rest easily on one another—'they pillow one another' (*na pa-lunna na wawi*)—this is a good sign. If, as one raises the 'lifted lobe' to look beneath, one finds that this is blemished on the underside, the diviner is hiding something. One also looks here for signs of the *marapu pa-deku* 'the following spirit,' a spirit of the in-laws' ancestors demanding brideprice. If the 'mat' is 'clean' (*na zingira teppe*), free of blemishes, this is a good sign.

The *maliti* 'banyan tree' is a short, thick lobe coming from the center of the liver (see letter G). Banyan trees are a symbol of the village, since they grow at its gate. Signs in this portion of the liver concern close relatives. If *na mballo maliti* 'the banyan tree is leafy' and this part of the liver is thick and full, this is good sign. If it is limp, there will be problems with someone close to the client.

If the *koko pandalu* 'the throat of the water jar' (see letter C), or more technically, the lesser omentum, has slits or notches in it, someone in the immediate household of the sponsor has done something wrong or will come to misfortune. One diviner told me that, after he conducted an *urrata* for a sick young niece of his one day, he saw this sign. Although Weyewa usually simply grunt, nod, or make a few brief comments when consulting an omen, this diviner was greatly agitated by what he saw, let out a yell, and threw the liver into the fire. The little girl died the next day in spite of his efforts to help her.

Moving to the right, one finds the *maredda* 'field' lobe (letter D), located on the 'right side' of, and opposed to, the *ate pawulla*. This lobe is associated with things outside the house—not personal fate—and foretells events such as blight, floods, drought. It is also an important location for signs from angry forest and lightning spirits. This liver flap has two parts to it: *maredda eri* 'sacred, prohibited field' (letter E), and *maredda koba* 'allowed field' (see letter F). Evidence of serious sins appears on the former, less important ones on the latter.

The *poddu* 'bile sac' (letter H) is a blue bag of bitter fluid. If full and bright blue, it foretells good luck and rains. If whitish, dry, and shriveled, it means drought and harder times. If the *nggollu* 'corral' (see letter I) known technically as the quadrate lobe, has a hole or blemish, then an animal will be stolen or die. A hole in the *nggollu* means *namawukke nggollu* 'the corral is open'—i.e., one is open and vulnerable to a catastrophe. A deep red blotch on this flap means that the *marapu muttu* 'the hot spirit' will soon send lightning, or some other form of mischief, to kill one's cattle.

Once, when an informant was discussing this lobe, he noticed just such a mark on the liver before us. He showed this to his brother, who was in charge of the ceremonies. The brother saw it and grinned sheepishly. He said he would sacrifice a chicken later on that day to whomever was angry and had sent this spirit. He was fairly certain, however, that the blotch had appeared because he had forgotten to sacrifice a chicken to the spirit of the fields before he picked some corn early that day. He shrugged, as one caught in the act, and went inside to tell his wife to catch another chicken out in the fields. A few minutes later, I heard the characteristic squawking of a fowl being slaughtered. He was atoning for his error.

Egg Omen

The clearest representation of inside/outside, and center/periphery, radial symbolism is reflected in the terminology and principles guiding the interpretation of chicken egg omens (*tollu manu*). The procedure is simple: the egg is cracked open into the palm of the diviner and the yolk and egg white are inspected for *kanurru* 'ominous spots.' The precise meaning of the spots depends on the kinds of questions asked in the divination. Often, however, an important question has to do with responsibility for the misfortune. In this context, the location of the spots can be taken as a response to a question about the identity of the culpable individual—that is, whether the guilty party is someone central to the social group of the victim, or someone more marginal to it. For instance, if the spots appear a bit further out into the egg white, the problem may lie with an affine or a *marapu pa-deku* 'following spirit' from one's wife-givers. The middle of the egg white itself is called the *maredda* 'field,' and it is here one looks for signs of disgruntled forest or lightning spirits.

Other Forms of Evaluation

Clients and onlookers do not always expect immediate relief from their problems, although sometimes they get it. According to Kaduku, sometimes when he performs a divination, the sick person becomes well immediately:

When I divine, if I 'connect with' [*wenna*] the thing that is causing the divination to begin with, even if I face the corner of the wall [and do not face the wall as is customary], whoever is ill may become well. [JK: Has this ever happened? K: Yes. JK: Tell me about it!] The woman, Koni Kanurru who lives in————: Well, I divined for the source of her illness. She was carried in during the night with urine flowing out of her, and runny feces. The urine and feces were all over the litter they carried her on. When they got her to the village of————, they came and got me. That same night she got better. . . . There were reasons [for her illness]: She and her family had been working several plots of rice, and . . . each time they promised to slaughter a water buffalo if they got a good harvest. . . . They harvested ten large silos of rice, and they failed to sacrifice. The 'water spirit' was angry, and caused her to have bad intestines. She was up and walking that same night.

A more complex evaluation, however, comes from the clients, their relatives, and onlookers. Sometimes these assessments are negative. They may express consternation to one another that particular hunches as to the source of misfortune were not adequately addressed. They may exhibit also some lingering doubts about the conclusions of the diviner, and sometimes there are even hints of malpractice. One man told me as we walked home after a rope divination that "I would never trust that kind of divination. You cannot see behind the [diviner's] fingers. What is he doing with those ropes? I don't know. With spear divination you can always see what he is doing." When they disagree with a diviner's conclusions, the latter is rarely confronted directly. Instead, Weyewa will seek a second opinion.

Evaluations of Weyewa divination are based on a variety of political, economic, and linguistic factors, factors that go beyond the purely technical features of the spiritual interview. Among Weyewa, for instance, clients, and bystanders may be dissatisfied with the size of the restitution necessary. They may quarrel about whether a simple chicken sacrifice following a divination will be enough to placate angry spirits or whether a placation rite or even grander ritual will be required to alleviate the problem. They may feel that the diviner did not properly address certain spirits, or made the matter worse by mispronouncing their names, or otherwise offended the deities. In some cases, they may feel that the diviner was not completely honest, that he was holding something back that he knew, and thus the divination would have to be performed again.

The diviner is expected to be verbally fluent and to speak with the intensity that such grave situations merit. Divination is itself expected to be 'hot.' In part this is because it represents a conflict between the spirit and human worlds, and is sometimes accompanied by anger and resentment on the part of the victims. The diviner's demeanor is expected to reflect this emotional climate. Diviners who treat the experience casually, who stop, chat, and joke in the middle of the event, are criticized by some of the older, more experienced, and renowned practitioners.

Conclusions

As the initial effort at "inscribing" the 'word' of the ancestors, *urrata* takes the form of a dialogic performance. This perspective permits us to appreciate the sophistication with which the diviner creates coherence, rather than requiring us to view him as simply manipulating technical media for a credulous audience. By constructing the discourse as dialogic interaction, the meaningful structure of the event unfolds through contrast and differentiation of distinct points of view of speaking individuals. This emphasis on segmentation and individuation is accomplished experientially, through indexical demonstrations of meaningful relations (e.g., using personal and demonstrative pronouns and quotations), rather than relying entirely on relatively arbitrary, decontextualized symbols such as myth recitations. At a time when the 'trunk' of the ancestral voice seems problematic and remote, the diviner effectively oscillates between the demonstrative power of the immediate contextualized discourse of the 'tip' and the more encompassing narrative discourse of reconciliation and atonement.

Notes

1. The ropes were said to have been discovered in the belly of a snake found underneath the village of Umbudenggu.
2. By spatial deictics, I mean those deictics that concern the specification of locations relative to certain culturally fixed anchorage points in the speech event (Levinson 1983:79). Rather than surveying the range of spatial deictic expressions in Weyewa, which would include adverbial expressons, deictic uses of prepositional phrases, and the like, I have chosen to focus instead on a morphologically discrete set of terms in Weyewa, partially described by Onvlee (1973:175–176), words that have the *primary* function of expressing spatial deictic relations.
3. Other, less important omens include the position of cowlicks (*kaliwura* or *urra*) in humans, horses (see Hoekstra 1948:178–180), and other mammals, the lines on one's hand (*urra limma*), and the cries of birds (*punni keila*). The behavior of many animals (especially rats, bats, birds, owls, and monkeys) can also be seen to portend future events, although these interpretations appear to be relatively unsystematic.
4. Blood which is multicolored or of overly thick or thin consistency is a bad sign, as are very small bubbles.

6

Songs, Gongs, and Oratory in *Zaizo* Placation Performances: The Poetic Accomplishment of Consensus

In many Weyewa myths, gongs and drums speak like humans. I once asked my friend Kaduku why these instruments no longer speak. He replied that back when the grass, earth, gongs, and drums still spoke (*ne ba na-panewe-po rutta tana, talla bendo*), every thing expressed its own opinion. No one could agree. When it would come time to perform rituals of sacrifice, unity was impossible because gongs and drums would not agree to be beaten, and animals would not consent to be killed, and they would flee across the 'stone bridge' (*lende watu*) that connected Sumba with other islands. There was so much confusion that the ancestors never got their due. It got so bad that people were not getting buried, and villages remained unconsecrated out in the forest. So the Creator Spirit struck the earth with lightning, breaking the stone bridge to the other islands. Animals and trees were struck dumb by the sound of thunder so that sacrifices and forest clearings could take place without dispute. But gongs and drums were not silenced altogether; instead, floor drums and hand drums were allowed to accompany singers as they spoke to the spirits, and gongs were permitted to carry the voice of spokesmen up to the spirits. As a reward, these instruments must be given offerings to 'cool them off' for enduring such a beating.

The tale associates the meaning of gong and drum music with the formation of consensus, movement toward agreement, and the fulfillment of responsibilities. In contrast to some strands of Western scholarship on the social meanings of music, which have dwelt on the capacity of music to create a transcendent experience of community (e.g., Zuckerkandl 1973:21–30; see also Langer 1942), Weyewa musical ideology seems to be preoccupied with the functions of music as a resource used by performers in particular situations in order to accomplish social goals. For them, music is not an abstract form so much as a tool that mediates between humans and the spirit world. The effort to create harmonious verbal and musical meanings is not only an interactional struggle, but a political one.

In the *zaizo* rite of placation, music and speech enact a dialogue. In this second, all-night stage of the ritual process of atonement—carried out if resources and determination permit—a gong- and drum-accompanied singer invites orators to 'supply' him with words of assurance and contrition that he can convey to the spirits. What follows is a richly meta-linguistic "dialogue about dialogue" in which orators and the singer debate in ritual speech about how to create consensus by speaking and performing in harmony; in the process of talk-

Table 15: The Structure of the *Zaizo* Performance

'*Step*' (nauta)	*Goal*	*Participants*
1) 'Support the buttocks, prop up the knees'	Consensus among participants	Singer, several orators, gongs, and drums
2) 'Reach the pallet, arrive at the hearth'	Re-affirm the 'words of the ancestors'	Main speaker, singer, gongs, and drums
3) 'Escort the spirits'	Expel the harmful spirits from the house, call the ancestral spirits back in: restore balance.	Singer, gongs, and drums
4) 'The bird completes its flight, the horse its race'	Conclude on a note of consensus	Several orators, singer, gongs, and drums
5) 'Offering'	Offer animal sacrifices to spirits to placate them	Singer or main speaker

ing about the proper procedures for achieving unity, they actually accomplish it. Then, drawing on the knowledge obtained in the divination, a single designated orator steps forward to describe the broken promises that led to the misfortune, re-affirms the collective commitment to them, and pledges to atone for the neglect. The singer responds to this account by inviting the ancestral spirits to forget their wrath and return to the house and village. He ends his performance around dawn by expelling the harmful spirits from the village (see Table 15).

The musical principles guiding the activities of the gong players, drummers, and singer cannot be viewed as a purely autonomous, abstract score, removed from the situated particulars of the event. Although the singer and his gong and drum ensemble are granted a certain privileged position spiritually, this does not result in interactional detachment. Indeed, the discourse of the singer is more subject to interruption, more contingent in terms of topic selection, and more likely to incorporate the voices of others than is the speech of the orators. Thus, while music is essential to the formation of consensus and spiritual harmony, this form itself is subject to multiple demands in the situation of performance. For instance, gong and drum music starts and stops according to the needs of the orators; musical and verse rhythms interact in complex ways; the melodic shape of the song must generally be congruent with the form of the couplets, many of which are supplied by the orators.

Ideally, this complex accommodation of musical form with interactional requirements must result in the creation of an authoritative, 'true,' and 'authentic' performance. This is not a purely aesthetic exercise or even a spiritual act of devotion. Such musical performances of placation rites are crucial for the ideological and political legitimation of particular households and individuals. It often causes extreme hardship for poor people to go beyond the initial divinatory phase of atonement and stage the feasts, buy or rent the musical ensemble, and hire a singer required for such an event; but if they fail to do so, and do so properly, the 'voice' of their ancestors must remain silent. Rather than admitting to such a poor, mute, and inanimate pedigree, Weyewa struggle to enact the 'true voice of the ancestors.'

Assembling and Performing the *Zaizo*: A Case Study

Malo Dunga did not want the voice of his ancestors silenced. He had struggled so hard to re-establish dialogue with his ancestral spirits (see Chapter Five) that he was interested when Mbani Mata, the diviner, and several of his agnatic kinmen suggested that he pursue and re-affirm the voice of his ancestors in a placation rite. Indeed, much of the discussion following the divination ceremony concerned what to do next in the atonement process. Talk eventually focused on a statement that emerged in the divination to the effect that if Malo Dunga paid his in-laws a water buffalo (a debt incurred originally by his father in paying brideprice), evil spirits would stop pursuing him. To make the exchange and settle the issue, Mbani Mata suggested a 'placation rite' (Plate Four) in which the history of relations between these two families could be aired and settled. Thus, even though they had identified through the divination, augury, and discussions the main causes of the misfortune, in many ways the most important task lay ahead—the task of re-stating what the promises were, and showing how their neglect accounted for these novel, stigmatizing, and disorienting events.

Assembling such a feast is a complex and expensive matter, and not to be undertaken lightly. Indeed, given the cost and difficulty, it is not surprising that many misfortunes are seen as requiring nothing beyond a divination ceremony. Sudden, intense, but usually non-fatal illness, such as dysentery or malaria, minor personal misfortunes such as a fall or broken limb, or a knife or horse accident do not generally necessitate a *zaizo*, especially if they occur relatively privately and do not have broad social implications. The following events, however, are almost sure to require more than a divinatory inquiry:

pare pa-tauda kamillaka	rice struck by lightning
pare pellida wangu	rice swept away by a flood
pare a muttu-na	rice that was burnt in a fire
pare a pa-kedu ata	rice that was stolen
ata mate maredda dana	person dying in the field
ata mate lara dana	person dying on the road
muttu-ngge umma	house burning down
muttu-ngge ingi	waistcloth catching fire
tama ata kedu	robbery [1]

Plate 4: Guests at a ritual. Ceremonial dress for men consists of decorative shoulder-, waist-, and headcloths, a sword, and a betel pouch.

For these misfortunes, to stop after the divination stage is to 'stop in the middle of the road.' When the startled ancestral spirits 'fly off' to the fields and streams' and 'stars and moon,' the dangerous wild spirits of lightning and forests enter the house, village, and body. To neglect the spirits in this state is a violation of traditional order, a rejection of their relationship to their ancestral past. To restore order, the spirits of their forebears must be 'summoned' and the 'hot' spirits escorted out into the fields, forests, and sky. Spiritual imbalances must be rectified and the associated fines and debts paid off.

For Malo Dunga, a man of only modest means, restoring the balance between the spirits of his in-laws and those of his own agnatic clan was costly. As the date for the *zaizo* approached, he checked with one of his relatives to make sure that a water buffalo was available for the event. With this assurance, he also began to make inquiries about borrowing the gongs and drums needed to perform the *zaizo*. Although the use of these instruments was not without expense, it was essential, for without them the *zaizo* would have to be postponed or canceled. A *zaizo* without the necessary musical accompaniment is impossible and, indeed, inconceivable.

The set of five tuned gongs (*talla*) required for a full performance of a *zaizo* is a prized item of family wealth that not everyone can afford. The "original" and most highly valued gongs for ritual events are brass *talla woddo* (literally, 'cat gongs,' so named for their high-pitched sound). In recent years *talla bei* 'iron gongs,' and even low-quality *talla tong* 'oil drum gongs,' are more commonly used and available for sale in the weekly markets. Each of the gongs has a name reflecting its function or sound. For instance, the name of one gong—*renda bendu* 'keeps time with the floor drum'—requires little explanation. This gong is also called *ndou tillu* 'the middle one.' The *pambale* or 'responder,' is so named for the way it is beaten in 'answer' to every other beat of the *renda bendu* gong. The *kawukeka* or 'tenor gong' has an onomatopoetic name which describes a lower midrange sound; variations in the beat of this gong provide a distinctive melodic shape to the polyphony. The *kabónguka* or 'hollow gong' has a name that is also onomatopoetic and refers to a deep, hollow sound. In the *zaizo* its beat alternates with that of the *renda bendu* and the drums. The last gong is the *kandurruka*, the largest 'bass gong.' This gong's beat follows the drums and *renda bendu*, but it is only struck every other beat.

When Malo Dunga had these gongs suspended from a horizontal bamboo pole, he had Mbani Mata say a prayer to the 'gong spirit' (*ndewa talla*), informing it of the upcoming event. In this prayer offering, in which a chicken is sacrificed and its meat given to the gong owner, the instruments are addressed as though they were hyperanimate beings, with special abilities to 'haul the speech, bring the talk' up to the ancestral spirits. When conducting a *zaizo cana* 'summoning zaizo' outdoors, Weyewa ritualists say such a prayer as they hang the gongs from a bamboo pole suspended from two four-foot high supports, known as a *landango*. When the event is conducted inside the house, the *landango* may be hung from the rafters, and the gongs in turn from it. Skilled young boys generally beat the gongs; I have never seen a girl or woman do so. During the initial stages of the *zaizo*, they dutifully stand while beating the gongs from the rack. As the night wears on, they almost always take the gongs off the rack and position them on the ground or floor while they find themselves comfortable places to lie in the vestibule.

Malo Dunga was able to get a *bendu* 'floor drum' and *bamba* 'hand drum' from his next door neighbor. The floor drum is a 40 cm high hourglass shaped drum made from readily available forest and animal products. It is a more common item in a household than gongs, but it is by no means universal, and its owner expected a small token of compensation at the end of the night from Malo Dunga. Older, elaborately carved ones with a resonant sound are particularly prized. In ritual speech, the *bendu* is also addressed as an agent and referred to as

a biluna	[he] who has in his waist
kaniki touda mbolo	three candlenuts
a landona	[he] who has on his forehead
wulu wailo manu	cock feathers

These couplets describe the three candlenuts that are placed in the body of the drum, and the cock feathers that adorn the head-tension strap. Since the drumhead is made of water buffalo hide, the floor drum is often associated with this animal.

a kacoro rutta	who grazes in the grass
a katattu tana	who stamps the earth
a manggiru ndende	who stands and rubs (against trees)
a manomba lara	who wallows in the path

Other couplets mention the materials out of which such a drum must be constructed. It must be round enough to 'roll'; it must be cut from the reddish-yellow corewood at the mid-section of a log, and the drumhead must be tied on with a *kawango* vine.

kadipu nggonggola	log-chunk [that] rolls over
kateri nggunggila	the middle section of a log
kazoza rara	the red corewood
kawángo lolo	the vine [that] binds

This drum is beaten by a young boy or man, or sometimes the singer himself, at a rapid but relatively steady pace with two 15 cm sticks, whenever it is the singer's turn to perform. Depending on the kind of *zaizo*, the floor drum is placed on a mat either in the courtyard in front of the house or in the vestibule inside. At the beginning and end of the event, the gongs and drums perform seven rounds of one or another of several special orchestral compositions. At this time, occasionally an older man with special expertise will step in and beat out, with great flourish, the complicated drum rhythms of these traditional musical compositions.

Like the gongs, the *bendu* has a 'spirit' (*ndewa*) which is given an offering at the end of a *zaizo* to 'cool' it down from being beaten all night and from contact with the 'hot' offended spirits. A small chicken is sacrificed and the meat given to the owner of the drum. The drum is one of the spiritual vehicles that the singer's voice 'rides' (*kalete*) up to the upper world to go and summon the spirits. While it is accorded special respect and is considered a minor deity in its own right, it is subordinate to the voice of the singer.

The second drum used in *zaizo* performances is also widely available. It is a shoulder slung tambourine with a long tubular sounding chamber. This 'hand drum' (*bamba*) has far fewer names than the floor drum and is not thought to possess a spirit, nor is formal compensation for its use required. Since its head is made of horsehide, it is often referred to as a 'horse' (*ndara*)—for example,

katámbo kiku	with a thick tail
manengge wonggo	a dense mane

It is generally held under the arm of the singer by a shoulder strap. The singer stands as he taps out a fast rhythm with his free hand. He adjusts the tempo and loudness to accord with the rhythm and emphasis of the sung verses.

Step One: 'Support the Buttocks, Prop Up the Knees'

While assembling the musical instruments is an essential part of any *zaizo* performance, even more effort is devoted to gathering and organizing human participation. During the post-divination discussion, Mbani Mata and Malo Dunga had tried to persuade the others to hold the *zaizo* that very night. They argued hard for it, saying that since almost everyone was already gathered, why not just continue? But they were unsuccessful, since Malo Dunga's in-laws would not agree to come on such short notice. To have the in-laws participate was essential, I was told, not only because tension between the families was identified as a cause of misfortune, but "because one's *loka* 'mother's brother' is one's [spiritual] source."

But Malo Dunga's *loka* refused to come unless he would receive a water buffalo (which was owed him by Malo Dunga's father anyway as part of an outstanding brideprice payment). When Malo Dunga agreed to do this, his uncle again stalled, saying that he was not yet ready to 'greet' Malo Dunga properly at the gate of the village with the obligatory counterprestation of a large pig and a couple of cloths. He could arrange such a greeting in two weeks' time, he said, contingent on the marriage of his own nephew, an event from which he expected to receive pigs and cloths as counterprestation.

So, three weeks later, at about four in the afternoon, a group of about a dozen men, women, and children, including Malo Dunga and Mbani Mata, waited outside my door. Malo Dunga had brought a water buffalo with which to 'greet' his in-laws' pig. I packed up my things quickly and joined them. We continued on for about another kilometer until we reached the village gate, where we were greeted by Dowa, a village elder and Malo Dunga's kinsman, with the ceremonial greeting (*pazimbala*):

dyoo appa ata-wu	halloo, what people are you
ta mbyali binna mone	at the male gate of the village
pu'u kawango ndazza?	at the trunk of the banyan tree?

Mbani Mata responded on behalf of Malo Dunga:

wali-nggo ndari tana	I have come from tilling the soil
mángu baba	in the lap of the land
wali-nggo mbatu rutta	I have come from weeding the grass
mángu lolo	with tendrils
nyakka ku-kowoka zakalla	thus I [arrive with] glowing red headcloths
nyakka ku-wanggara zaloki	thus I [arrive with] shining shoulder bands

Mbani Mata continued, saying that they were seeking a blessing for one who had experienced misfortune and that they were bearing gifts for this purpose.

After two more such exchanges, Dowa declared, *Na-wukke binna!* 'The gate is open!' A small chicken was sacrificed, a coconut was split and its contents sprinkled on Malo Dunga and the gate, and we all entered the village. While waiting for Malo Dunga's in-laws to arrive, we sat and chatted on the veranda. At about 8:00 p.m., their maternal uncle finally arrived, and a chicken and a small pig were sacrificed and prayed over. The chicken was consecrated to Malo Dunga, the unfortunate man. He began by informing Mbili and Koni, the ancestral pair who were responsible for making certain 'promises' and who had been offended when Malo Dunga, their descendant, neglected to fulfill them. Mbani Mata tossed some kernels of dry husked rice toward each corner of the house and proclaimed:

natti karere rai wollamu	your cucumber flower offspring there	
natti karobbo rai uwa	your gourd fruit descendant there	
na dukki-na mawo ro'o kawendo	he arrived at shadow of the house eaves	
na toma-na katonga	he arrived at the porch	
ne ba ku ponggo-ngge	and if I cut the tree	5
wazu ndukka pu'u	to its base	
ne ba ku-wei-ko-ngge	and if I search for water	
we'e ndukka mata	to its source	
ndau kamboro-ka beto	don't hide the source of red ants	
ndau katimbu-ka-ngge teri	don't hide the fish in a bamboo jar	
		10

Addressing the spirits Mbili and Koni, Mbani Mata asked that they accept the arrival of their descendant, the client Malo Dunga ("cucumber flower") to the house ("the eaves, the porch"). He then asked for a blessing on his analysis of the misfortune, asking that, if he tried to get to the 'base' of things, the other participants might not hide from him what their true message was. He concluded by offering a chicken as a welcoming gift to Malo Dunga for making the journey to the village and 'climbing up the house ladder' in the hearth area:

nakka manu	This chicken there by him
pa-opi wai we'e kapurreta	to wipe off his sweat;
lunggu-minggi ne ba hinna	I say to you right now
ka pa-ndekke-ni nauta	so he climbs the house ladder
ka pa-pala-ni koro	so he crosses over into the hearth area

He then sacrificed a small pig, asking a blessing on the *zaizo* ceremony about to take place.

ka na seda-ngge ana manu-ngge	so the baby chicken is about to die
ka na mate-ngge ana wawi-ngge	so the piglet is about to die
ka na pato'o waina li'i Inna	to help us listen to Mother's voice
ka na pato'o waina li'i Ama	to help us listen to Father's promises

He continued:

ndai pa-ele-nggai lara	do not deviate from the path
ndai pa-temba-nggai teko	do not raise your sword at me
	[and block the path]
lunggu ne ba hinna:	I say this now:
"dyeimba wai pongu-ni	"receive this truly
limma kawana-mi"	with your right hand"

By the time the chickens and piglet were slaughtered, their omens inspected, and the food cooked, it was already 10:00 p.m. After the plates of food were cleared away, a boy was sent to go and fetch another gong (one had been lent out and was not yet returned) and another boy was sent out to cut some new drumsticks.

It was decided that this would be a *zaizo umma* 'house zaizo' in which the goal was to *pa-rénge-na li'i* 'to make [the spirits] hear the voice'—that is, to reaffirm their commitment to the 'word.' Since this event did not involve the summoning of the spirits of persons who had died outside the house, nor the spirits of rice carried away by flood, but rather communication with angry ancestral spirits, it was felt that this matter could be handled inside the house rather than in the courtyard, where the performance is called *zaizo cana* 'yard zaizo.' It is also worth noting that this event took place in the month of July—the dry season—when nights are clear but very chilly indeed in the Weyewa highlands. Although no one mentioned the greater comfort of an indoor performance, it seems possible that this may have been a factor in the decision. In any event, the drummers and gong players began to arrange the mats and blankets in the vestibule to make themselves comfortable for a long night.

Mbani Mata began to warm up for his role as the singer. As the meaning of the title of the singer (*a zaizo*, lit.'he who zaizos') might suggest, he is considered to be integral to the event as a whole. It is he who mediates between the orators and the spirit world. Often relatively young (usually under fifty years of age), and always male, he is chosen for his competence, his stamina, and his knowledge of, and sympathy for, the case at hand. His 'voice' must also be pleasing: valued voice qualities include *li'i katerreka* 'high-pitched, ringing voice,' *li'i kalada* 'great [deep] voice,' and *li'i nggellara* 'throaty voice;' unpleasing voice qualities are *nggerre* 'raspy' and *mbuwwa* 'cracking.'

In general, the singer is accorded many names during the ritual event, but the most frequent mention his connection to the ancestral objects with which he is associated during the performance.

a pa-zadidi pa-rawi Inna	who is alongside the works of Mother
a pa-zangera pa-wolo Ama	who is beside the works of Father

He also has several names that describe his skill and style of delivery:

Plate 5: The floor drummer keeps time with the singer in a placation rite.

ana manganne ate dana	child with an expert heart
ana manelo wiwi ndeta	child with clever lips
a ndondo pa-zila	who sings affectingly
a ngi'o pa-zali	who weeps melodically
a kawula timbu teri	who calls out [when] smelt [are running]
a ka-aula zodo nale	who shouts out [when] sea worms arrive

The prominent ritual speaker Lende Mbatu once told me that he prefers to have a non-relative for a singer when he delivers the main speech: "Because the specks of grass in my own eye, I cannot remove. Another person removes them for me. Even if my own brother knew how to sing, or my own son, I would take a non-relative singer to work with me." Lende Mbatu sees the role of the singer as one who poses hard questions, who asks for debate and is aware of the details of procedure. He says that once, when he performed as a singer, he asked such hard questions that no one dared to speak the whole evening.

Signaled by a quick flourish on the drums, the gongs began to play together according to a musical composition distinctive to the village. After a prescribed number of beats, the men let out a deafening 'whoop' (*kabuara*), which consisted of one man emitting a trilled *lalalalalalalalaaaaaaaa*, the prolonged last syllable of which fell in pitch, joined by a thunderous *Yow!* in unison with all the other men. This was repeated again and again until after the seventh time, two of the gongs dropped out, the syncopated rhythm of the drums was replaced by a monotonous steady beat (Plate 5), and the singer began to sing.

The Formation of Consensus: A Meta-Pragmatic Exercise

Mbani Mata made clear that his 'song' was not a fixed, rigid script which he simply enacts, but rather a collaborative accomplishment for which he required the consensual support of others. His dialogue with the orators can be viewed as a discourse about how to engage in discourse. This "meta-pragmatic" discussion is essentially an inventory and description of the procedures and instructions for using speech and music in *zaizo* performance so as to create consensus (cf. Silverstein 1981). In the course of this debate about how to perform the song, they actually accomplished it.

Mbani Mata's song and the actual *zaizo* performance itself began immediately by singing about singing. Mbani Mata listed the obligatory components of the performance—gongs and drums—and stated that they were 'complete'; He then urged that no one should sing 'with a different melody' and 'no one should gallop at a different pace.' In so doing, he not only describes the wholeness of the collaborative, polyphonic effort between the gongs and drums and singer, he is exemplifying it as well.

yo malla malla o-o	well, well, come on o-o	1
ho malla malla o-o	well, well come on o-o	
ha malla malla o-o	well well come on o-o	
yo malla malla o-o	well, well, come on o-o	
ho malla malla o-o	well, well come on o-o	5
ha malla malla o-o	well well come on o-o	
mai-ngge Yoli	come, Yoli	
hu ole milla	ho humble friend	
mai-ngge Pyeda	come, Pyeda	
hu ole dara	ho sorrowful friend	10
hu nyakka ngurru	so that there are rumbling sounds	
ka mawo wengga	in the cool shadow of the house	
hu nyakka nyángi	so there are tinkling sounds	
ka Loko Toza	from the river Loko Toza	
ka ryanda kenda	the waistcloths are carved	15
kambolo uwe	g-strings fastened with rattan	
ka lénga mattu	because your faces	
o-o -dumi mata	are complete	
ka lénga tanga-	because your lips	
o-o -dumi wiwi	are paired	20
ndau tarra	don't compete	
touda-ka-ni wale o-o . . .	for a turn to answer . . .	
ngga'i ka wiwi	so that the lips	
o-o renda mera	o-o speak in harmony	
ngga'i ka ate	so that the hearts	25
o-o renda zama	meld together	

In the preceding text, 'humble friends/sorrowful friends' refers to the participants and 'rumbling sounds/tinkling sounds' to the gongs, while 'waistcloths/g-strings' is a reference to the drums (actually, to the head-tension straps on the drums). After establishing the participation of these elements, Mbani Mata goes on to exhort them to coordinate their efforts and not to compete for a turn to answer one another.

This coordination was accomplished musically as well, as Figure 8 shows. In general sung *zaizo* verses are characterized by multiple musical phrases linked by a 'step-wise' descent of pitch (cf. Feld 1982:99–100). Weyewa ritualists call this *na pa-nauta-ngge li'i-na* literally 'he makes a ladder of his voice.' In the example, Mbani Mata employs musical phrases in which the initial beat has stress, as do the final two. The melodic form may be adjusted in a number of ways in order to fit the requirements of the couplets. While the phrases all illustrate an orderly, step-wise descending melodic contour, on lines 21–22, Mbani Mata suddenly modulated the pitch, tempo, volume, and rhythmic pattern for emphasis. Although Mbani Mata frequently adjusted the musical form to accommodate the couplet and verse requirements, he also took some liberties with ritual speech in order to fit the musical pattern he had established. For instance, in the full couplet form of one of the embedded couplets is:

*hu nyakka ngurru-**ngurru***	so that there are rumbling **sounds**
ka mawo wengga	in the cool shadow of the house
*hu nyakka nyángi-**nyángi***	so that there are tinkling **sounds**
ka Loko Toza	from the river Loko Toza

Boldface indicates words omitted in the actual performance. In the actual performance, onomatopoetic reduplication of *ngurru* 'rumble' and *nyángi* 'tinkle' was omitted so as to fit with the five syllable verse pattern he has established.

Words can also be segmented in various ways so as to accommodate the requirements of musical performance. On lines 17–20, for instance, Mbani Mata broke apart the verbs *mattu-du-mi* 'to complete your . . .' and *tanga-du-mi* 'to pair your . . .' so as to accord with the rhythm of the song.

ka lénga mattu	because your faces
o-o -dumi mata	are complete
ka lénga tanga-	because your lips
o-o -dumi wiwi	are paired

Suddenly, about ten minutes into Mbani Mata's song, the first orator of the evening cut in, shouting *dyoo zaizo!* 'hail singer!' in a loud voice. The drums and gongs immediately stopped, and the singer acknowledged the request for the floor, shouting: *malla!* 'well,' or 'come on!' The speaker then continued on the

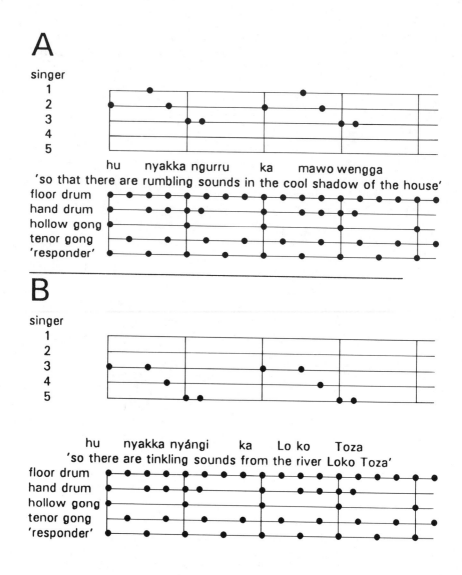

Figure 8: The melodic shape of the *zaizo* song.

C

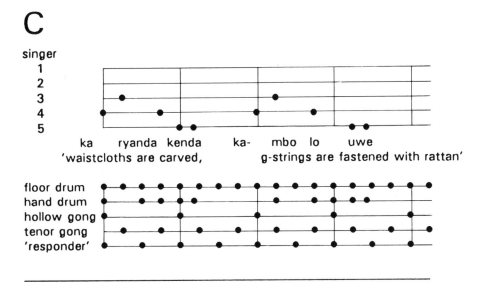

singer
1
2
3
4
5

ka   ryanda kenda   ka-   mbo lo   uwe
'waistcloths are carved,   g-strings are fastened with rattan'

floor drum
hand drum
hollow gong
tenor gong
'responder'

D

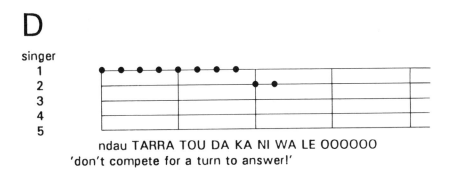

singer
1
2
3
4
5

ndau TARRA TOU DA KA NI WA LE OOOOOO
'don't compete for a turn to answer!'

floor drum
hand drum
hollow gong
tenor gong
'responder'

meta-pragmatic theme of how to conduct the *zaizo* in such a way so as to create consensus. Notice how he framed his entire speech as a quote which he would like to attribute to the singer:

tena!   [it is] true [what you say]!   1
   "ba pa-renda witi kako-wu   "make your legs dance and go
   ba kambolo bindo ndende-wu   make your waist garment hold you erect
   ka tema-ngga kere kede-nggu   and support my buttocks
   ka rukka-nggandi kundo kako   and prop up my knees   5
   ka ku mbokota pa-ro'o   so that I am richly foliated
   ka ku mbidura pa-uwa"   so that I am laden with fruits"
      lummu-do-na   if you say that [it is proper and true]
         a zaizo!   hail singer!

The singer replies:

malla!   come on!   10

The speaker continues:

ne'e-ko nya-ngge   perhaps
   koko pa-kalallu   there is a tempting throat
      a mattu mata ndandara   among the attentive completed faces
   ate pa-kapadana   there is a teasing heart
      a tanga wiwi pullu   among the paired, clever lips   15
         tema-nggo kere-mu   I support your buttocks
         rukka-nggu-ndi kundo-mu   I lift your knees
ne yauwa   as for me
   nda ku bongga kedu ate   I am not a coy dog
   nda ku manu baza koko   I am not a cock all puffed up   20
      zaizo tau!   singer, go!

This orator, because he spoke first, had a special responsibility to monitor the formation of consensus and respond if anyone spoke with a discordant voice. It is also his duty to be the last one to speak at dawn, so that his speeches are 'even,' not 'odd.' He is called:

a kawúnga punni nggirri   the first to sound at twilight
a kawúnga yaka male   the first to peep in the evening
a kangali wúnga woti   the wall that was first built
a kadoke wúnga timbu   the banyan that first grew

In the speech above (1–20), he expressed his support for the singer. He said the singer was right to ask others to get ready and to want to be "foliated" (with support) and supported from the buttocks. Although there may be some who are doubting, he, for one, is not being coy.

Other men soon joined in, waiting their turn. In general, the elder males of the group function as monitors, making sure that the details of ritual procedure are properly adhered to. Conventionally, these men are referred to in their ritual capacity as those who:

a totoka pa-ngadu	who observe from below
a nggeloka pa-redda	who oversee from above

Such individuals insure that everyone speaks an 'even' (*nggenna*) number of times before the 'main speaker' begins the *li'i marapu* the 'promises of the ancestors.' They also lend their support, with the message that, as one man put it during the performance:

mbyali monno mbyali	on one side and the other
byondo monno lyola	above, and below
ba ulle mera zadda-wa-nda	we all were same-sized tusks,
kadu mera ndende-wa-nda;	we all were same-length horns;
ka ta muttu mirrita maredda	so we are a field burnt to the ground
ka mbuka mbillira kandawu	so we are a forest leveled
ndau kedaka Lawonda-ka-na	do not make riddles like Lawondans
ndau lawiti Wanokaka-ka-na	do not sing [cryptic] Wanokakan songs

Unlike divination, in which the obstructions to the 'word' were portrayed as sensory and perceptual, in placation rites the obstacles to the completion of the event are more social in character. Indeed, the main concern of the orators during the initial two hours of the placation rite is consensus. These short orations, usually no more than five minutes long, are concerned that no one be overly timid or cautious, that everyone be sincere and in agreement.

In Mbani Mata's supplications for orators to relieve him, he sometimes pleaded that

na ndoli-bai ndara-nggu	my horse is tired
na ndoda-bai asu-nggu	my dog is exhausted
na kari dodo lomma	the little water buffalo is panting
na ndara wura kambu	the horse has a foaming underbelly

As is usual, to combat this fatigue and *kouka* 'raise up' the spirits, women performed *pakallaka* or ululations. The term *pakallaka* is derived from the word *kalla* 'to keen, to wail.' It is a sound which some observers feel resembles a high-pitched and rapid version of the so-called "war-whoop" in the media depictions of American Indians. The trilling effect, however, is achieved with the tongue and not with the hand. It is delivered by 1–5 adult women at intervals apparently unrelated to the rhythm of the gong and drum, but which are about one or two minutes apart. It only occurs while the orchestra and singer are performing.

Step Two: 'Reach the Pallet, Arrive at the Hearth'

After everyone had spoken twice, Mbani Mata began to re-frame the discourse by suggesting that a main speaker come forward and 'cross over' to the interior of the event, both literally (by stepping over into the hearth area) and figuratively (by discussing matters of core importance to the participants). He sang:

ho mai pa-kako-mu o-o	ho come, let us go o-o	1
ho ole dara o-o	ho humble friend o-o	
ho ne pa-ndende o-o	ho stand up o-o	
ho ole pera o-o	ho my peer o-o	
ho toro nduwa o-o	ho grasp this well o-o	5
ho malla toma o-o	ho come and reach o-o	
ho neka tandingo o-o	ho the pallet by the fire o-o	
ho ana api o-o	ho [by the] little fire o-o	
ho aromowe o-o	ho turn your face to it o-o	
ho newe tullura o-o	ho the cooking stone o-o	10
ho la kateti o-o	ho which is leaning o-o	
ho mata api ladu o-o	ho the blazing fire o-o	
ho pala inu o-o	ho cross over the tracks o-o	
ho ne ba hinna o-o	ho right now o-o	

Through his song, Mbani Mata was asking that the 'main speaker,' or 'lord of the center' (*mori pu'u*) stand up and cross over the low wall (*koro*) to sit by the fire and begin the delivery of the *li'i marapu*. The person he was referring to was an elderly, famous ritual spokesman named Ngongo Tadu, Malo Dunga's uncle on his father's side. The latter stood up from where he was sitting, yelled *dyoo zaizo!* to get the floor, fished out a handful of betel and areca nut ingredients from his bag, and handed it to Mbani Mata, saying:

ne ba hinna-ngge	and now	1
"buala tekke-mu	"lift up your head	
palengge mata-mu	raise your eyes	
nena bau palai koro	there by you cross the wall	
kau toma tandingo ana ladu	and you reach the pallet by the fire	5
kau palai koro	so you cross over the wall	
kau dukki rabuka kaliddora"	and you arrive at the narrow hearth"	
lummu nya zaizo!	you say that singer!	
Singer:		
malla!	come on!	
nenati ba hinna-wi pa-mama	there now by you is the betel quid	10
tapala panewe	which divides up the talk	
nenati ba hinna-wi watu	there now by you are the stones	
like la kandauke	which separates this speech from	
	others	

Plate 6: The 'main speaker' in a placation rite sits inside the hearth area as he delivers the 'words of the ancestors.'

With that, Ngongo Tadu stepped over the wall and sat down next to the 'hearth' (Plate Six) and the *pari'i urrata* 'the divination post' of the house. Now the *zaizo* had essentially become a dialogue between the singer and the main speaker.

After this turning point in the ceremony—this 'speech boundary' (*tapala panewe*)—Ngongo Tadu's speeches grew more lengthy and profound, analyzing the misfortunes of the clients in relation to their neglect.

dyoo zaizo!	hail zaizo!	1
haa newera	ah, we are here	
nyakka ku-dyulango kandauka	so I create with talk	
nyakka ku-pyandango panewe	so I repeat by speaking	
hidda a ma-para wali pu'u	those who were struck from the base	
		5
hidda a ma-pobba wali lawi	those who were slapped from the tip	
takka newera	but here	
a kazaza wai pa-mbulla-na	there is something sunken and forgotten	
a ando wai pa-lénga-na	there is a stake left behind in the field	
ka ba nya-ko,	and if that is it,	10
wa'i-ngge	there are those who	
pa-kandauka rowi ndou-na	speak with their own lips	

wa'i-ngge	there are some who
panewe tudda wekki	speak to display their bodies
nda kanangganipi-ki-we	it is not a dream 15
dappa pa-tobo-ngge	[but] instead one can directly
panewe denga-ni	speak to him
nati pa-pana-na Nyani	the one who gave birth to Nyani
dappa panewe dénga	directly speak with them
wali ate-ni	from the bottom of one's heart 20
"hauwa nga'a nda ku-nga'a	"As for me, I received no food
ne'e-ngge kuru koba kaka	since I was kept under the coconut shell
we'e nda ku-binu-ki	I received no drink
ne'e-ngga kambu limma bendo	there covered as I was under a hand
nya-ki-we	so 25
ku-kapa kualo	I beat my wings like an eagle
riwu ana nggengge	and disturb my thousands of
	descendants
ku-zoda rande	I peck like a duck
pyoku ana rawa"	at my own ten thousand little chicks"
hinna	he said 30
ba na panewe rowi ndou-na	when he speaks with his own lips
ba na kandauka tudda wekki	when he speaks using his own body
mbarra-na kudda koko	to the tender-necked [descendants]
mbarra-na mbera lipi	to the shaky-shouldered
	[descendants].

In this speech, Ngongo Tadu said he was re-telling (lines 3–4) the case of the unfortunate victims of calamity (lines 5–6); but in so doing, he noticed that there was a neglected promise in their past (cf. the abandoned "stake", lines 8–9). He hinted at disunity among the descendants on this matter (cf. lines 12–14), but claimed that direct and sincere communications revealed the true voice (lines 15–20) of their ancestor: 'the one who gave birth to Nyani.' This ancestor was quoted as saying that he received no sacrifices, or celebrations (lines 21–23, "food" and "drink") associated with housebuilding and thus began terrorizing his own descendents (lines 26–29).

Not all the 'voices' of the ancestors are discordant ones, or complaints. In some cases, more recent ancestors are themselves guilty of neglect for which their descendants must atone. In this sense, *li'i* also means 'promises' that were neglected. In the following oration, Ngongo Tadu recounted how, when Mbili and Koni (the recently deceased parents of Malo Dunga, the client) prayed to their ancient ancestors, they promised to stage large celebrations for them and "feed" them, but that these plans were never realized: the promises contained in the quote (lines 5–11) remained like a stake not yet carved from the core of tree, like ongoing discourse that never reached completion (lines 12–15).

ba na toma-na	when they encountered 1
zuzu wai karere	the breasts of the cucumbers

ba na dukki-na	when they reached
kenga ana woza	the thighs of the crocodile child
"hoo	"oh yes 5
ku-pa-nga'a-kuminggi a muttu	I will give you hot food
ku-pa-riwo-kuminggi we'e loko	I will bathe you in river water
ku-pa-nga'a-kuminggi a muttu	I will give you hot food
ku-kuddo-kuminggi nu'u koko	I will rub you with coconut milk
ku-pa-lunna-kuminggi wawa	I will give you a pillow below 10
ku-pa-zande-kuminggi zoro	I will give you support in front"
ne'e-po-ngge katoda ate ritta	but all this remained in tree's core
kandauka inda bode	speech that was never completed
ne'e-po-ngge kere milu mandungo	but it was only a plan
panewe inda bonnu	talk that was never fulfilled 15

Notice that in these last two speeches, the focus of the talk had shifted away from an account of the troubles described in the divination rite—the death of Malo Dunga's wife and water buffalo—to an account of the neglect and other transgressions which lay behind it. Unlike the early stages of ritualizing disaster, placation rites in general have very little to say about the actual events of the misfortune itself. Rather, the focus here is on moralizing the narrative.

Even with such a shift in perspective, in many cases the transgressions themselves are handled delicately, and referred to only in allusions. For instance,

enu we'e mángu nggengge	drinks water with spiders in it
nga'a rutta mángu ndabbo	eat grass with poison in it

and

utta pa-kedu	stolen betel fruit
winno pa-kedu	stolen areca nut

were metaphorical expressions used during the evening to refer to incest committed among members of the same clan as a possible source of misfortune which was never elaborated.

Step Three: 'Escorting the Spirits'

In courtyard zaizos, the singer and the orators stand "outside" in the 'yard' (cana) to bring the domestic spirits back 'inside' to the house. In the 'house' zaizo, however, although no ancestral spirits are believed to be flying about outside the house, there are "outside" spirits who have penetrated the interior of one's domestic space who must be expelled.

As dawn approached, Mbani Mata took on the task of escorting the dangerous spirits outside the village to the forest and sky. To do this, he recruited the services of the messenger spirit, Tawora Karaki (discussed in Chapter Three). If Ngongo Tadu moralized the narrative, Mbani Mata spatialized it.

yemmi kaina-ngge o-o	you too o-o	1
newwe nya-na o-o	right here and now o-o	
pa-kondo kiku kako o-o	escort the tail o-o	
"nyakka zanga-wangga	"escort me on the shoulders of	
bale wosa o-o	the crocodile [ancestors] o-o	5
tara bindo ndende-nggu o-o	with protective thorns o-o	
kalete-wangga towo rara o-o	who rides on my red head[cloth] o-o	
ya, a palewa-ngga o-o	who sends me out o-o	
nggidu nggoda o-o	here and there o-o	
a pa-wenda-ngga o-o	who orders me o-o	10
pilu pata o-o	everywhere o-o	
ngge yemmi kai-na o-o	you also o-o	
nyakka ngurru o-o	thus [you] rumble o-o	
mawo wengga o-o	beneath the cool shadow o-o	
nyakka nyángi o-o	thus [you] resound o-o	15
Loko Toza o-o	from the River Toza o-o	
ne ba hinna-ngge o-o	and now o-o	
newe nya-na-ngge o-o	that it is so o-o	
ta-ndeke-na o-o	we step o-o	
iru wa'i-na o-o	in the footprints o-o	20
ta-pa-terre-na o-o	we grasp one another o-o	
koko limma o-o	hand in hand o-o	
ne ba hinna-we o-o	and now o-o	
hiddi pa-pa-talla o-o	we hold out o-o	
randi limma o-o	with open hands o-o	25
kondaka pa-rénda-ngge o-o	we sing together like *kondaka* birds o-o	
terre-na kiku ndara o-o	hold the tail of the horse o-o	
nando kere zope-mi o-o	follow like knife sheath-holders	
newe nya-na o-o	now, here o-o	
pa-buala tekke-mi o-o	lift up your head o-o	30
pa-lengge mata-mi o-o	raise your eyes o-o	
a kadia tutu tera o-o	[you] bark-cloth pounding board o-o	
ama Ndairo o-o	[you] father of Ndairo o-o	
kapaka-nggu laingo mate o-o	[you] oasis tree in the barren sand o-o	
inna Leda o-o	[you], mother of Leda o-o	35
ndilu-we tillu o-o	incline your ear o-o	
kualo-we mata o-o	fasten your eyes o-o	
ama Ngongo o-o	to the father of Ngongo o-o	

A litany of ancestral names follow, each of whom is directed to "face" the others. Once this roll-call is complete, the ancestors instruct the messenger spirit, Tawora Karaki,

pa-katanga ngenge ngora o-o   to fasten his headcloth chinstrap o-o   1
ne ba hinna-we o-o   right now o-o
pa-lengge Tawora Pinda Leti o-o   take off, Tawora Pinda Leti o-o
ka ka zili o-o   and clear the way o-o
Karaki Pinda Namu o-o   Karaki Pinda Namu o-o   5
kana dingi-pona dodango o-o   so that dark clouds recede
   ne ka bilu-ngge bengge o-o   so he puts in his waistcloth o-o
    mama pa-pa-ndalara o-o   the betel and areca nut [offerings]
   ne ka wunggu-ngge limma o-o   so he puts in his hand o-o
    kutta pittu nggazu o-o   seven betel catkins o-o   10

ne ba hinna-we o-o   and now o-o
   ne ka toma-ngge o-o   so that he arrives at o-o
    tiddi wai manera o-o   the side of the *manera* waters o-o
   ne ka dukki o-o   so that he reaches o-o
    ndonga wai lapale o-o   the side of the *lapale* waters of o-o   15
     na'i watu pa-pa-ndende o-o   the [village altar] erect stone o-o
     na'i wudi pa-pa-mulla o-o   the [altar of] fig tree o-o

ne pa-woti-na panewe o-o   you then carry your speech o-o
   lero laingo deta-mi o-o   as a flag across the desert o-o
ne aila-mi kandauka o-o   you then haul your talk o-o   20
   kappe ndara rara o-o   as on a saddle of the red horse o-o
kau pa-lengge-wa o-o   and you send [Tawora Karaki off] o-o
   ka toma tiddi wai manera o-o   so next he reaches the waters of o-o
   ndonga wai lapalena o-o   and the banks of o-o
    a dawa binna kiku o-o   he who guards the 'tail' gate o-o 25
    a kandi binna ngora o-o   and he who guards the front gate o-o

ka na-wukke-minggi binna o-o   then he opens the gate for you o-o
ka na-bowa-minggi lara o-o   then he clears the road for you o-o
   ne ka toma-ngge o-o   so that next he arrives at o-o
   ne ka dukki o-o   so that next he reaches o-o   30
    ta mbyali binna mone o-o   the other side of the male gate o-o
    pu'u kawango ndazza o-o   and the foot of the banyan tree o-o

ne ka toma-ni o-o   next he arrives at o-o
   tiddi wai manera o-o   the side of o-o
   na'i nya-nangge o-o   that there o-o   35
    watu pa-pa-ndilli o-o   altar of displaced stones o-o
    watu pa-pa-kai o-o   altar of the removed rocks o-o

ne kalete pando penne o-o   on to the hills twice climbed o-o
   mawo mara loko o-o   and the spirit of dry rivers o-o
ne ka ndoba pando mburu o-o   on to the valley twice climbed o-o   40
   ninno wai karingina o-o   the reflection of cool waters o-o

ne ba neti-ngge o-o   so that what departs are o-o
   a madala manu muttu o-o   the hovering scorched chickens o-o
   a matomba wawi mbera o-o   and the breakaway wild pig o-o
    ba na kandandaka o-o   that caused the quivering o-o   45
    odo kambu ndara o-o   of the horse's chest o-o

ba na kabakku wiwi Inna o-o	and the Mother to bite her lip o-o
ba na kalelapa o-o	and caused the dizziness o-o
mawo koba mata o-o	of the spirit of one's "face" o-o
ba na kabula-ngge mata Ama o-o	and Father's eyes to bulge o-o 50
ne ba hinna-we o-o	and now o-o
a matanda ana ranga o-o	a small animal is picked out o-o
ne ba wa'i-ndi o-o	and now available are o-o
ne pa-benu-ma o-o	things to drink o-o
ne pa-nga'a-ma o-o	things to eat o-o 55

As is usual, in this narrative, Tawora Karaki's journey takes him past the village altar ("erect stone and fig tree"), past the village gate, past the garden altars set up for the stones they removed, and out into the streams and mountains. Out there, the hovering spirits, who have been running about wildly, are set free. They caused the ancestors to quiver, bite themselves, and lose face. Now, we are assured, animals have been set aside to feed and give them drink.

Step Four: 'The Bird Has Completed Its Flight'

When this journey is complete, and the Karaki spirits have returned to their place by the door of the house, then the main orator speaks up again, with the message that

na winggirai ndara	the horse turns around
na dikkirai bongga	the dog turns directions

This verbal frame indicates that the *zaizo* can now take on a new course, namely its conclusion.

In the case study at hand, the 'first speaker' of the evening spoke again at about 5:30 a.m., recommending that

keila ndukka lera	the bird has completed its flight
ndara ndukka malle	the horse has finished its race

and that everyone rest. Mbani Mata agreed, responding in song:

malla malla peina?	come, come on, how about it?	1
malla malla peina?	come, come on, how about it?	
malla malla peina?	come, come on, how about it?	
malla malla peina?	come, come on, how about it?	
ndende ndara peina?	shall the horse stop, how about it?	5
ngaru bongga peina?	shall the dog rest, how about it?	
na delaka-ngge tana, peina?	it is light out now, how about it?	
na wanggara-ngge loddo, peina?	the sun is up now, how about it?	

The main speaker finally brought the performance to an end by shouting *dyoo zaizo* 'hail singer,' and simply saying 'it is finished!' (*ndukka-bana*).

Step Five: 'Offering'

While Mbani Mata and the other speakers rested, and many of the children curled up and went to sleep, the women began preparing rice and coffee. Some young men went to get the larger animals ready for slaughter. As soon as word came that the animals were prepared, Mbani Mata sat up and prayed over several chickens and a pig. One was dedicated to the ancestral spirits of Malo Dunga's house, which were referred to indirectly as

lambe mbelleka	the wide house post collar
pari'i a kalada	the great house post

followed by a series of praises and assurances that there would be grand feasting soon. The next was to the spirit of Malo Dunga's wife's lineage, so that

ngga'i ka nda na ndunni oro	so that he does not retrace his steps
ngga'i ka nda na bali wewe	so that he does not retrace his tracks

The third was to the lightning spirit,

ka nda na wolo-ka-na	so that he does not make
katura riti kangga	sharp sticks as booby traps
ka nda rawi-ka-na	so that he does not make
kasoba tana rara	holes in the red earth

and so that there might be fertility in the gardens, and no disease. The children and heirs of the house were then fed the livers of the slaughtered chickens, and the placation rites were complete.

Comparison of Placation Rites with Divination

Uses of Dialogue

Placation rites are verbal dialogues concerned with misfortune. The focus of these relatively complex events, however, is markedly different from that of the divination ceremonies. While both interweave narrative structure and dialogue, in divination the goal is to identify and differentiate distinct semantic contributions of others into a dialogue, while in placation rites the goal is the opposite. In the *zaizo*, the distinctiveness of the dialoging partners is minmized and they are urged to 'support' and 'prop up' one another in order to re-affirm the neglected 'word.'

In placation rites, the healing ceremony moves one step closer to narrative monologue. While both divination and *zaizo* justify their claim on the audience's attention with reference to the extraordinary nature of the calamitous events, in divination, such a justification is used to legitimate a dialogic performance, an emergent question and answer exchange. In placation rites, the preoccupation with the extraordinary nature of calamitous events is used to justify the re-telling of the tale. This emphasis in placation rites on re-telling is especially clear in the actions of the singer. His task is to repeat, restate, and reproduce in song the words of the orators. The orators, for their part, also emphasize the repetitive and routine character of their discourse:

nda ku-tura tana pamba	I don't cultivate new rice fields
nda ku-poka ala oma	I don't clear new jungle

Furthermore, the orators emphasize that they are drawing on prior discourse, such as that in the divination account:

tana oro ledu-na Inna waika	this is land trod by our Grandmother
rutta oro iwwu-na Ama umbu	this is grass stepped on by Grandfather

It is this emphasis of structured repetition of prior discourse which marks the beginnings of what I call entextualization.

Uses of Narrative Structure

Narrative orientation in placation rites is no longer achieved here by contextualized indications of persons in the immediate audience, but rather by reference to persons by their proper couplet names, or in terms of the place they originate from. One man with the name of Mbora Kenda, for instance, in ritual contexts is referred to by the singer as *Mbora umbu Kenda, Kenda wazu umma,* 'Mbora, lord Kenda, Kenda of the Wooden House.' People and places are more often referred to with proper names, not indexed with pronouns.

In the scenes of narrative complicating action, in which the 'voice' of the ancestors is described, in divination performances one sometimes finds references to disaffected or 'coy' ancestors who are 'hiding' or being 'tricky.' Furthermore, there is often some ambiguity as to the authorship of the different 'voices' being reported. In the *zaizo*, by contrast, the main speaker quotes directly and extensively from clearly defined ancestral voices, even without framing the statement with locutive verbs. When quotation frames are employed, they often appear in more conventionalized form, as quotations framed in couplet form, such as the following:

nya li'i kamezi-na	thus saith the sweet voice [of]
nya li'i malangi-na	thus saith the blessed voice [of]

or as statements that one's speech follows the law of

ukku Benge Modu	the law of Benge Modu
pata Lero Dinga	the way of Lero Dinga

As in most placation rites, the one that followed Malo Dunga's divination gave a somewhat less personal account of the misfortune than one finds in the divination itself. While the account of the misfortune in the divination rites is often highly personalized—touching on the particularized concerns and discourses of the headman, and Koni and Mbili, and so on—one of the main themes of the early speech-making in the placation rite is the abandonment of individual, dissonant voices and the formation of a consensus. Although in practice they do not always achieve this, this goal is expressed by orators in couplets such as:

maingge	come on	1
mattu mata	all you eyes	
tánga wiwi	[and] pairs of lips	
ka ta-rukka kundo kako	let's support the knees to walk	
ka ta-tema kere kedde	let's support the buttocks to stand	5
ka tamuttu ka ta-mirrita maredda	let's burn the fields black	
ka tambukka mbillira kandawu	let's clear the forest clean	
nda'iki bongga kedu ate	there are no dogs of fickle heart	
nda'iki manu eka bei	there are no chicks of other hens	

The image of consensus is here evoked by the completed sets of eyes and lips, who support one another to 'walk' on the path, the image of the totally burned fields, the completely cleared jungle, and finally the absence of any dissenting voices.

The Uses of Sensory Experience

Another key difference between *zaizo* and divination rites pertains to the role of the imagery of sensory experience. While in divination, the misfortune is described in terms of hot and cold, numbness and sensitivity, in the *zaizo* the imagery focuses on more conventionalized, moral commentary. By *moral* here I mean that the speaker describes the event using the collective standards by which the group evaluates behavior. The description of the misfortune itself, which the main speaker finally begins to address at about 2:30 or 3:00 in the morning, makes no mention of specifics of the illnesses, fevers, deaths, and other experiences, but rather focuses on the moral infractions that led up to them. An example of such commentary from the placation rite which followed the divination for Malo Dunga is provided below.

newwe a pa-beti-na	here, what was thrown off,	1
pa-mbulla-na Mbili	forgotten by Mbili	
newwe, pa-tumba	here, what was tossed	
pa-lénga-na Lyende	far away by Lende	
ánga nda pa-ánga	neglected	5
pullu nda pa-pullu	ignored	
nyakka	and that resulted in	
wa'i-ngge a	people who were	
pobba wali pu'u	struck at the base	
para wali lawi	throttled from the tip	10

The Imagery of Inside and Outside

In divination performances, the relationship between the imagery of inside and outside is complementary, antagonistic, and relatively static. Spirits are identified in terms of their position in this inside/outside scheme. Spirits associated with the interior of the house might be asked:

ne'e-du tullura kateti	Are you among the hearth stones?
ne'e-du rabuka kalido	Are you among the hearth ashes?

while those associated with the "outside" fields and forests are queried:

ne'e-du ta-nggyionga maredda	Are you out in the fields?
ne'e-du ta ala kandawu	Are you off in the jungle?

That is, these spirits are merely being identified, not being asked to move.

The symbolic themes in a *zaizo* are more dynamic, narrative, and transformative than those in rites of divination. Particularly in *zaizos* held out in the courtyard, the relationship between inside and outside is re-established by summoning wayward spirits back into the house and chasing away intrusive ones. In such outdoor events, as proof of the spirits' return, the ritualists look for footprints in an ash-filled coconut half-shell—a sort of miniature hearth—placed at the end of a bamboo ladder leading from the eaves of the house. The angry ancestral spirits are implored to return from their hiding places among the "stars" and "sun," climb down the roof of the house, via the ladder, and resume their usual resting place inside the cool house. Thus the speaker pleads:

ndau kapairo-ka-na mburru	do not be slow in descending
ndau katumba-ka-na kedde	do not be late in departing

The singer, in his turn, narrates the journey by which the return proceeds:

inu li pa-mane-ngge e-e-e	the tracks that were followed e-e-e	1
lara li pa-lina-ngge e-e-e	the path that was travelled e-e-e	
bau katenggi binna wanno	as you gaze up at the village gate	
bau tangara nauta umma	as you look at the house ladder	
ba Mbili	if you are Mbili	5
ba Koni	if you are Koni	
takka-du	truly	
ne pa-mbona-ba-ngge mburru-ngge	and you come straight down	
ne pa-deku-ngge tolaku manila	along the soaring house tower	
ne pa-mane-ngge bawe ta kamberu	along the Kamberan center rafters	10
ne pa-mbona-ba-ngge tana-ngge	and you come down to the ground.	

The dangerous spirits, on the other hand, are verbally "escorted" away from the house by the singer, with the help of the envoy spirits, Tawora Karaki:

yemmi	you	1
Tawora pinda lete	Tawora traverses mountains	
Karaki pinda namu	Karaki traverses valleys	
kau pa-kondo	may you escort [them away]	
kau pa-ngíndi	may you bring [them away]	5
kau pa-lengge-wi	to make them leave	
kau pa-kako-wi;	to make them go;	
pa-lewa nggidu nggoda	order them here and there	
pa-wende pilu pata-wi	command them several ways	
nyakka na kambodo tana dana	so that they are like earthworms	10
nyakka na kamauta tonggo wazu	so they are ants on the tops of trees	

The final evaluation and conclusion appears when the main orator prays over the animals to be sacrificed to the angry spirits and asks that no more misfortune threaten them, no more booby traps await them, no more danger strike them in the road, no more shocks in the middle of the night; and furthermore, he asks, may they have good harvests, pest-free fields, and days free of illness.

When the placation rite sponsored by the unfortunate Malo Dunga and his clan brothers finally came to a close, guests and hosts parted ways with a feeling that not all was yet resolved and many disputes lingered. One thorny issue centered on the account of misfortune that emerged over the course of the ritual. Mbani Mata's account of Malo Dunga's crop failures, illnesses, and bereavement laid the blame squarely on the grieving man. Mbani Mata implied, however, that if Malo Dunga resolved the outstanding issue of unpaid brideprice, then his claim to his father's patrimony would be strengthened. This last point was something that his competitors for that property were not so willing to concede; this case was still being discussed when I visited during the summer of 1988.

The Use of Music

Perhaps the most obvious difference between divination and placation rites in terms of their capacity to evoke the 'words of the ancestors' as an enduring text is the use of music. Unlike the diviner, who bears the sole burden of creating discourse coherence through the 'sorting' of distinctive dialogic positions, the performers in a *zaizo* draw on the redundant conventional rules for coordinating relations among participants and the strophic, repetitive character of the musical stanzas as a resource in the creation of coherence. By discussing how they plan to orchestrate their diverse roles, they accomplish the unity they seek. While it has by no means lost its emergent character, this stage of the process of ritual atonement nonetheless does evoke the image of relatively structured, rigid, but shared patterns of cooperative behavior. In contrast to the themes of individuation that pervade the divination, the musical aspects of *zaizo* are associated in both myths and actual practice with a heightened form of sociability and collaborative behavior.

This oscillating pattern of signification in the *zaizo* between the emphasis on emergent indexical accomplishments of coordination and unity through performance and the symbolic expression of ready-made, conventional narratives and metaphorical relations is a fundamental rhetorical strategy that shifts in orientation as the ritual process of atonement moves toward the textualized pole of ceremonial meanings. In the following chapter, I examine the ways in which narrative, music and symbolic meanings saturate the performance frame as singers and sponsors attempt to free themselves of the contextualized particulars of calamity and celebrate an authoritative, enduring image of the 'voice of the ancestors.'

Notes

1. *Zaizos* are on rare occasions held to 'curse' (*mazazara*) someone who is believed to be causing one harm. According to Mbulu Renda, a ritual spokesman, the songs employed in these *zaizo* have a distinctive rhythm and melodic shape.

7

Unity and Exchange in Rites of Fulfillment: The 'Word' as Monologue

In a particularly moving series of Weyewa tales, an orphan boy draws on the power of song and narrative to compel the fulfillment of broken 'words' of promise. As the story begins, an infant boy named Mada Luwu is abandoned in the jungle when his older sister and caretaker, Kyazi, finds a husband. Before departing for her new village, she charges him with the 'word' (*li'i*) that when he grows up, he must seek her by following a trail of yarn that she will unravel behind her on her way from her past to her future home. With the help of a magical dog and an enchanted toy top, he manages to survive to adulthood, and he begins to search for her. Despite many trials along the way, through verbal cleverness and magic Mada Luwu eventually prevails and tracks his sister down. When at first she refuses to believe that his name is really Mada Luwu, he attempts to prove it by engaging in a contest with the magic top that she entrusted to him as a child. He wins, but in the process he destroys his opponent's top and wrecks his sister's crops as well. She drives him away, and he sits alone on a stone and weeps affectingly as he sings the tale of his sad history of broken promises. When she is eventually so moved that she recognizes his 'voice,' at the same time she also remembers her 'word' to him. With grand feasting and lavish gifts, Mada Luwu's identity and 'name' are re-established as being those of her true brother and the rightful recipient of her marriage payments.

In the story, Mada Luwu does not resolve his destiny through spoken dialogue or negotiation. The tale illustrates instead the power of monologic, sung narrative, in which the thread of memory links—with a magnificent play on the two senses of *li'i*—a present performance of the voice with a promise of the past. To forget the 'word' is to allow the hot and wild agents of calamity to crash through and penetrate the boundaries of one's social and symbolic space, as Mada Luwu's sister Kyazi discovers to her dismay when she fails to recognize him. In Weyewa ritual life, sudden death, devastating fires, crop loss, and the like all set in motion a verbal and ceremonial process, by which the violated promise is identified in divination, re-affirmed in a *zaizo*, and, if resources and determination permit, fulfilled through feasting and song so that fertility, growth, and exchange can continue. As these ceremonial stages unfold, the dangerous and unstable forces of disunity of the outside are expelled, and the true word of the ancestors is restored to the inside by unifying the divergent voices into one single 'trunk' of discourse. The contrastive character of oppositions between ancestors and descendants, wife-givers and wife-takers, and verbal form and content are minimized through vital, life-giving ritual exchanges and performative involvement.

Authoritative, narrative songs or chants are performed in the final steps of the atonement process, in what may be called "rites of fulfillment."[1] These rituals 'fulfill' in two senses: first, they 'make good on a promise to the spirits' (*na-ponnu-we li'i marapu*) made in a preceding ritual event such as a divination or *zaizo*; and, second, they offer 'personal fulfillment' (literally, 'fill the body') and renown for the individual sponsoring the event. Weyewa understand both senses as motives for undertaking these elaborate spectacles. The three most important rites of fulfillment are dragging a tombstone (*téngi watu*), building an ancestral house (*rawi umma rato*), and a 'celebration feast' (*woleka*). Although not specifically seasonal in nature, these ceremonies tend to occur during the comparative leisure of the dry season, following harvest. None are obligatory; indeed, only very wealthy, ambitious men manage to perform all three in a lifetime.

Sociologically, all three are elaborate feats of organization, requiring complicated exchanges of labor, food, animals, and forest and mineral products, as well as other resources. Smooth cooperation among the diverse groups of participants is a paramount concern for the sponsor. Representations of these ceremonial relations in ritual speech stress their mythical origins as enactments of an ancient cosmological order. For example, the actions of quarrying the stone for a tomb, extracting the lumber for a housebuilding ceremony, and harvesting the rice for a celebration feast are spoken of as reflecting a primordial, harmonious, marriage-like union between the wife-giving spirits of the earth, forest, and fields and their wife-taking human occupants. The cooperative relations among elder and younger clan segments and their affines are also represented as reflexes of ancient, preordained alliances and customary obligations.

While these ideological reasons for participation are important, individuals also contribute cattle, pigs, and other resources to the feasts of a powerful person because they view it as a kind of insurance against harder times. If misfortune should strike, it is good to have someone powerful in one's debt, whom one can call on in times of distress. In the nineteenth century during the height of the slave trade, people willingly offered their labor and resources in exchange for protection under the 'banyan tree' of wealthy and charismatic rajas who lived in walled, fortified villages. Poor people still try to stave off agricultural and other misfortune by cooperating with the housebuilding, stone-dragging, and feasting of more wealthy and powerful individuals, who demonstrate their abilities through speech and economic activities.

In rites of fulfillment, the paramount verbal genre through which ritualists express both lineage ideology and their own individual oratorical abilities is a category of charter myth that is closely guarded and cloaked in 'sacred authority' (*erri*). This essentially monologic style known by the cover term *kanúngga* consists largely of a series of place and personal names which evoke the story of the ancestral migration from the past to present, during which the major patterns of Weyewa social life were established. Unlike divination and placation rites, in which verbal form consists of dialogue, question and answer, or debate, the *kanúngga* narratives of rites of fulfillment—*oka* 'chants' and *we'e maríngi* 'blessing songs'—are delivered by a single individual who acts on behalf of the 'voice' of the ancestors, whose words he directly conveys. Coherence is created through spatialized narrative structuring, in which clauses are linked by a rhetoric of cause and result through discourse markers such as *nyakka* 'so that' and *ngga'ika* 'in order to.' Unlike the *zaizo*, the singing in rites of fulfillment is uninterruptable, and embedded almost entirely in fixed conventional couplets. There appears to be little room for improvisation, personal asides, or individual opinion.

As the ultimate example of the 'voice of the ancestors,' the *kanúngga* form of discourse accomplishes its relation to these prior discourses—its "intertextuality"—partly through a systematic denial of its situated character. Performers of these narratives scorn the dialogic contingencies that characterize rites of divination and reject the preoccupation with complex feats of musical and oratorical coordination displayed in the *zaizo*. Thoroughly saturated in a frame of performance evoking ancestral times and ancient places, 'blessing songs' and chants nonetheless subtly accommodate the participation structure of the event through intonational cues and rhetorical elaborations. Thus the interactional detachment of chants and blessing songs can be viewed in ideological terms, as a way of minimizing the relation of the performance to the actual event by directing comparisons with other texts, other times and other places—the authoritative realm of the ancestors.

While the performances of the *li'i marapu* 'words of the ancestors' in rites of fulfillment are the most authoritative forms of ritual speech in Weyewa ceremonial life, this claim is not based on the exact and precise replication of the supposed actual words attributed to the ancestors. To make this claim would be seen as a haughty effort to usurp the original ancestral authority. Speakers reluctantly admit that omissions may occasionally occur in songs or chants, but evaluate performances in relation to the overall restoration of order sought by the ritual. Obvious lapses are usually interpreted either in bodily terms—as failures of stamina, or temporary incapacity of the vocal chords or sensory faculties—or as a serious spiritual fault due to ritual neglect, a curse, or ritual impurity.

Promises

Fulfilling 'promises' is at the heart of all climactic feasting events in Weyewa. As has been repeatedly emphasized throughout this book, the notion of 'promising' is closely bound up with ideas of verbal performance and economic exchange. One of the important senses of *li'i* 'word, voice,' for instance, is 'promise,' as in 'plant the word' (*katukku li'i*). There are also two words that explicitly refer to 'promising' in Weyewa—*kira* 'promise, reckon, arrange (an appointment)' and *ndandi* 'promise, agree.' The first, more commonly used, term, *kira*, has temporal connotations, implying a time frame for its fulfillment.

It is often used in conjunction with a verb that carries spatial-locative connotations, such as *tau-ngge,* 'to place, to put' or *bondala* 'to set down'; faithfulness to such promises is described in terms of immoveability and fixity. A common way of initiating promises to exchange things, or agreements to meet at a certain time, is *kata tau-ngge kira,* literally 'let's place a promise.' Dates and terms are suggested, and if, by signifying with a nod and an *O'o* 'yes,' or some other symbolic gesture, the parties agree, the promise is considered binding. It is awkward (although grammatically possible) to performatively pronounce, 'I (hereby) promise to do so-and-so.'

In couplet speech, *kira* pairs with *ndandi,* as in *kira wulla, ndandi ndou* 'promise a month, agree on a year,' which refers to a promise to perform a ritual at some future date. *Ndandi,* which appears to be related to the Indonesian *janji* 'to promise, to agree' and has roughly the same range of meanings, is far less commonly used.

Covenants with *marapu* spirits consist of a kind of exchange agreement: in return for a smooth recovery from an illness, the cessation of calamity, a bounteous, pest-free harvest, or some such blessing, the descendants agree to stage a feast, build a house, or drag a tombstone in their honor. Holding up one's end of the bargain is crucial; failure to do so will result in punishment.

Mbulu Kulla, an ambitious middle-aged man, worked hard at fulfilling promises to his ancestors. I asked him why he decided to stage a large temple-building ceremony. He replied:

> We experienced many misfortunes. With tears in our eyes and mucus in our noses, we asked the spirits what they wanted, and we saw that there were spirits who 'had not eaten rice, and had not drunk water' [i.e., no celebration had been held in their honor]. Not even a chicken had been given to them! So we held a ceremony [*zaizo* 'placation rite'] to bring back these spirits, and stop all the deaths in our family, so we could close up the graves, and start to live our lives again.

According to Mbulu Kulla, the calamities that resulted from the neglect of these wrathful spirits were not his fault to begin with. Rather, the misfortunes were linked to his father, who died young, leaving unfulfilled promises that he told no one about:

nda'iki li'i pa-na'u	there were no final orders
nda'iki li'i pa-nanggo	there were no dying wishes

So his children inherited his neglect and began to suffer calamities until they discovered the promises he had made and met the obligations.

Promising is a speech act (Austin 1962; Searle 1969), but one that takes place in a complex interactional setting. While much has been written on the logico-relational features of such speech acts from the perspective of the sender, less is known about the larger cultural context of communicative exchange and negotiation by which such promises are accomplished. Although the particulars of these events vary widely among Weyewa, a common context in which such promises are made is the following: the morning after a 'divination' and all-night *zaizo*, the participants to the rite and their kin and co-resident villagers gather on the veranda of the house where the ceremonies took place for a post-*zaizo* feast. Mats are spread out and as people arrive they sit and enjoy a betel and areca nut chew with their relatives and co-villagers. As soon as the key awaited guests and important feasting ingredients are all in place, the 'main orator' (or some other individual with authoritative knowledge of the afflicted family's history sits on the right side of the veranda and asks for everyone's attention. One such scene I recorded in the fall of 1978:

Mbulu Kulla: [In a loud voice] IN ORDER TO [pauses, waits for quiet], in order to describe for all of you here, those things . . . [the recent events in the family which we were discussing] and the approval of Ndabi Ndende, Ndappa Rawa [our shared ancestors], there remain a few things to say.

Regarding the ancient past, when the pig was old and the dog was aged, these matters have already been raised up to the spirits, and placed by the side of the Mother, by the side of the Father, who are truly like upright roosters.

But now, if that is so, and I along with you have arrived here, in the shade of the eaves, at the edge of the veranda, if that is so, my brethren, we [are here] with tears in our eyes and mucus in our noses, and our Mother and our Father are here, too, who arrived last night; all because we forced our bodies and drove our selves;[2]

Regarding all of this, because "we ate no rice, and we drank no water" and "we were ignored, and we were neglected" if that is said by them [the ancestors] to me, then let us talk and pose questions, let us discuss and set a date [for a feast in their honor]

Lende Mbatu: So that,—that's all right—as I see it, as I see it for example, we don't break new ground here. In accordance with tradition, we must encircle the house, [so] the [ancestors] come back to the village courtyard, and arrive at the doorstep once again. All this before we finally "roast and slaughter" . . .

Mbulu Kulla (the main orator) began by offering his summary of the reason for the gathering; it concerned matters of the ancient past that had been recently discussed with the spirits, on account of which people suffered ("tears in the eyes") and struggled ("drove our selves"). To stop the neglect, Mbulu Kulla proposed that they set a date on which to atone. Lende Mbatu, one of Mbulu Kulla's kinsmen and a ritual spokesman, then proposed the exact form which the promise could take: invite the spirits back to the village and to the house through a *zaizo* and *woleka* 'celebration feast' ("roast and slaughter").

In the discussion that ensued, the male heads of families, many with their wives sitting next to them, raised questions about how soon the necessary cattle could be accumulated, who should contribute, and how much (although this latter was left somewhat vague), and whether all the right people were there to make a decision of this kind. After about an hour of talk, the first speaker raised his voice once again and proposed that they sacrifice a chicken to the spirits and test the proposal that they hold the feast on a certain date. The sign of approval or disapproval would be in the chicken's entrails.

The ritual spokesman went up into the house, prepared an offering, and about five minutes later came out with the opened chicken carcass and the duodenum ready for inspection. He handed it to the main orator who proclaimed 'the chicken has spoken,' meaning that there was ancestral approval for these plans. He handed it to the others sitting on the veranda. As the others looked at the entrails and discussed them with one another informally, the main orator told the young boys to prepare for the slaughter of the pigs and water buffalo that had been brought for the gathering.

The promise was reiterated by the main orator in a prayer. The prayer excerpted below was delivered in the house as the animal offerings were readied for slaughter in the courtyard. In it, he requests that the spirits provide pest-free and abundant harvests so that he and his kinsmen can fulfill his promise.

ne ba hinna	and now	1
wolo-ba-ngge kira	we have made a promise	
rawi-ba-ngge ndandi	we have reached an agreement	
ne'e kira a touda ndou-na	for a date three years from now	
ne'e nya-langge neweti	it will thus occur here	5
monno hinna-ki-do-ngge	and thus it is so	
ka na-dadi-ko-ngga	therefore may there be	
we'e parekka	bountiful water for me	
ka na timbu-ko-ngga	may there grow for me	
we'e parandi .	water that is plenty	10
ngga'i-ka-na	may there be	
mane-ko-ngga pola-na	thick strong rice stalks	
ngga'i-ka-na	may there be	
mandaupa-ko-ngga pola-na	fat and long rice stalks	

Housebuilding

In the prayer above, Mbulu Kulla promises to return to the ancestral village in three years, swearing that he will first 'descend to the rice fields' to 'work the fields, and pull out the weeds' (*ndari tana, mbatu rutta*) in order to accumulate the wherewithal to stage the costly feast. In prayers and song, these upcoming years of preparation are depicted as a 'descent' and migration out from the social environment of the village to that of the isolated and undomesticated gardens and fields. Couplets represent this as a 'hot' time, due to the exertion of hard labor and the proximity to dangerous autochthonous spirits in the forests, watercourses, and fields. Another common image for this period is 'bitterness' (*poddu*), signifying the prohibition on the slaughter of livestock to be accumulated for the upcoming feast (see also Kuipers 1984a). It is seen as a time of great effort and personal sacrifice: 'I drive my body, I push my self' (*ku-zoka tou-nggu, ku-mbole wekki-nggu*).

It is during this period of 'bitter' hard work and self-denial that Weyewa ritual leaders begin to pull together the resources to fulfill their promises to the ancestral spirits. To build an ancestral house, it is necessary to obtain hundreds of bamboo and hardwood poles from the forest, as well as several tons of grass thatch (or nowadays, corrugated, galvanized tin [*seng*]). Cutting the four main posts of the house nowadays requires a legal permit from the Department of Forestry, as well as the permission of the 'lord of the forest' (*mori kandawu*). The latter is obtained by providing a prayer offering of shavings of gold and silver wrapped in banana leaves (*marata*), along with some coconut meat, and a small live chick and puppy, which are let free in the woods. If the trees to be cut down are on someone's land, the negotiations for the wood are conducted like marriage negotiations. The owner takes the part of wife-giver, and receives horses, buffalo, and spears as payment, and if there is a countergift, it consists of pigs and cloths. Once the timber is removed, the forest must be 'closed' again with an offering to the spirits and to the owner.

Nowadays, the task of hauling the logs and bamboo from the woods to a point near the ancestral village can be accomplished by truck. As of 1987, however, there was still no direct road access to most ancestral villages, and dragging the four main house pillars (*pari'i*) the final few kilometers into the village itself still required crews of dozens of young men using ropes and long vines. The worksongs sung by the young men as they drag the heavy logs represent the pillar as a young woman—a bride—with a 'slender waist, and beautiful complexion,' whom they are bringing home to stay in the village. At the gate of the village, a ceremonial greeting (*pazimbala*) is performed between the 'lord of the village' and the spokesman of the pole dragging group in order to obtain permission to enter.

During the course of the housebuilding procedure, themes of blood sacrifice, male-female sexuality, and hot and cold are interwoven through ritual speech, ceremonial practice, and mythology. While present to some degree in all housebuilding ceremonies, these images are particularly salient in the rules and behavior associated with the re-building of *rumata* 'sacred temples' (cf. Kapita 1976b:271ff.). These were especially sacred, collectively owned and maintained houses inhabited by descendants of a low-ranking clan of slaves and war captives who were said to have been used as sacrificial victims as part of the final stages of the re-building ceremonies. It is said that their skulls were planted beneath the house poles in order to atone for the transgressions of Mbora Pyaku. Since this practice has been discontinued, a small water buffalo is now substituted, with the caveat that these are the procedures of *nggokko rato* 'spotted priests'—impure ritualists. The imagery of human sacrifice, as an ultimate demonstration of hierarchical domination, contrasts with the institutionalized licentious and egalitarian behavior on the eve of the slaughter, when unbridled sexuality is permitted and men and women may have intercourse with whomever they choose.

The 'heat' thus generated by torrid sexuality, combined with the sweaty hard work of construction, the feverish intensity of sacrifice, and the proximity to spiritually dangerous forest products, requires resolution through 'cooling off' the following day with a formalized, highly structured narrative song known as *we'e maríngi* 'blessing song' (literally 'cool water'). Such songs are a necessary accompaniment at several key moments in the very final stages of the fulfillment of a housebuilding promise so that the resident spirits may return to re-inhabit the dwelling. In the song excerpted below, an elderly male performer sings a stanza of couplet verse ending with *we'e maríngi-o-o-o* 'cool water o-o-o.' This line is then repeated once by a chorus of young males, whereupon the singer produces another stanza and the procedure is repeated until the whole story is told.

Although no *rumata* remain in Weyewa, the 'blessing song' excerpted below was performed to consecrate the rebuilding of a small, uninhabited temple (*kabubu*) devoted to the bones of human sacrificial victims slaughtered in the past for the *rumata* in the ancestral village of Lewata. As a powerful symbol of clan unity and hierarchy, the temple and its rebuilding offered an occasion for members of the various lineages to gather and work cooperatively. Representatives from each house brought a few bundles of green bamboo, some sheaves of freshly cut and tied imperata grass (*ngaingo*) for the roof, and chickens and pigs for slaughter. The old temple was 'demolished' (*tettera*) after a brief offering, the old wood and thatch cleared away, exposing the fragments of bleached white bones and what appeared to be buffalo horns. All representatives contributed a shaft of bamboo to the new structure, which was erected in about an hour. Before the grass thatch was in place, a singer stood on top of one of the nearby stone sarcophagi, and began to sing.

We'e manggabbo oooo!	Fresh water oooo!	1
He?	Hey?	
. . . ka ndu wale ya?	. . . why aren't you responding?	

After this admonition, the singer began again, after which the chorus finally joined in (the overlap is indicated with brackets):

We'e maríngi oooo!   Cool water oooo!
        [
chorus: *ooooo!*   ooooo!   5

The song began with a caveat alluding to the lack of proper human sacrifices in the present day, and the general loss of status in the Lewata clan. It then
proceeded to describe the journey of the lineage's ancestral figure, Mbulu
Nggollu Wolla, as he invites the ancestors of other village residents to attend the
feast for the partially fulfilled promise of sacrifice and rebuilding. In describing
the itinerary, the singer also reproduced the spatial arrangement of the original
village settlement, which reflects the hierarchical structure of relations among
the descendants.

Tukku rewooo rara-ngge   The red torch was smashed
puwa tammeee moro-ngge   the green blowpipe was shattered

The singer thus began with the disclaimer that the clan has been rendered de-
fenseless by calamity. Their weapons shattered and smashed, the clan members
can no longer carry out rituals in the proper manner. Despite this sorry state,
they proceed with the 'gathering,' asking how the village and indeed all of Weyewa (referred to here with the couplet name, Nyura Lele Mayongo, We'e Paboba
Yarra) has become so quiet and impoverished in ritual activity.

ba na kapondiii ana rato-ngge   thus the gathering of the children of
                                                                           princes
na kapozi ana nggenggeeooo   and there is a cluster of spider children
                                                                           oooo
                   [
chorus: *ooooo!*   ooooo!   10

Peiya-mo-we newe?   How could this happen here?
Nda pa-kuku-da-we manu-ngge   No more clucking chickens
nda pa-weka-da-we wawi-ngge   no more squealing piglets
    Nyura Lele Mayongo   in Nyura Lele Mayongo
    We'e Paboba Yarra-nggeeoo   in We'e Paboba Yarra ooo
                   [
chorus: *ooooo!*   ooooo!

His disclaimers completed, the singer begins to describe the journey of the ancestral figure Mbulu Nggollu Wolla as he makes his way around the village,
inviting other households to attend the temple-building feast, of which the present event is an example.

Nyakka-na lolungooo malawo-na   Thus we proceed like rats in a row
nyakka-na burungooo tawewe-na   thus we parade like pheasants in formation
    ngara ndukka oleee Innanggu   all of our Mothers
    ngara ndukka oleee Amangguuooo   all of our Fathers oooo   20
                   [
chorus: *ooooo!*   ooooo!

Nyakka-na tanga tilluuu dommo-ko
nyakka-na mattu mataaa we'e-ko
   ngara ndukka anaaa pondi-ngge

   ngara ndukka anaaaa nggenggeooo
        [
chorus: ooooo!

All the ears are paired
all the eyes are complete
all the children of the hallowed
      gathering
all the spider children ooo   25

ooooo!

Nyakka-na wolongooo tarenda-ngge
nyakka-na ngginggaraaaa pa-redda-ngge
   ngara ndukkaaaa ana pondi-ngge

   ngara ndukkaaa ana rato-nggeoo
        [
chorus: ooooo!

So we all work together
we quickly see the road to embark on
all the children of the hallowed
      gathering
all the children of the priests ooo   30

ooooo!

Nyakka-na pa-zamako-nggeee lawi-na
nyakka-na pa-merako-nggeeee pu'u-na
   newe woloooo Inna-ngge
   newe rawiiii Ama-nggeooo
        [
chorus: ooooo!

So the tip is matched
so the trunk is parallel
these deeds of the Mother
these works of the Father oooo   35

ooooo!

Teda-mu-niii nawwa-ngge
   Mbulu Nggolluuu Wolla-ngge
   a longge-na kadippu rundaaaa rangga
   kadippu mbaliiii mbonnu-nggeoo
        [
chorus: ooooo!

Wait for this one [named]
   Mbulu Nggollu Wolla
   whose hair is silver dewangga cloth
   a piece of gold from abroad ooo   40

ooooo!

A mángu kangangoooo aro umma
   a mángu katodaaa tillu natara
   a mángu kabubuuu Rato Pengu
   Mbili Maneee Mbyali-nggeoo
        [
chorus: ooooo!

Who has a spirit altar in front of his house
who has a skull tree in the courtyard
who has a spirit temple of Rato Pengu
   Mbili Mane Mbyali oooo   45

ooooo!

Nyakka-na pawuzzaaaa nggaddi kako
nyakka-na patoriii nggoko nggaiwe
   newe woloooo Inna-ngge
   newe rawiii Ama-nggeoo
        [
chorus: ooooo!

So he was boiling with an urge to go
so he earnestly attended to this and that
to the relics of the Mother
to the relics of the Father   50

ooooo!

Mbittaka-daaaa tana-na-ngge
nggunggila-daaa watu-ngge

The land is flattened out
the stones are cut to shape

a toma-du-niii nawwa-ngge	he reaches this place
Ngongo Mawooo Ninno-nggeooo	Ngongo Mawo Ninno ooo 55
[	
chorus: *ooooo!*	ooooo!

Thus the first to be invited is the ancestor of the We'e Melli lineage.

Dukki-du-niii nawwa-ngge	Thus he arrives here
Mbili Mawooo Kombo-ngge	to Mbili Mawo Kombo's
Kyoni Ndendeee Ngara-nggeooo	Kyoni Ndende Ngara's ooo
[	
chorus: *ooooo!*	ooooo! 60

The next to be invited is also an ancestral pair from We'e Melli.

Toma-du-niii nawwa-ngge	And next he arrived here
Winni Lendeee Ndima-ngge	at Winni Lende Ndima's
Lyali Ndelaaa Ramba-ngge	at Lyali Ndela Ramba's
a zadidi wiwiii Inna-ngge	who attends to the lips of the Mother
a zangera wiwiii Ama-nggeooo	who is next to the lips of the Father 65
[	
chorus: *ooooo!*	ooooo!

mbitta-ka-daaaa tana-na-ngge	the land is flattened out
nggunggila-daaa watu-ngge	the stones are cut to shape
ne kambyataaa We'e Melli-ngge	in the plaza in front of We'e Melli clan house
ne Tanjongaaa Kambu Watu-nggeoo	of the Tanjonga Kambu Watu ooo 70
[	
chorus: *ooooo!*	ooooo!

ne ba na-pa-lengge-weee lawi-na	so he embarked from the tip
Mbyulu Nggolluuu Wolla	Mbyulu Nggollu Wolla
ne ba na-pa-kedde-weee pu'u-na	so she got up to go from the trunk
Winni Tendaaa Zapaooo	Winni Tenda Zapa ooo 75
[	
chorus: *ooooo!*	ooooo!

The narrative proceeded for 229 more lines, listing house names in the village of Lewata. Most of the stanzas consisted of couplet names, each alluding to the history and status of a lineage within the village. The order in which the singer performed the names corresponds to the mythical 'path' of the ancestral figure Mbulu Ngollu Wolla as he invites the lineages of the village to attend the event. In enumerating the members of the village, the singer rhetorically constructs an image of the unity of the group.

Text and Context in the Blessing Song Performance

In Blessing Song performances, the singer relentlessly emphasizes the *unity* of the diverse components of the village. Unlike the *zaizo*, in which orators acknowledge explicitly that alternative points of view (albeit undesirable) do exist, in these performances, such references to possible sources of tension within the audience are not even admitted into the text. Instead, the singer is emphatic that the 'tips are matched, the trunks are parallel' and the diverse components of the clan, young and old, recent and ancient, low and high status are all in harmony with one another. Differences have all been evened out, so that the 'land is smooth, the stones are flattened.' The unitary nature of the characters in the story is an icon of an ideal of sociability that the singer wishes to promote among the participants in the event. He suggests that the audience itself is unified, unlike the competing factions represented in the discourse of both the divination and placation rites.

Melodic structure contributes to the rhetorical unity of the text (see Figure 9). Unlike the *zaizo*, in which successful performance requires a relatively complex rhythmic and semantic coordination and adjustment with gongs, drums, and other orators, this song is the responsibility of a single individual who follows a more or less ready-made, redundant, and formulaic melodic and semantic pattern guiding the structure of the stanzas. Not only does the stanza consist of couplets, but coherence is created *across* lines of couplets by melodic parallelism between all but the last phrases of a verse, which is itself parallel with other stanza endings. The stanza in lines 11–15, for instance, is constructed of four melodically parallel lines, each ending on the tonic, or first pitch of a three note scale. The final phrase of the last line is signalled formulaically, only by rhythmic, syntactic, and semantic parallelisms, but with a melodic schema: instead of resolving the melody into the tonic pitch as in the other lines, the last word is extended on a second note of the scale as a signal for the chorus to join in and bring the note down to the first pitch of the scale. Since this same pattern is repeated in all the other stanzas, it creates coherence not only within the stanzas, but across them as well.

In schematic form, the melodic pattern of the stanza in Figure 9 might be represented as follows:

```
[singer]                         112-311
                                 112-311
                                 112-311
                                 112-311
                                 112-322-
                                        [
[chorus]                                -2-1
```

where numbers represent pitches, hyphens represent extended pitch, and the open bracket represents the chorus's overlapping contribution in the final line.

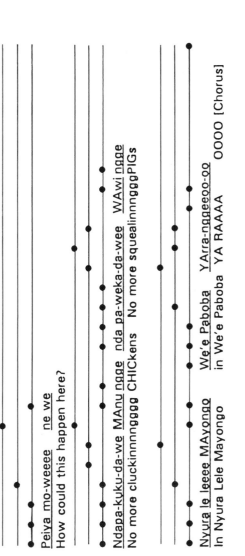

Peiya mo-weeee   ne we
How could this happen here?

Ndapa-kuku-da-we MAnu ngge nda pa-weka-da-wee WAwi ngge
No more cluckinnnnggggg CHICkens   No more squealinnngggPIGs

Nyura le leeee MAyongo   We'e Paboba   YArra-ngqeeoo-oo
In Nyura Lele Mayongo   in We'e Paboba YA RAAAA   OOOO [Chorus]

Figure 9: The melodic shape of the blessing song.

Although the number of lines varies somewhat throughout the performance, the basic melodic pattern establishes the stanzas as a structural unit, and creates a vocal image repeated throughout the text.

The redundant, formulaic, and stereotypical character of the performance creates such a powerful image of thoroughly entextualized performance that it is easy to overlook the ways in which the singer modulates features of the delivery and content in order to accommodate his audience. He *does* contextualize the narrative in at least two important ways: (1) by adjusting the performance in relation to his chorus and, more importantly, (2) by elaborating on the problematic status of certain lineages.

The singer must adjust his song to accommodate the differential competence of the audience in the 'blessing song' genre. In the example above, when he began with the cue 'fresh water o-o' he was greeted with silence, as the chorus of approximately ten young men failed to respond. He admonished them:

He?	Hey?
. . . ka ndu wale ya?	. . . why aren't you responding?

After a pause of a second or less, the singer began again,

We'e maríngi oooo!	Cool water oooo!

and a prominent young man took a deep and audible breath, cueing the others to join in:

chorus: *ooooo!*	ooooo!

At this point, the speaker finally began the narration of the text.

Tukku rewooo rara-ngge	The red torch was smashed	5

Since the chorus of young boys was far less familiar with the structure of the narrative than the singer, the performer cued them intonationally as to when they should respond by singing the 'cool water o-o' line.

These pitch cues can be crucial even for an experienced audience, because, while many discourse features of the song call attention to its densely structured *textual* character—for example, the rigidly parallel couplet forms and pragmatically demarcated stanzas—the number of lines making up a stanza is not al-predictable (compare, for example, the 3-line stanza on lines 57–59 versus the five-line stanza in 61–65), and stanza boundaries do not always coincide exactly with couplet boundaries. On line 52, the singer begins with a couplet, but ends with two independent lines, both of which could have been paired but were not:

Mbittaka-daaaa tana-na-ngge	The land is flattened out
nggunggila-daaa watu-ngge	the stones are cut to shape

| *a toma-du-niii nawwa-ngge* | he reaches this place | |
| *Ngongo Mawooo Ninno-nggeooo* | Ngongo Mawo Ninno ooo | 55 |

While the use of the narrative result-marker *nyakka* 'so that' implies a certain logical coherence, fixity, and inevitability to the relationships in the song text, in fact the order in which the singer mentioned the places in some cases indexed current status struggles. For instance, when the singer mentioned the name of the house of the lineage of Umbu Tirrika, he then proceeded to make an outer arc in his journey, inviting the ancestors of the house of a slave lineage, Ndappa Roka–Ndappa Lawa, and then another slave lineage, Mawo Wunnuta, before returning to the center of the village. Through this juxtaposition, not only were the lineages of Ndappa Roka–Ndappa Lawa and Mawo Wunnuta linked to one another by their shared low status, but also, as a result of its narrative proximity to the low status lineages, Umbu Tirrika was represented as a slave-guardian lineage. At the time of the performance, the status of Umbu Tirrika was a sensitive issue because a young man from that lineage had begun to make inquiries about marriage with a woman from a high status lineage and wanted moral and economic support from his fellow clan members. Thus the spatiotemporal ordering of the place names connotes not only ancient obligations and hierarchical differences, but indexes some contemporary social relations as well.

The degree of elaboration of stanzas can vary contextually depending on the audience (cf. Bauman 1986:78–111). In this case, in order to emphasize and call attention to the low status lineages, the singer stretched the name of the slave group across two stanzas, something not done in any other part of the song:

nyakka dukki-du-niii nawwa-ngge	thus he arrived here	
Mbili Ndappaaa Lawa	Mbili Ndappa Lawa	
Myoda Mbaliii Rara	Moda Mbali Rara	
Manu Ndappaaa Lawa-ngge-oo	Manu Ndappa Lawa oo	195
[		
chorus: ooooo!	ooooo!	

nyakka na toma-du-niii nawwa-ngge	thus he arrived here	
Mbili Ndappaaa Roka	Mbili Ndappa Roka	
Pyeda Ngokkooo Rato	Peda Nggoko Rato	
Tollu Ndappaaa Roka-ngge-oo	Tollu Ndappa Roka oo	200
[		
chorus: ooooo!	ooooo!	

By dwelling markedly on the name of this low status lineage, the singer created a frame against which the subsequent names were juxtaposed. By listing the name of the Umbu Tirrika clan next, he effectively made a comparison.

Rather than simply ending the tale when all houses were mentioned, the singer concluded with a moral evaluation on the state of the village:

| *ndappa kuku-da-weee manu-ngge* | no more chickens crow here |
| *ndappa wekka-da-weee wawi-ngge* | no more pigs squeal here |

ne Nyura Leleee Mayongo	here in Nyura Lele Mayongo
ne We'e Pabobaaa Yarra-nggeooo	here in We'e Paboba Yarra ooo
[	
chorus: *ooooo!*	ooooo!
Nyakka-na marota-ndiii kawendo-ngge	Thus the house eaves are dilapidated
nyakka-na pa-lummuta-ndiii ondi-ngge	thus the sarcophagi are covered with moss
ba hinna-we newwe wolooo Inna-ngge	thus it is here by the relics of the Mother
newwe rawiii Ama-nggeooo	here by the relics of the Father
[	
chorus: *ooooo!*	ooooo!

Despite the tremendous effort involved in cooperating to rebuild the temple, the singer reminded his audience of the current state of deterioration and impoverishment of the village. The village sarcophagi remain neglected, the houses still are dilapidated, and the village silently awaits the renewal of noisy ritual activity.

Thus the re-telling of the narrative of the gathering of the 'princes and priests' (i.e., the tale of the journey of Mbulu Nggollu Wolla) is less a re-creation of a changeless social order (following a standard functionalist interpretation) than an effort by the singer to mark the limits of disorder and neglect. The spectacle of monologic song, followed by lavish exchange and consumption is not viewed as a *re-enactment* of the glorious days of Mbulu Nggollu Wolla and his wife Winni Tenda Zapa, in the hopes of re-creating or somehow restoring those times, so much as an attempt to halt the forgetfulness, dilapidation, and deterioration of their spiritual and social life in a dynamic spirit of reproduction and renewal. Neither the 'word' in the song nor the economic transactions that follow it are regarded as exact copies of prior ancestral arrangements. Instead, they minimize the differences between the ancestral order and their own ritual practice as a way of rejecting promiscuous, untidy, and negligent conduct that leads to misfortune and blocks the path to creative growth.

Stone-dragging (*Téngi Watu*)

While stone-dragging is a significant rite of fulfillment for Weyewa, and an impressive undertaking, since there are no unique genres of ritual speech exclusively associated with this ceremony, I will describe it only briefly here.

Like housebuilding ceremonies, stone-dragging typically begins with a 'promise.' One man described to me how his father came to him in a dream and complained of his cramped and uncomfortable grave in front of the house. The man then promised to make a tombstone, and re-bury the bones of his father the following year. Nowadays, however, many prominent men ensure that they will be buried with renown by dragging their own tombstones.

Traditionally, the toadstool-shaped tombstones consist of two pieces often described in gendered terms: a hollow rectangular 'female' base (*bei*) as sepulchre, and a flat rectangular lid or 'leaf' (ro'o), linked with maleness. They are cut with machetes and heavy knives out of soft, white, wet limestone, which dries and hardens in the sun as it is dragged with ropes and vines on a tackle of logs to the destination, usually in the center of a village. Once inside, a wide variety of images may be carved into the leaf and base, but typically these include images of wealth possessed by the deceased: water buffalo horns, gongs, horses, spears, *mamuli* pendants, even pigs and knives.

Since about the middle of the 1970s with the increasing availability of Chinese-owned trucks for hire, few sponsors are willing to bear the cost and risk of having a large stone dragged any distance across the rugged Weyewa landscape, despite the prestige and attention that such an elaborate act of organization generates. Many people, indeed, have foresworn stone-cutting altogether and replicate the traditional design with concrete molds.

As with wood-cutting ceremonies, the spirits of the earth must be asked for permission to remove the stone. They are given an offering of *marata* gold and silver scrapings. If the stone is extracted from land owned by someone else, the owner may also require a marriage-like payment, consisting of horses and knives, for which the countergift is pigs and cloth. As the stone is dragged along the earth, a singer is hired to encourage the young men pulling on the ropes. As with the dragging of the house pillars, the stones, particularly the 'base' (*bei*), is represented in *padengara* 'dragging songs' as a female, as a beautiful bride to be carried into the village. At the village gate, the 'lord of the village' and the 'lord of the stone' engage in a ceremonial dialogue in which the stone-draggers are asked to state formally their purpose in entering the village before permission will be granted.

Celebration Feasts (*Woleka*)

The most prestigious ritual culmination of all ceremonial endeavors—stone-dragging, housebuilding, marriage arrangements, harvesting, or whatever—is a *woleka* 'celebration feast.' As the ultimate occasion for the fulfillment of a promise to the ancestors, these three- or seven-night pageants are actively and anxiously anticipated as occasions to dance, sing, play gongs, 'eat meat,' and ostentiously display ancestral heirlooms and personal wealth in the village 'courtyard' (*natara*). While the final day of these gatherings is often the scene of bitter quarrels and fierce competition over status, expressed in meat division and the exchange of livestock, the night and morning preceding it are the occasions for the reproduction of some of the most life-affirming and sacred verbal traditions among Weyewa.

At about 10 o'clock in the evening, after an animal has been slaughtered for the arrival of guests, the ancestral spirits notified, and the meal dishes cleared away, the first peals of the gong orchestra ring out with a characteristic *woleka* rhythm signifying that the celebration has officially begun. The first four evenings of a seven-night *woleka* typically consist only of gong playing and dancing lasting one to two hours.[3] Adolescent girls and young women, who are often the sponsor's daughters, nieces, or neighbors, dress in elegant sarongs and bright headcloths, heavy ivory bracelets, and ancient gold and silver pendants. The women 'dance' (*nenggo*) counterclockwise around the courtyard with straight-backed shuffle-steps and lowered eyes and with their partly outstretched hands open and rotating at the wrist in slow, flowing circles. For women, the vehicle of expressive movement is their bodies. This contrasts with expressive foci of the 'men's dance' (*kaba*) accompanying them, which are the heirloom objects brought down from the sponsor's attic—spears, swords and buffalo-hide shields—which they menacingly brandish, shake, and thrust as they twist at the waist and jerk their heads about with rolling eyes.

On the fifth night, following a performance by the dancers lasting about an hour (or seven rounds of the gong rhythm), young orators and a singer begin a ritual speech dialogue very similar to the initial phases of the *zaizo* 'placation rite.' The main difference is that the singer, addressed as *a ndondo* 'one who sings,' delivers his song unaccompanied by gongs or floor drum. The only ac-companiment permitted is a rhythmic jingling of small finger cymbals (*lang-goro*), or sometimes, a hand drum (*bamba*). Since it is brief and an opportunity for young men to practice their ability in ritual speech, this first night of ritual speaking is known as 'young fish playing, young turtles frolicking' (*manggeko ana iya, maranggo ana wonnu*).

The initial hours of each subsequent evening performance also include ludic, even parodic elements, elements largely quite absent from divination and placation rites. Quite often, dancers in the courtyard will temporarily adopt the dancing style of the opposite sex in order to get a laugh. In one feast I attended, a young orator poked fun at Weyewa declamatory style. He called for the speak-ing floor by shouting out the customary *dyoo! a ndondo* 'hail singer,' and once he was acknowledged, he created a dramatic pause in which he arranged his shoulder cloth with mock seriousness, simply said "I support you. Amen!" and turned his back to the audience, who convulsed in laughter at his unexpected brevity. In another feast, a young man began dancing behind the courtyard singer and imitating his motions, to the howls of the young children and the shouted imprecations of the elders (cf. Boon 1984). Such levity is less common in rites of placation.

After the fifth night, performances increase in duration, intensity, author-ity, and explicit mention of mythical precedents. On the sixth night, preceding the ritual dialogue between singers and orators, for instance, a spokesman tosses out rice into the courtyard and, after shouting "ooo-yau" three times, begins a trembling monologic chant (*oka*) informing the spirits of the village, of the land, of the gate, and in the heavens of his reasons for performing the feast. This is called 'sweeping the courtyard, cleaning the ring' (*wambo natara, ware tawurru*) in preparation for upcoming sacrifices. In it, he invokes the names of ancestors who taught Weyewa how to eat rice, how to feast, and how the evening's performance fulfills the promises made by ancient ancestors. Following this approximately twenty-minute performance, the ritual dialogue begins.

On the seventh night of a *woleka* performance I attended in the ancestral village of Lewata, the chant (*oka*) began when a designated person called out, 'handfuls of rice, hoorah!' (*doppola nga'a, yau!*) in memory of the ancestor, Yonggara Dendara, who taught them how to eat rice with their hands and not straight from the plate, like dogs. He then called out 'bring forth and strike the source, and the offspring, hoorah!' (*pakedde kamboli bei, kamboli ana, yau!*), alluding to the imminent sacrifice ('strike') of a young female water buffalo ('source') owned by the sponsor to the ancestral spirits. Unaccompanied by gongs and drums, these chants are not associated with symbolic instability and transition (e.g., as in the *zaizo*; cf. Needham 1967) so much as with the display of lineage unity, symbolic resolution, and ancestral authority.

The following *oka* chant was recorded on the evening prior to the final day of feasting in the ancestral village of Lewata, August 23, 1987. The chant usually delivered on this evening is described in terms of its purpose, which is to 'bring forth the reasons, sprinkle the courtyard with rice' (*ndullaka wangu, yaza-we natara*); that is, ritualists inform the spirits of the village of the reasons for the feast. In the chant, the speaker Malo Winno—who was also the sponsor of the feast—began by recounting the original migration to the hilltop village through the voice of the founding ancestors (the "I" of the chant) and how it was settled by a group of three and a group of four. As wealthy and high-status figures ('pearl-necklaced bottles'), they were summoned by the original inhabitants of the domain, a pair named Lende Nyura Lele and his wife Kioni We'e Paboba.

Oooo . . . . yau!	Oooo . . . . hoorah!	1
Oooo. . . . yau!	Oooo . . . . hoorah!	
Eia awa-doni	We beg your pardon	
"wolo engge"	"let's goof off"	
inda lunggu	I don't say that	5
Eia awa-do-ni	We beg your pardon	
"rawi ndeta"	"let's have fun"	
inda lunggu	I don't say that	
Eia awa-do-ni	We beg your pardon	
newe wolo Inna	because of these creations of the Mother	
		10
nyakka ku-deku-na	I follow	
rukku ndara Lewa	the tracks of the horse from Lewa	
Eia awa-do-ni	We beg your pardon	
newe pa-rawi Ama	because of these creations of the Father	
nyakka ku-mane-na	I follow precisely	15
wata [. . . .].	the groove [inaudible].	
Na'i, ba ku-toma-ngge	As I arrive here	
newe lete a mandetā-na	at the hill so high	
ba ku-dukki-ngge	as I reach	
newe ndoba a mandalē-na	the valley so deep	20

Eia awa-do-ni	We apologize
na'i a kawula-ngga ndobā-na	to the one who calls us from the hills
eia awa-do-ni	we apologize
na'i a kaaula-ngga ladaka-na	to the one who calls us from the mountain
Nya-we ka nyakka	And so 25
ba ku-kedde mangu Inna	as I proceed with my Mother
ne'e Kambiata Lai Tangiobba	to Kambiata Lai Tanggiobba
ka nyakka ku-kedde mángu Ama	as I proceed with my Father
ne'e Parioro Lele Nammu	to Parioro Lele Nammu
ka nyakka ku-toma-ngge	and so I arrive 30
Lewata Mandiangga	at Lewata the Tall
ba ma-tullura ka-touda	as three upright [men]
ka nyakka ku-dukki-ngge	and so I arrive
Kaliaki Winno Wole	at Kaliaki Winno Wole
ba ma-wolo-na kambatu mbittaka	as we create a smooth village plaza 35
ka nyakka newe-na mbyali	and so now on the other end [of the journey]
ka nyakka wa'ini	here are
ole nggozi rewa koko-nggu	my fellows of the pearl necklaced bottle
na'i pata mbua kabani	these four men
ne ba na-kawula-ngga ndoba-na	he called us from the valley 40
na'i Lyende Nyura Lele	Lyende Nyura Lele
ne ba na ka-aula-ngga ladaka-na	when she called us from the mountain
na'i Kioni We'e Paboba	Kioni We'e Paboba
oooo . . . . yau!	oooo . . . . hoorah!
oooo. . . . yau!	oooo . . . . hoorah! 45

The rest of the chant described how the ancestors were neglected and how the current performance atones for that neglect. In this case, when the ancestral temple houses were allowed to fall into disrepair, it made the spirits angry. Thus, with the performance of the present feast, the performer Malo Winno claimed the descendants have 'descended to the courtyard and risen up into the house' to feast and praise the ancestors to atone for their neglect, and to fulfill their original promise. By recounting the 'word' of the ancestors,—the original promises and obligations for which the feast constitutes a fulfillment—the chant attempts to legitimate the performance.

As in the blessing song, this performance by Malo Winno stresses the serious, unified, and authoritative character of the performance. Consciously constructing the text as a communicative event, Malo Winno emphasizes that there are no voices leading them astray:

Eia awa-doni	We beg your pardon
"wolo engge"	"let's goof off"
inda lunggu	I don't say that 5

Eia awa-do-ni	We beg your pardon
"rawi ndeta"	"let's have fun"
inda lunggu	I don't say that

Along similar lines, he emphasizes over and over the precedent for the performance: that everything that is done and said 'follows the tracks/follows the
groove'—that is, the rules and procedures set by the ancestral spirits. These
protestations on the part of the speaker appear to be consistent with the relatively
monologic participation framework, the use of narrative form, the rigid couplet
and intonational structure, and the frequent use of proper names that evoke
powerful ancestral personages.

Despite this emphasis on the rigidly conventional nature of the chant, this
performance indexes its audience in significant ways. In this instance, a major
problem facing the sponsor Malo Winno was not the unity of the participants,
but whether the conduct of the ritual was legitimate and correct. There were two
reasons for this concern. The first was that since the sponsor had suffered a
number of rather embarrassing economic setbacks in recent years, there was
some question about his ability to carry out such a ritual competently. A second
factor in the sponsor's sense of insecurity about his ceremonial status was the
presence in the audience of a renowned ritual spokesman, a person who had a
penchant for questioning openly the authority of ritual performances.

Some felt that Malo Winno expressed this insecurity by over-emphasizing
the ancient and encompassing character of this performance. Critics pointed to
the presumptuous use of the names of the ancestral pair considered to be the
founder of the entire Weyewa region.

ne ba na-kawula-ngga ndoba-na	he called us from the valley
na'i Lyende Nyura Lele	Lyende Nyura Lele
ne ba na ka-aula-ngga ladaka-na	when she called us from the mountain
na'i Kioni We'e Paboba	Kioni We'e Paboba
oooo. . . . yau!	oooo . . . . hoorah!

Critics pointed out that the speaker simply mentioned the name without
providing any detailed genealogical connection to other ancestral spirits. They
implied that had he spelled out the connections, his claim to be directly descended from those who heard the 'call' or voice of these founding ancestors
might have been challenged. They argued that he included such a prestigious
name to forestall the criticism that the ritual performance was not properly conducted. While some considered the use of this name a questionable insertion,
supporters emphasized that it gave the narrative an inclusive character: "he
wanted to say 'this is a source village for all of Weyewa.'"

The next morning, after all the *loloka* 'guests' have arrived with their buffalo
and pigs, a speaker surrounded by gaily decorated dancers offers these animals to
the spirits in sacrifice. The speaker asks that these animals be received as 'food
and drink,' and as a message or supplication 'carried in the waistcloth, carried in

the hand' to the Creator Spirit. Of the Creator, the speaker requests prosperity: that he make 'the horse tails plump, and the cattle horns full.' Thus, rather than viewing the fulfillment of the promise to feast as a completed act, the chant describes a wish for fertility, well-being, and growth. Such a wish for fecundity implies a hope for change and contains the seeds of future exchanges between the living and the dead.

Spectacle and Exchange

The successful performance of the 'word' in blessing songs and chants is both condition and outcome of the fulfillment of the 'word' through exchange of animals. The ability of a sponsor to perform the chant himself (or to have it properly performed) suggests a certain rhetorical competence, an essential ingredient in successful economic negotiations. Such a chant also necessarily implicates the sponsor in a wide net of kin relations, suggesting powerful family and lineage connections. These factors combined to make Malo Winno a good "investment" for those who were invited to contribute animals. For poorer people looking for a safe place to invest an animal in expectation of future return, a charismatic individual who is well connected, a 'source' of authority, and powerfully linked to the 'trunk' of Weyewa genealogical discourse is likely to be regarded as an reliable trading partner with many branches of support. On the other hand, without such investments of animals, the demonstrations of skill cannot take place. Gaining control of a potentially vicious circle—animal exchange does not happen without competent performance, but performance cannot occur without investment of animals—is a high-stakes game that only a few individuals can master.

In the case of Malo Winno's feast, the exchanges that occurred not only could be justified as an enactment of ancestral 'words' of promise but also represented entrepreneurial efforts on his part to rebuild his lineage and regain a position of prominence for himself and his family. To understand the relationship between the verbal performance of the 'word' and its fulfillment through exchange, it is important to provide a description of the wider context of feasting and slaughter.

Shortly following the chant, the spectacle of animal slaughter and meat division begins (Plates 7 and 8). Buzzing crowds of men, women, and children sit jammed onto the creaking and overloaded verandas of the houses which overlook the courtyard as their hosts scurry about proffering betel and areca nut, and otherwise attending to the guests' needs. Cheers and shouts arise as a designated man dances about the courtyard brandishing his sword, watching for an opportunity to 'slash' (*teba*) the throat of a water buffalo, whose horns are tied with at least two twenty-foot lengths of rope gripped by groups of young men on either side of the animal. After the initial cut, the terrified beast invariably kicks and bucks, shaking its sharp horns dangerously close to the seated crowds. If, as

Plate 7: The slaughter of a buffalo. Animal sacrifice represents an important climax in a rite of fulfillment.

Plate 8: The butchering and exchange of meat in a rite of fulfillment. Division of meat is carried out according to precise rules.

occasionally happens, a water buffalo breaks loose, pandemonium ensues as laughing and screaming onlookers scramble over one another to avoid the pan-icked and half-dead animal with its partially severed head.

Still, a struggling animal is regarded as a propitious sign. Other omens are found in whether it finally rests on its left (bad) or right (good) side, the kind and number of death screams it makes (the more the better), and the configuration, color, and irregularities in the liver. Pigs are killed with far less spectacle; they are laid on their side with their legs tied together and a spear is 'stabbed' (*ndak-ura*), or more accurately, shoved, between their ribs. The body hair is then quickly singed off with torches.

Before the meat division begins, all animals must be killed. This may take several hours, depending on the number of water buffalo to be killed and the problems encountered. The head and right foreleg of the slaughtered pigs and buffalo are customarily given to the sponsor of the feast, who then dries the horns and jaws and hangs them as trophies on the veranda in the front of the house. The rest of the meat is carefully divided according to the amount of gift brought. Large contributors may return laden with a leg and a flank, or even several of them. Everyone attending the feast, regardless of whether he or she brought anything, receives a share of meat.

Participation in celebration feasts tends to be structured around affinal, marriage-like alliances. When Malo Winno sponsored an important celebration feast in 1987, I asked him to identify the guests who brought animals, their relationship to him, the kind of animal brought, and the kinds of debts the exchange engendered. In this case, although the crowd attending was well over two hundred, there were only twelve official 'guests' (*loloka*)[4].

1. Umbu Tawi is a Lolinese man whose rice fields adjoined those of the sponsor, Malo Winno. Umbu Tawi is considered a wife-taker (*lazawa*) since his son married a Weyewa woman from the same patriclan as Malo Winno. He brought a male water buffalo, considered to be an exchange for a large tusked hog brought by Malo Winno to Loli the previous year.

2. Mbulu Dairo is the nephew (MBS) of Malo Winno and was raised by him. When he later married, he joined his wife's clan which lacked males. He brought a large hog to Malo Winno as a token of appreci-ation of the care and concern that was shown him while growing up.

3. Bulu Ama Pare of the Lewata clan is a neighbor (no close family con-nections) who brought a large pig carried by four persons. This repre-sented a first time exchange between the two.

4. Mbulu Rato is the nephew of Malo Winno (MBS). As a representative of a lineage that stands as 'wife-giver' to Malo Winno, he brought a large sow (carried by four persons) in exchange for one exactly the same size given to him last year by Malo Winno.

5. Ngongo Ama Toro could be considered a wife-giver through distant

family relations, so he brought a pig; but he explained his connection as being primarily a 'neighborly' one, since he and Malo Winno have huts near one another in the Waikelo rice fields.

6. Mbulu Kaka brought a large hog carried by eight persons: he is both a cousin and a wife-giver to Malo Winno's brother and has received many animals from both of them.

7. Lende Dungga Meza is a 'wife-giver' (*pa-wera*), since his daughter is in the process of marrying one of Malo Winno's sons. Since he had already received a large number of horses from Malo Winno's family, he brought a large pig.

8. Daud Pila is a potential wife-taker (*lazawa*). He had recently returned from the hospital and stopped by Malo Winno's house; Malo Winno gave him a sarong and a waistcloth and a small pig as gifts. In exchange, Daud brought a stallion.

9. Ngongo Luku is a cross cousin (MBS), and thus a 'wife-giver' to Malo Winno. Their families claim to have an ancient and ongoing alliance as co-villagers in the greater village of Lewata. He has in the past provided two water buffaloes to Malo Winno, and brought a medium sized pig to this feast. Malo Winno has reciprocated in the past with a large pig.

10. Mbulu Mere is Malo Winno's brother-in-law, a 'wife-taker' (*lazawa*). Since he did not have the water buffalo that is the customary gift of a *lazawa*, he brought a large pig instead, calling it "sugar and coffee" (*kopi gula*), that is, domestic assistance not to be calculated under normal rules of reciprocity.

11. Dadi Mezango is Malo Winno's mother's brother (*loka*) and co-villager; he brought a large tusked pig which was immediately exchanged for a large bull water buffalo. The number of exchanges between them was too numerous for Malo Winno to recount; he did remark that when Dadi Mezango arrived to attend a feast of any kind, Malo Winno always met him at the gate with a countergift.

12. Mbulu Mori occupies the position of nephew, or father's brother's son. He brought a large pig and received in return a large share of buffalo meat. He is also a member of the Lewata patriclan although the former status of his lineage is the subject of whispers and indirect remarks.

Nine of the twelve guests claim an affinal connection with the sponsor. Of these, six occupy a kinship category glossed as 'wife-giver' (*pa-wera*), a group that traditionally provides pigs in exchange for cattle in the context of feasts. Of the three 'wife-takers' (*pa-lazawa*), who traditionally provide cattle in exchange for pigs and cloths, one brought a water buffalo, one brought a horse, and one, with apologies, brought a pig. Most of the guests brought pigs (10); but since water buffalo sacrifice is an essential feature of any *woleka* feast, five were slaughtered, of which four belonged to the host[5].

Common Characteristics of Rites of Fulfillment

The Affinal Idiom of Exchange

The marriage idiom that dominates the exchanges accords well with the themes of fulfillment, fertility, and growth in the celebration chants and songs. In ritual speech, marriage is represented as a source of replenishment and fertility for the lineage, and as a way of extending its reach into new territories. During the marriage negotiations, the bride is referred to as 'rice seed' (*winni pare*), while the groom's natal village and clan are described as a 'field' ready for planting. By extension, the relation between the two families is described as one that promotes fertility and growth through extension: 'thick vines of cucumber, plump tendrils of the gourd.'

The imagery of marriage and affinal relations also has special significance for Weyewa notions of misfortune. As we have seen in Chapter Three, misfortune is often viewed as a violation of the social and spiritual boundaries of the inside and outside. Marriage relations are also often represented in ritual speech as a way of routinizing the relationships between outsiders, who are in some case potential enemies, and the members of one's own lineage represented as "insiders." Weyewa speak of the entire process of conducting affinal relations as one of motion between social boundaries. Affines are called *loloka ndomma*, literally, 'regular guests.' They are outsiders who come in and out of one's social space with some frequency and routine. Negotiations between these two parties are characterized in terms of the action of the spokesmen

ndikkita pa-la'o	who go back and forth
noneka pa-mai	who run in between

The final stage of marriage, in which the transaction is finally complete, is called *pa-ndikki minne* 'to move the woman.'

In the context of discussions about misfortune, this formalization of relations of inside and outside in marriage can be and is seen as a means of minimizing the contrastive character of the opposition. In concrete social terms, this amounts to a prevention[6] of tensions. As one newlywed man expressed it, "Soon I will have troops to fight for me." What he meant was that he would soon have supporters, in the form of in-laws, and eventually children, to help him guard his gardens and house at night, fulfill his ritual duties, and maintain alliances. Children and affines are sources of labor, economic, and even military support. Through marriage alliances, one acts to reduce the insecurity of relations between inside and outside. Thus, unlike rituals of misfortune which focus on accounts of the past, the themes of marriage found in *woleka* celebrations are forward looking and concern the future. If rites of divination, placation and house blessing are responses to disorder and death, celebrations feasts for Weyewa concern perpetuation, reproduction, and continuation—the "flow" of life.

Of the affines, only the wife-givers (*pa-wera*) are specifically associated with the amelioration of misfortune. While the mother's brother is throughout eastern Indonesia linked with fertility and botanical imagery (cf. Fox 1980), what is less often remarked on is how such life-giving attributes are invoked in specific contexts. Among Weyewa, in times of calamity, the victim's mother's brother (*loka*) is among the first to be summoned and his very presence is held to maintain a sense of order. Divination, placation rites, and blessing songs, to say nothing of *woleka* celebrations, cannot begin until a representative from the house of the mother's brother is present. In ritual speech, the *loka* is represented with the image of the protective banyan tree, a symbol of security ('the leafy banyan tree, the wide branched banyan tree' *maliti a pambewa, kadoke a pa-nganggo*). Perhaps even more telling is the standard custom that when a negative omen is discerned in pig, chicken, or liver augury, it is the *loka* who is called in to sacrifice another animal whose omen will be inspected in an effort to *kouka* 'raise up their spirits.'

From Opposition to Unity

Successful performances of rites of fulfillment triumph over oppositions between ancestors and descendants, wife-givers and wife-takers, and verbal form and verbal content. Performers and participants, by standing amid the ancestral hierlooms and ancestral villages, seek to minimize the distance between themselves and their forebears by wearing their clothing, speaking in their voices, and walking along their paths. And while the participants themselves tend to be clearly distinguished in oppositional terms as wife-givers and wife-takers, the import of these contrasts is directed towards the creation of fertile, life-giving unities through marriage-like exchanges rather than on separation and differentiation.

As the distinctive speech events constituting the final stages in rites of atonement, 'chants' and 'blessing songs' show a preoccupation with achieving *proximity* to, if not identity with, the 'voices' of the ancestral spirits. This is reflected in the oft-repeated desire on the part of the speaker to get 'closer' to the spirits, or to be 'at the side of the Mother and Father':

ngga'i ka ku-toma	so that I arrive
tiddi wai manera	at the banks of the *manera*-waters
pa-wolo Inna	by the creations of the Mother
ngga'i ka ku-dukki	so that I reach
ndonga wai lapale	the shore of the *lapale* waters
pa-rawi Ama	by the works of the Father

One important way of accomplishing this unity with the ancestral spirits discursively is through the formalization process itself. The consistent use of such *formal* features as repetition, parallelism and redundancy in ritual speech is as-

sociated in Weyewa ceremonial ideology with the ancient and ancestral character of the *content* of the discourse. Expressed in Saussurean terms, speakers thus
minimize the distance between, and indeed create a kind of semiotic fusion of,
the *signifiers* of ritual speech (the verbal form) and its *signifieds* (the true 'voice'
of the ancestors; cf. Briggs 1988:330; Saussure 1959:115). Thus the 'true' *li'i
marapu* 'voice of the ancestors' is a blending of the present form of the 'voice'
with the ancient 'promise' through an involved, authentic performance.

The pervasive use of names of ancestral persons and places also minimizes
the contrast between signifier and signified. In Chapter Four, I discussed how
Weyewa naming practices express a privileged and close connection between
names and the person or place denoted. Thus children are believed to possess a
special and intimate association with their *tamo* 'namesake.' If a child is sick, it
may be because his or her name does not fit, or because his or her *tamo* is angry.
By using couplet names, names which evoke *types* of persons who stand for
clans, regions and social groups, this *tamo* relationship is in effect extended to
include whole groups. The meaning of the name of the pair of ancestral spirits
Lyende Nyura Lele, Kioni We'e Paboba (lines 40–43), for example, is not so
much a word denoting a specific individual as a name of one who symbolizes
the unity of the entire region. Descendants, as 'tips' to the ancient 'trunk,' can
identify with this source and indeed *merge* with it.

Monologic Discourse

An important way in which Weyewa performers talk about the goals of
social harmony and cooperation in rites of fulfillment is in terms of discursive
interaction. In divination, the repeated calls for the necessity of dialogue reflect
the very lack of social solidarity that speakers hope to overcome in the course of
placation rites. In rites of fufillment, however, performers describe the unity of
the social group in terms of achieving a single unitary voice with no dissenters.

The verbal genres in 'blessing songs' and 'chants' are semantically monologic but pragmatically dialogic (cf. Urban 1986). That is, while there is some
turn-taking, the role of the chorus is simply to ratify the discourse of the singer
and plays little role in modifying it. The semantic content of the discourse of the
singer and chanter is not contingent on the responses of the chorus of responders.
Performers are constrained pragmatically, however, by the length and timing of
the response. While these affect the structure of participation, they do not affect
the structure of ideas in the narratives.

The role of the individual in monologue is quite complex. During the performance itself, singers tend to speak through the voice of the ancestors. But
when performers are asked about it afterwards, their comments suggest a more
dynamic interplay between the artistry of individual performance and the traditional generic requirements. For instance, some Weyewa ritual speakers consider
the achievement of conventional monologue to be a personally creative act, an

expression of individual verbal prowess and interactional politics. One prominent ritual spokesman, Lende Mbatu, told me that

> It has never happened that I have been completely hung up while speaking. . . . Nor have I ever been stopped by anyone else in any of my performances . . . and if someone wants to better himself at my expense, to make himself appear superior, he had better just watch out. When I face the crowd [and begin to speak], the gongs stop. And when I sing or pose questions, even if all the big men are angry and excited, they stop and listen. (Lende Mbatu II:224)

Monologue for Weyewa is an ultimate expression of solidarity, unity and harmony. Unlike Jakubinskij (1979) who sees monologue as an unnatural, "artificial" state, Weyewa performers see it as a desirable goal. Monologue is not the result of the "suppression" of natural impulses to interrupt and respond (cf. Jakubinskij 1979:330–31), so much as an act of creating order out of disorder through verbal domination by an individual. By "individual" in this case, I mean a collaborative production that draws on the charisma of the individual performer and the traditional authority of the ancestors whose 'voice' he mediates.

Innovation of Meanings

Despite the deep involvement of the performer in the enactment of a rigid, unitary, and monologic 'voice' of the ancestors, the comic and ironic elements of the event continually strain at the boundaries of the performance frame. Even as the singer or chanter stands atop a tombstone to express respect for the hierarchical and univocal 'word of the ancestors,' this takes place amidst the backdrop of lively exchange, negotiation, and individual display. Occasionally during such performances, dancers in ceremonial dress launch into a parody of their role to the hoots of the onlookers, or an sacrificial animal breaks free from its tether provoking laughter. Although in the blessing songs and chants of the rites of fulfillment, the monologic 'voice' of the ancestors emerges relatively unhampered by the "noise" and tangled disunity among the various tip-like branches of the clan, these feasts are manifestly occasions for expressions of individuality, parody, poker playing, and unrestrained self-aggrandizement by both sponsor and the guests. In many ways it is a veritable cacophony of voices.

Many Weyewa claim that in the past such lack of unity and respect was not common. Then, in *tana mema* 'the original world' a single powerful man could silence all dialogues and create unity between both humans and the spirit world and among humans themselves by controlling the resources of women, cattle, and land with which exchanges of the 'word' are made. Concentrating wealth in his hands, he would use the slaughter of cattle to re-affirm and re-create the obligations of those subordinate to him. In this way, he also consolidated his control over the 'word,' expressed in rites of fulfillment as the monologic recitation of narrative *kanúngga* histories, re-enacting his status as a 'trunk' of history. Even today, when a sponsor successfully stages all three rites of fulfillment, admiration is expressed for the person in terms of his control over the 'word': A common form of praise is to say 'nothing more can be said [about him]' (*nda pa-tekki-ba ata*); in effect, he demonstrated his greatness by quieting all dialogue, gossip, and alternative points of view about him, compelling all to acknowledge his accomplishment.

The question of how, or if, this image of a single, powerful 'trunk' embodied in an individual is rooted in history is beyond the scope of this book. Among the Weyewa of the latter 1980s, however, it seems clear that the monologues in which these hierarchical relations are reproduced must be viewed with what Bakhtin calls a "sideways glance" (1981). The *kanúngga* models of history and social relations are now challenged by the small, but increasingly powerful Christian minority, who possess authority backed by the Dutch Reformed and Catholic churches, and the military might of the Indonesian armed forces and national bureaucracy. As contexts for engendering 'words' of economic obligation and exchange, *woleka* feasts are threatened by the increasing commercial independence of farmers who sell their surpluses in local and interregional markets. No single Weyewa can hope to dominate all transactions through the traditional framework. As the singer stands alone atop the sarcophagus to deliver his monologue, other restless voices clamor for a hearing.

Notes

1. Kapita (1976b:366), for instance, glosses *woleka* as 'fulfillment of a covenant.'
2. The ancestral mother and father "arrived" the previous night when they symbolically descended to the house by leaving small tracks in an ash cup (see Chapter Six). Their arrival was described as being the result of great effort by the descendants.
3. *Woleka* celebrations last seven nights in the ancestral villages, but only three nights in the garden and 'corral' settlements.
4. Since, in some cases, the information recorded here is sensitive, I have used pseudonyms.
5. The number of buffalo slaughtered in Weyewa feasts appears to be lower than in neighboring Kodi. One of my assistants suggested that Weyewa place special value on water buffalo in preparing flooded pond fields, a form of rice field nearly absent in Kodi, and so are reluctant to part with them. Raising water buffalo for purposes of meat production alone is relatively rare, partly because of severe constraints on pastureland.
6. In some cases, marriage is in fact a culmination of a series of rites of misfortune. For instance, when a calamity takes place and the diviner determines that certain spirits are angry, then the guilty party may sometimes respond by declaring certain fields, cattle, and even his daughter *poddu* 'bitter' (cf. Kuipers 1984a). In order to release this prohibition, a *woleka* celebration must be staged before the cattle can be slaughtered, the rice consumed, or the girl married off.

8

Conclusions

With great passion and at considerable expense, Weyewa ritual spokesmen construct a textual image of their social and religious life. In their rites of atonement, they struggle to identify, re-affirm, and enact the *li'i* 'words of the ancestors'—by which they mean a connected body of teachings, promises, and obligations set down—fixed—by the ancestors and expressed in narrative form. The imagery of these texts suggests a preoccupation with coherence, unity, resolution, and consensus, described in part as an absence of dialogue, discordant voices, or playful levity. The stated goal of such performances is to follow the 'tracks and spoors'—the inscriptions, as it were—laid down by the ancestral spirits.

An appreciation of the entextualization process in Weyewa rites of atonement, however, requires that the text model of society outlined by scholars such as Becker (1979), Geertz (1983b), and Ricoeur (1981) be extended to confront issues of power, authority, and material interests. For Weyewa, these complex ritual events are not merely acts of "fixing" meaning; they are carefully orchestrated efforts to *control* it. Since personal fortunes and individual reputations can rise or fall depending on how these 'words' of obligation are interpreted and enacted, the issue of how such meanings are established is not an intellectual or mystical one for Weyewa: it is a public spectacle in which power and authority are at stake. By gaining control over the meanings of the promises embodied in the words of his ancestors, Malo Dunga, for instance, was able to use this knowledge as a strategy in mobilizing the resources (cattle, pigs, cloth) of his kinsmen to help fulfill a covenant. By demonstrating that he was a man of his word, he was able to confer further prestige on himself and his family, as well as on other participants to the event. Thus entextualization cannot be viewed as a purely aesthetic process among Weyewa; it is intimately linked to the interests of performers and audience alike.

If we are to focus on how Weyewa texts come to be authoritative and acquire a kind of binding power, we must direct our attention to the nature of *performance*. Viewed out of context, as isolated documents, formal poetic structures, rigid genres, or authorless enactments, Weyewa ritual speech activities are easily misunderstood and their compelling significance is lost. When Weyewa ritual speech is examined in its context of use, however, new kinds of data come alive that shed light on the entextualization process.

Close attention to actual ritual speech performances reveals a wide variety of verbal structures, not just formal poetic ones. Although this finding occasionally surprised and even dismayed my assistants, ritual speaking does not consist of pure couplet speech, but is in fact rich with deictics, locutives, and discourse markers which link speech to its context of use. This is a point made repeatedly by Bauman (1984) and Hymes (1981), but news of it has been slow to penetrate studies of the texts of the Indonesian archipelago. In part this is due to a long (and in many ways venerable) tradition in Western scholarship on the area, which in focusing on the formulaic, couplet-based "ceremonial languages" re-ifies these styles of speaking as formally or functionally autonomous phenomena. Most of the late nineteenth- and early twentieth-century research on Indonesian poetic languages and parallelism, for instance, was carried out by philologically inclined European linguists (e.g., Hardeland 1858; Kern 1956; Van der Veen 1965), or by structurally oriented ethnologists who linked the stylistic differentia-tion of speech varieties to historical differences in social groupings such as dual sovreignty or priesthoods (e.g., Adriani 1932; Fischer 1934). Both groups of scholars saw ritual speech as a relatively separate and independent "language" whose autonomy is guaranteed by either the internal formal structure of the style or the structure of society. Since language in this view exists apart from the events in which it is used, there was relatively little information on the perform-ers, the setting, the delivery technique, the role of the audience, and the emer-gent features of the performance itself.

But as the Weyewa ritual speech events show, the use of parallelism cannot be viewed as a formally or functionally autonomous stylistic phenomenon apart from the performances in which it occurs. This is true for at least two reasons. First, many couplets have important meanings which only emerge in the context of performance. Thus the "cooking fire"/"hearth" image in a couplet such as

toma tandingo ana ladu	reach the pallet by the cooking fire
dukki rabuka kalido	arrive at the narrow hearth

not only refers to familial and spiritual intimacy, but also functions as a "keying" device that signals a shift towards a more serious contextual frame, one which excludes children and women from the discourse as it approaches the "hearth" of the matter at hand.

Second, couplets such as the example just mentioned are themselves often part of larger discourse units. While Weyewa do indeed see speaking in pairs as the definitive characteristic of these performances, they also recognize that cru-cial to the organization of any performance is emergence of larger supra-couplet structures of discourse. The boundaries of such larger units may be signaled by couplets, but often they are marked by particles and pauses, discourse markers made familiar in pioneering work by Hymes (1981) and Tedlock (1983).

The Weyewa data on rites of placation also highlight the importance of music and its relation to the building of texts in oral performance. Since the organization of the verbal materials often depends crucially on the interaction of rhythm, melody, and verse constraints, it is important for linguistically inclined scholars to pay close attention to the musical context of such verbal performances. These uses of music are not abstract or cosmic; among Weyewa, they are less concerned with the creation of a transcendent experience of community than with the construction of a consensus so that the performance can proceed. The harmonious melding of voices among gongs, drums, and singing is indeed a lofty goal which guides the participants; it is also a practical, interactional accomplishment in actual performances.

Once consensus is achieved through rites of placation, Weyewa fulfill the promises to the ancestors through the performance of authoritative monologues. Despite repeated statements by the performers denying the dialogic, contextualized character of the narratives (e.g., "'let's goof off' we don't say that"), it is clear from careful attention to the actual speech that these too are situated acts that subtly accommodate audience input. In Weyewa, however, the *irreversibility* associated with this context/text continuum (as well as to the associated continua—garden/village, tip/trunk, periphery/center) is a powerful *ideological* construction. By insisting on a discourse that is not endlessly negotiable, malleable, and transformable, Weyewa set limits on disorder and accomplish, at least for a time, the harmony, unity, and monologue they so desire.

Thus conceived as a form of verbal practice, the textualization process also sheds light on conceptions of power and authority. Geertz, for instance, draws on a textual model of social life to examine how leaders "justify their existence and order their actions in terms of a collection of stories, ceremonies, insignia, formalities, and appurtenances that they have inherited" and how these symbols "mark the center as center and give what goes on there the aura of being not merely important but in some odd fashion connected with the way the world is built" (1983b:124). By examining such political performances he hopes to shed light on how key concepts such as charisma get constructed in particular societies.

While the role of performance, pageantry, and display in constituting the "centers" and "peripheries" of Indonesian political systems has been a significant theme in the scholarly literature (e.g., Anderson 1972; Geertz 1980; Errington 1989), the role of language in such interactive events has not been explicitly addressed. The Weyewa data suggest that the progress toward the "centers" of power and authority that one finds in rites of atonement constitutes a series of performance "frames" into which one can be relatively saturated, or from which one can be relatively detached. Among Weyewa, the uses of quotations, couplets, and deixis are crucial to signaling how "central" a performer thinks his performance is.

Entextualization and the Study of Institutional Authority

The study of entextualization has relevance well beyond eastern Indonesia. In its broadest sense, wherever the relationship between situated conversation and decontextualized discourse is an institutionally structured and legitimated, and interactionally accomplished *process*, the concept can be fruitfully applied (Bauman 1987; Kuipers 1989). Examples of such transformations of contextualized talk into formal texts include the relation between patient-doctor encounters and the medico-legal record (e.g., Pettinari 1988), the relation between mediation and adjudication in legal settings (cf. Brenneis 1986), and the relation between taped recordings and transcriptions (e.g., Urban 1987). This gradual objectification and decontextualization of discourse from its immediate situation of utterance exercises power by extracting, appropriating, and reporting the speech of others, detaching it from whatever meanings prevailed at the time of its original utterance and re-defining it in a new context (Bauman 1987; cf. Bakhtin 1981, 1986; Volosinov 1971).

The end result of this process is a stretch of talk which *appears* to be removed from the 'here and now' of audience interaction. But as Pettinari's studies of surgical reports show (1988), even the most authoritative, scientific, and highly structured reports exhibit evidence of the powerful structuring effect of the audience. In this sense, "entextualization" can be viewed as a linguistically and pragmatically structured cultural *ideology* about the irreversibility of the relationship between context and text, even though in fact the process is dialectical at each moment.

An important first step in analyzing this process of "decentering" or extracting discourse from its contextual surroundings is to recognize the *stylistic* characteristics of discourse in such settings. This requires close attention to the ways in which language is seen to become its own context, reflexively calling attention to its own formal structure through heightened rhetorical or even literary patterning (on verbal style in medical and legal settings, see Cicourel 1981; O'Barr 1982; Shuy 1976). Once the formal stylistic features of such institutional discourse have been identified, then a next important step is to compare discourse types across contexts. In the medical domain, Cicourel (1974, 1975, 1983) has investigated how the experience of interviewing is transformed across contexts into a formal record of notes and into a medical document. He observes that these records (whose compositional principles must be learned informally) are like a "folk practice" where stories are told in fairly standardized ways even though the original experience might not have happened in quite the same way. In the legal profession, a comparable process occurs as courtroom dialogue is extracted, appropriated, and transformed into the monologic discourse of adjudication and sentencing. Within more artistic pursuits, the "versioning" process involved in musical and theatrical rehearsals may represent gradual stages of decontextualization and appropriation.

While such work provides a valuable understanding of the cognitive and linguistic tasks of learning, processing, and structuring of institutionally important genres of communication, many dimensions for comparison remain for future researchers to explore across the text-building contexts. Among these are the ways in which participants in construction of such authoritative discourse exploit generic resources for the creation of ambiguity and contradiction, as well as authority, status, and social control. Also worth exploring are variations in the bureaucratic and institutional processes by which access to such richly entexted discourse is structured.

Viewing medical and legal discourse *across* contexts in relation to a bureaucratically and ideologically arranged process of "entextualization" has a number of connections with other lines of investigation currently under way. In Habermas's terms (1984), entextualization might be viewed as a "colonization of the lifeworld," in which the systemic imperatives of bureaucratic rationality absorb and dissolve the client's self-understanding of, e.g., a medical complaint. He advocates the emancipatory move of achieving more humane care by empowering the patient. For those who cast their work in relation to the philosopher Gramsci (see Frankenberg 1988), the notion of cultural hegemony (see Lears 1985) might be particularly useful in explaining the ways in which entexted medical discourse gets re-centered and re-contextualized in ways that obscure its authoritative character, e.g., in middle class health magazines, science shows, and school textbooks. [1]

There are no doubt many other applications of the notion of entextualization in institutional settings. The few suggested here, however, reinforce the idea that the inscription of meaning is a fundamental and powerful force in the patterning of discourse and the social cirumstances that discourse organizes. In its broadest terms, it is a cultural activity concerned with the fixation of meaning from the flow of events—"history from what happened, thought from thinking, culture from behavior" (Geertz 1983b:31). This book celebrates the power of performance in that process.

Epilogue: Innovation and Convention in a Changing Weyewa Society

What is the future of the textual model of Weyewa society? How long will the image of ancestral 'words' have the power to constitute the center? While ritual leaders remain devoted to a description of the central acts of religious and economic exchange in their society as the production, distribution and fulfillment of ancestral words, other images, media, and rhetorical strategies are competing for attention with increasing volume. If, as the government urges, slaughter and exchange of cattle and cloth will be viewed less as a fulfillment of a promise than in terms of the numerical, monetary imagery of profit and loss.

The ban on ritual speech performances enacted in December of 1987 (see Introduction, p. 1) is but one moment in the recent history of declining authority for the *li'i* 'word' of the ancestors. Indeed, Weyewa ritual speech now appears to be gradually losing its place to the Indonesian national language (*Bahasa Indonesia*) as the idiom of religious, legal, and moral authority. While this decline in ritual speaking seems to linked to modernization in the agricultural, educational and bureaucratic system, the rise of Bahasa Indonesia cannot be viewed in simple terms as a matter of transformation from "oral" to "print" culture. The case is illustrated with an *surat perjanjian*—a legal 'letter of promise'—which is an important local genre of bureaucratic communication written in Indonesian that has come to supplant the 'word' of the ancestors in some legal contexts.

While systematic challenges to indigenous structures of authority began with arrival of the Dutch troops of the Netherlands East Indies, they have taken on new forms since independence through the bureaucracy and state ideology (*Pancasila*) of the Republic of Indonesia. *Pancasila* calls for national unity through, among other things, "belief in one god" and "social justice." The former stipulation permits Islam (Indonesia's majority religion) to coexist with Christianity, Confucianism, and even Balinese Hinduism, but does not authorize ancestor worship or animism—categories to which the Sumbanese *marapu* practices have been assigned. The "social justice" component of *Pancasila* was employed as one justification for disbanding the "feudal" (*feodal*) institution of raja in 1962 as well as the dismantling of the authority of other, traditionally powerful lineage leaders. Co-existing with the system of indigenous leadership—and now gradually eclipsing it—is a complex, centralized bureaucratic hierarchy backed by a largely non-Sumbanese military force.

One major event which illustrates the weakening of the authority of the lineage was the construction of an irrigation system and hydroelectric dam at the site of the sacred gushing spring at Waikelo in the mid 1960s. According to a former official in the local Department of Agriculture, prior to the construction of the facility, the spring watered some 300 hectares of rice fields, whose cycles of cultivation and fallowing were regulated by certain lineage elders carrying out the 'words' of the ancestors. After the project was built, over 1500 hectares were available for continuous irrigation. Not only were traditional leaders unprepared to oversee and control this increase in scale of production, but government officials took the initiative by encouraging farmers to abandon the ritual schedule of planting and harvest by trying new high-yield, hardy, and fast-growing varieties of rice which permitted two or more plantings per year. According to oral accounts of witnesses, the ownership of the new and ambiguous categories of land which emerged from irrigation were often assigned to individuals, not lineages. When disputes arose, government employees (such as police, judges, or district heads) increasingly mediated the disputes, and enforced the settlements.

Such official challenges to the political role of the lineage (and the ancestral spirits who legitimate it) are reinforced by Indonesian programs of mass education, which are now indoctrinating a second generation of students. Aided by the doubling of the elementary school buildings in the Weyewa district (from 29 to 60) in 8 years, approximately 95% of the school age population hears the message of *Pancasila* in daily classes on the subject from the aggressively Christian, Indonesian-speaking teachers.

Given these challenges to the authority of the lineage and the 'words' of the ancestors, fewer and fewer Weyewa appear to be willing to invest large amounts of cattle, pigs, cloth, and time into identifying, re-affirming, and fulfilling those ancient 'words' of ancestral obligation. As they say in couplets:

wulla eka ounda	the moon rises differently
lodo eka tama	the sun sets in a different place

i.e., there has been a drastic, cosmic reorientation of their world.

There are now government incentives for Weyewa to forsake their native ritual practices altogether and convert to Christianity. While most Weyewa remain primarily subsistence farmers, employment by the state as a teacher or bureaucrat is a prestigious goal for the rapidly growing numbers of elementary school children. All teachers and employees of the state are now effectively required to be Christians, and are explicitly forbidden to participate in feasting. Furthermore, children who wish to continue their education beyond elementary school must obtain a birth certificate (*surat akte kelahiran*) signed by either a Catholic priest or a Protestant minister, a requirement which virtually compels them to convert. With such support from the government, the rate of conversion to Christianity has accelerated. According to church officials I spoke to, in 1955 the Christian church (both Protestant and Catholic) could claim little more than 5% of the population. In 1978 a little more than 20% had converted. By 1986, however—a mere 8 years—the number had reached 47%, and is fast approaching a majority. Once converted, Weyewa are forbidden to address the ancestral spirits, or to eat *kana'a marapu*—meat which has been offered in a ceremonial exchange to the ancestral spirits. The Protestant church has been more rigid about compliance with these requirements than the Catholic church, but both have the strong backing of the Indonesian government on this matter of feasting.

Increasingly, the effective language of political and religious authority in Weyewa is *panewe dawa* 'Indonesian' and not *panewe tenda* 'ritual speech.' When disputes arise, the matter is now less likely to be viewed as a reflection of a neglected *li'i* 'word' but a neglected *perjanjian* 'promise.' This latter word is Indonesian, and reflects the fact that the court proceedings are increasingly conducted in Indonesian, and the final report is written up in Indonesian. Since most of the police stationed in Weyewa are not natives to the area, the language of law enforcement is Indonesian. School is effectively conducted in Indonesian from the first grade, even though it is not a requirement until the third grade. Indonesian is also the language of the Christian churches. Although there is a Weyewa language New Testament, all Catholic services and most Protestant services employ the Malay Bible and the Indonesian language. I recently (1988) attended a funeral service for a Christian Weyewa woman, in which at least 99% of those attending were Weyewa but the language employed was nonetheless Indonesian.

The following case illustrates how one important function of the *li'i* as a traditional obligation or 'promise' now increasingly shares a place with the written, Indonesian language *perjanjian* 'promises' composed by elected or appointed officials of the legal and political bureaucracy.

Shortly after the rainy season began in November of 1987, brothers Zairo Palla "the Elder" (*Matto*), and Zairo Palla "the Younger" (*Ki'i*) had a falling out. During that month, when the elder moved his family from his village to his garden hut in order to plant corn, rice, and root crops in the nearby field, he discovered that a clump of thatch had been tied in a circle and hung from the eaves of the house. Such a *weri* or 'prohibition' denies entry except to those willing to risk supernatural punishment. Zairo Palla Matto grew angry when he learned his brother, who had been using the land for the past seven years, had placed it there to keep him away. The brothers faced off menacingly on the border of the land and traded accusations, each backed by supporters armed with spears, rocks, and knives. The elder claimed that his younger brother had leased him the land in exchange for a water buffalo the latter needed for a burial feast when his mother-in-law died. Since the elder brother did not use the land, Zairo Palla the younger continued to cultivate it. When the latter heard that his elder brother planned to begin using it, he hung a 'prohibition' on the garden hut near it to warn him off. It was this sign that led to the dispute.

Like many other Weyewa in similar predicaments, instead of settling it with a clan elder, they went to the 'village headman' (*kepala desa*), an official of the Indonesian government, who listened to both sides of the case. After negotiating

Indonesian language 'letter of promise'

Surat Perjanjian   1

Kami yang bertanda tangan dibawah ini masing-masing bernama:
1. Zairo Palla Matto, alamat We'e Panoka, dusun Kalimbundaramane III,
R.U. Kanai Gole, desa Kalimbundaramane.
2. Zairo Palla Ki'i, alamat Tara We'e, dusn Kalimbundaramane III,   5
R. U. Kanai Gole, desa Kalimbundaramane.
     Kami kedua oknum ini yang tercantum namanya di atas ini, menyatakan
dengan sungguh-sungguh dan tulus-ikhlas di hadapan pemerintah desa, bahwa
sekembali kami dari sini, dini hari juga tgl 8-12-1987 kami akan mencabut
weri yg kami perdirikan di kareka keni (didlm kalionya Zairo Palla Matto).   10
Sebab weri yang kami perdirikan ini menjadi masallah dengan (Zairo Palla
Matto) Bulu Kalli.
     Mengingat demi terjamin nya kembali kerukunan ~~kembali~~ kekeluargaan
kami maka weri ini kami cabut dengan secara sadar dan ikhlas, tanpa
dipaksa oleh pihak manapun.   15
     Demikian surat perjanjian ini kami buat dengan sebenar-benarnya, dan
apabila kami melanggar pernyataan ini kami kami bersedia dituntut dihadapan
yg berwenang sesuai dengan pelanggaran kami.
Kalimbundaramane 8-12-87

Yang Membuat Pernyataan: 20

(Zairo Palla Matto)   (Zairo Palla Ki'i)

Saksi-saksi:

Kepala Dusun IV   Kepala Dusun III

1. (L. Nada)   2. (B. Padede)

Mengatahui   25
Kep. Desa Kal. Ndaramane

(Z. M. Lete)

with each party, mostly in Indonesian, he proposed a solution, which both accepted. Both parties were asked to sit outside his office while he wrote out, using the Indonesian national language, a document called a *surat perjanjian*, literally a 'letter of promise' in which parties swore to abide by the settlement. They were invited back inside to listen as the village headman read the document to them. The two litigants sacrificed a chicken, informing the ancestors in ritual speech of the new *li'i* 'word' of agreement. After checking the chicken's entrails for approval, the two men then placed their thumbprints at the bottom of the page.

English translation

Letter of Promise   1

We the undersigned, respectively named
1. Zairo Palla Matto, address We'e Panoka, village of Kalimbundaramane III,
R.U. Kanai Gole, subdistrict Kalimbundaramane.
2. Zairo Palla Ki'i, address Tara We'e, village Kalimbundaramane III,   5
R. U. Kanai Gole, subdistrict Kalimbundaramane.
   We two individuals whose names are attached herein state sincerely and
honestly and straightforwardly in front of the government of the subdistrict, that upon
our return from here, this day also 8-12-1987, we will remove the ritual prohibition
which we erected in the garden hut (in the garden of Zairo Palla the Elder).   10
Because the ritual prohibition which we erected occasioned a dispute with (Zairo
Palla the Elder) Bulu Kalli.
   In consideration of the return to peacefulness ~~return~~ in the family,
thus we will remove the ritual prohibition, consciously and freely,
without being forced by any party.   15
   This letter of promise has been hereby duly created, and
if we transgress this statement, we are prepared to be prosecuted before
the authorities in accordance with our transgression.
                        Kalimbundaramane 8-12-87

                        The Makers of the Statement: 20

(Zairo Palla Matto)   (Zairo Palla Ki'i)

                        Witnesses:

Village Head IV   Village Head III

1. (L. Nada)   2. (B. Padede)

                        Understood by   25
                        Kep. Desa Kal. Ndaramane

                        (Z. M. Lete)

As a concrete example of the changes in discursive practice with respect to
the 'word,' the structure and the content of the *kepala desa*'s document are in-
structive. Except for the names, which have been altered, everything else is
exactly the same.
   Viewed ethnographically as a cultural phenomenon, the Indonesian language 'letter of promise' (and the dozens like it issuing out of the same office
each year) does not in itself represent a radical transformation of consciousness
so much as a resource in a complex multimedia performance. While the written

word shares the stage with ritual speech, the document symbolizes (although does not always accomplish) discursive control over the situation of the two brothers by powerful people.

Like many such Western-style legal documents, this example is quite rich in rhetorical devices supposedly linked to "oral cultures" (Ong 1982:39ff). It relies heavily on formulaic speech ("We the undersigned," line 2; "whose names are attached herein, line 6; "honestly and straightforwardly," line 7; "this letter of promise has hereby been duly created," line 16; etc). These clauses are linked less by an analytic or syllogistic rhetoric of cause and result than by an "aggre-gative" clause structure (except for the "Because" on line 11), a paratactic piling of phrases one after another. Finally, while the use of dates, full names, places, and signatures suggests a rhetoric of "distanced objectivity" (Ong 1982:45ff), the writer exhibits his own point of view clearly by gradually shifting the reference of the first person plural exclusive pronoun 'we' (*kami*, lines 2, 7, 9) from index-ing *both* the elder and younger brothers (lines 2 and 7) to referring only to younger brother as the one who erected the prohibition (line 9). The reported 'voice' in the document becomes that of the younger brother, and the elder becomes the addressee.

While it is clear that this written document is guided by a sophisticated logic derived from a unique set of a cultural and historical circumstances, it cannot be said to be *inherently* more logical, objective, de-contextualized, or abstract than the spoken genres it replaces. How does one measure such things as the relative "efficiency," "practicality," or "precision" of a style of communi-cation? Perhaps it is absurd to evaluate the two genres comparatively at all; what is important for Weyewa is that the written mode of discourse is backed by pow-erful people.

What will become of 'ritual speech' in the future? Will *panewe tenda* be-come aestheticized as 'literature' (*sastra*),—and thus taught in schools—as one official suggested, or will it become 'folkore' and remain a primarily oral phe-nomenon displayed in "folk festivals" for visiting dignitaries (Lutz n.d.) and the occasional marriage ceremony? In either case, as Fox has observed, it is likely to be assigned to the realm of 'culture' (*kebudayaan*), a category that is increasingly separated from 'religion' (*agama*) and 'politics' (*politik*) (Fox 1988:20). As the Christian religion and the Indonesian government take over the latter two cate-gories of endeavor, it seems likely that ritual speech will also become increasingly sentimentalized and marginalized: a 'voice' from the distant past.

New performance frames for the creation of authority are in the process of being built, and the role of ritual speech in constructing them is open to ques-tion. Whatever role it plays, it seems clear that verbal performance in some form will remain central to their participation in social and religious life. In a discus-sion with his client prior to his performance in a divinatory inquiry, a spokesman named Mbulu Renda received a question about recent challenges to the author-ity of ritual discourse. What is striking (but characteristically Weyewa) about his answer is the passionate commitment to achieving authority through authentic performance:

> Now since I am a priest, that which is called 'priesting' if we really mean it, let's do it; . . . if we are going pray to the *marapu* ancestral spirits, then we must *really* pray; otherwise, we should just become Christians, and *really* do that . . .

Notes

1. Cultural hegemony, according to one definition by Gramsci, is "the 'spontaneous' consent given by the great masses of the population to the general direction imposed on social life by the dominant fundamental group: this consent is 'historically' caused by the prestige (and consequent confidence) the dominant group enjoys because of its position and function in the world of production" (Gramsci 1971:12, cited in Lears 1985:568). This ideology, which is a kind of "contradictory consciousness" is embodied in the "language itself." Thus discourse plays a central role in the domination of one group by another.

References

Adams, Marie Jeane
  1969 *System and Meaning in East Sumba Textile Design: A Study in Traditional Indonesian Art*. New Haven: Yale University Press.
  1970 Myths and Self-Image Among the Kapunduk People of Sumba. *Indonesia* 10:80–106
Adriani, Nicolaus
  1932 Indonesische Priestertaal. In *Verzamelde Geschriften van dr. N. Adriani*, Vol. 3, pp. 1–12. Haarlem: F. Bohn.
Anderson, Benedict
  1972 The Idea of Power in Javanese Culture. In Claire Holt, Benedict Anderson and James Siegel, eds., *Culture and Politics in Indonesia*, pp. 1–69. Ithaca: Cornell University Press.
Austerlitz, Robert
  1958 *Ob-Ugric Metrics*. Helsinki: Suomen Tiete Akademia.
Austin, John
  1962 *How to Do Things with Words*. Cambridge, MA: Harvard University Press.
Bakhtin, Mikhail M.
  1981 *The Dialogic Imagination*. Ed. Michael Holquist, and trans. Caryl Emerson and Michael Holquist. Austin: University of Texas Press.
  1986 *Speech Genres and Other Essays*. Ed. Michael Holquist, trans. Caryl Emerson and Michael Holquist. Austin: University of Texas Press.
Banfield, Anne
  1973 Narrative Style and the Grammar of Direct and Indirect Discourse. *Foundations of Language* 10:1–39.
Barthes, Roland
  1967 Le discours de l'histoire. *Social Science Information* 6.4:65–75.
  1972 The Structure of the *Fait-divers*. In *Critical Essays*, pp. 185–196. Evanston, IL: Northwestern University Press.
Bateson, Gregory
  1972 *Steps to an Ecology of Mind*. New York: Ballantine Books.
Bauman, Richard
  1984 [1977] *Verbal Art as Performance*. Prospect Heights, IL: Waveland Press.
  1986 *Story, Performance and Event: Contextual Studies of Oral Narrative*. Cambridge: Cambridge University Press.
  1987a The Role of Performance in the Ethnography of Speaking. In Richard J. Parmentier and Greg Urban, eds., *Performance, Speech Community and Genre*, pp. 3–12. Chicago: Working Papers and Proceedings of the Center for Psychosocial Studies no. 11.
  1987b The Decentering of Discourse. Paper delivered at the 86th Annual Meetings of the American Anthropological Association, Chicago.

Bauman, Richard and Joel Sherzer, eds.
  1974 *Explorations in the Ethnography of Speaking.* Cambridge: Cambridge University Press.
  1975 The Ethnography of Speaking. In *Annual Review of Anthropology* 4:95–119
> Becker, Alton L.
  1979 Text-building, Epistemology and Aesthetics in Javanese Shadow Theatre. In
    A. L. Becker, and Aram Yengoyan, eds., *The Imagination of Reality: Essays
    in Southeast Asian Coherence Systems,* pp. 211–243. Norwood, NJ: Ablex
    Publishing Co.
Bell, Catherine
  1988 Ritualization of Texts and Textualization of Ritual in the Codification of Taoist Liturgy. *History of Religions* 27(4): 366–392.
Ben-Amos, Dan
  1982 *Folklore in Context: Essays.* New Delhi, Madras: South Asian Publishers.
Benveniste, Emile
  1966 *Problems in General Linguistics.* Trans. Mary Elizabeth Meek. Coral Gables,
    FL: University of Miami Press
Bernstein, Basil
  1971 *Class, Codes and Social Control,* Volumes One and Two. London:
    Routledge.
Bloch, Maurice
  1975 Introduction. In Maurice Bloch, ed., *Political Oratory and Traditional Society,* pp. 1–28. New York: Academic Press.
Boon, James
  1984 Folly, Bali and Anthropology, or Satire Across Cultures. In Edward Bruner,
    ed., *Text, Play and Story: The Construction and Reconstruction of Self and
    Society,* pp. 156–177. Washington, DC: 1983 Proceedings of the American
    Ethnological Society.
Bourdieu, Pierre
  1977 *Outline of a Theory of Practice.* Cambridge: Cambridge University Press.
Bowen, John
  1989 Poetic Duels and Political Change in the Gayo Highlands of Sumatra. *American Anthropologist* 91:25–40.
Brenneis, Donald
  1986 Decontextualization and Recontextualization in Legal Discourse. Paper presented at the 85th Annual Meetings of the American Anthropological Association, Philadelphia, PA.
Brenneis, Donald Lawrence and Fred R. Myers
  1984 Introduction. In Donald Lawrence Brenneis and Fred R. Myers, eds., *Dangerous Words: Language and Politics in the Pacific,* pp. 1–29. New York: New
    York University Press.
Bricker, Victoria
  1974 The Ethnographic Context of Some Traditional Mayan Speech Genres. In
    Richard Bauman and Joel Sherzer, eds., *Explorations in the Ethnography of
    Speaking,* pp. 368–388. Cambridge: Cambridge University Press.
Briggs, Charles
  1988 *Competence in Performance: The Creativity of Tradition in Mexicano Verbal
    Art.* Philadelphia: University of Pennsylvania Press.
Buehler, Karl
  1982 The Deictic Field of Language and Deictic Words. In Robert J. Jarvella and
    Wolfgang Klein, eds., *Speech, Place and Action: Studies in Deixis and Related*

Topics, pp. 1–30. New York: John Wiley and Sons. (Originally published in German in 1934.)

Chafe, Wallace
1981 Differences Between Colloquial and Ritual Seneca: or How Oral Literature is Literary. In Alice Schlichter, Wallace Chafe, and Leanne Hinton, eds. *Reports from the Survey of California and Other Indian Languages*, no 1, pp. 131–145. Berkeley: University of California at Berkeley, Department of Linguistics.
⌐ 1982 Integration and Involvement in Speaking, Writing and Oral Literature. In Deborah Tannen, ed. *Spoken and Written Language: Exploring Orality and Literacy*. pp. 35–53. Norwood, NJ: Ablex Publishing Corp.

Chafe, Wallace and Johanna Nichols, eds.
1986 *Evidentiality: The Linguistic Coding of Epistemology*. Norwood, N.J.: Ablex Publishing Corp.

Chomsky, Noam
1965 *Aspects of a Theory of Syntax*. Cambridge, MA: MIT Press.

Cicourel, Aaron
1987 Cognitive and Organizational Aspects of Medical Diagnostic Reasoning. *Discourse Processes* 10(4): 347–369.
1983 Hearing is not Believing: Language and the Structure of Belief in Medical Communication. In Sue Fisher and Alexandra Dundes Todd, eds., *The Social Organization of Doctor-Patient Communication*, pp. 221–239. Washington, DC: Center for Applied Linguistics.
1981 Language and Medicine. In Charles Ferguson and Shirley Brice Heath, eds., *Language in the USA*, pp. 407–429. Cambridge: Cambridge University Press.
1975 Discourse and Text: Cognitive and Linguistic Processes in Studies of Social Structure. *Versus* 12(2): 33–84

Clifford, James
1986 On Ethnographic Allegory. In James Clifford and George Marcus, eds., *Writing Culture: The Poetics and Politics of Ethnography*, pp. 98–121. Berkeley: University of California Press.

Clifford, James and George Marcus, eds.
1986 *Writing Culture: The Poetics and Politics of Ethnography*. Berkeley: University of California Press.

Coser, Lewis
1975 Two Methods in Search of a Substance. *American Sociological Review* 40: 691–700.

Couvreur, A. J. L.
1917 Aard en Wezen der Inlandsche Zelfbesturne op het Eiland Soemba. *Tijdschrift van het Binnenlands Bestuur* 52:206–219.

de Haan, J. H.
1938 Rapport Betreffende De Grondrechten In de Onderafdeeling West Soemba, 2 Juni 1938. In G. H. Riekerk, ed., *Memorie van Overgave van het Onderafdeeling Soemba*. Unpubl. archival manuscript.

de Josselin de Jong, P. E. ed.
1977 *Structural Anthropology in the Netherlands*. The Hague: Martinus Nijhoff.

Dempwolff, Otto
1934–1938 *Vergleichnede Lautlehre des Austronesischen Wortschatzes*. Berlin: Dietrich Reimer.

Derrida, Jacques
1974 *Of Grammatology*. Trans. Gayatri Spivak. Baltimore: Johns Hopkins University Press.

Dorst, John
1983 Neck Riddle as a Dialogue of Genres. *Journal of American Folklore* 96: 413–433.
Downs, R. E.
1955 Headhunting in Indonesia. *Bijdragen tot de Taal-, Land-, en Volkenkunde* 111:40–70.
Du Bois, John W.
1986 Self-Evidence and Ritual Speech. In Wallace Chafe and Joanna Nichols, eds., *Evidentiality: The Linguistic Coding of Epistemology*, pp. 313–336. Norwood, NJ: Ablex Publishing Corp.
Duranti, Alessandro and Elinor Ochs
1979 Left Dislocation in Italian Conversation. In Talmy Givon, ed., *Syntax and Semantics*, vol. 12: *Discourse and Syntax*, pp. 377–416. New York: Academic Press.
Duranti, Alessandro and Donald Brenneis, eds.
1986 The Audience as Co-Author. *Text* 6(3)
Dyen, Isidore
1965 A *Lexicostatistical Classification of the Austronesian Languages*. International Journal of American Linguistics Memoir 19. Bloomington: Indiana University Press.
1978 The Position of Languages in Eastern Indonesia. In S. A. Wurm and Lois Carrington, eds., *Proceedings of the Second Austronesian Conference*. Pacific Linguistics Series C, no. 61, pp. 235–254. Canberra: Australian National University, Research School of Pacific Studies.
Ede, D. A.
1964 *Bird Structure: An Approach Through Evolution, Development and Function in the Fowl*. London: Hutchinson Educational.
Erikson, Kai
1977 *Everything in its Path: The Destruction of Community in the Buffalo Creek Flood*. New York: Simon and Schuster.
Errington, Shelly
1989 *Meaning and Power in a Southeast Asian Realm*. Princeton: Princeton University Press.
Ervin-Tripp, Susan
1972 On Sociolinguistic Rules: Alternation and Co-occurence. In John Gumperz and Dell Hymes, eds., *Directions in Sociolinguistics*, pp. 213–250. New York: Holt, Rinehart and Winston.
Evans-Pritchard, Edward E.
1937 *Witchcraft, Oracles and Magic Among the Azande*. Oxford: Clarendon Press.
Feld, Steven
1982 *Sound and Sentiment: Birds, Weeping, Poetics, and Song in Kaluli Expression*. Philadelphia: University of Pennsylvania Press. Second edition with interpretative reading by its original subjects, 1990.
Fillmore, Charles J.
1982 Towards a Descriptive Framework for Spatial Deixis. In Robert Jarvella and Wolfgang Klein, eds., *Speech, Place and Action: Studies in Deixis and Related Topics*, pp. 31–60. New York: John Wiley.
Fine, Elizabeth
1984 *The Folklore Text*. Bloomington: Indiana University Press.
Fischer, D. Th.
1934 *Priestertaalen: Een Ethnologiese Studie*. s'Gravenhage: Martinus Nijhoff.

References   185

Forth, Gregory L.
    1981 *Rindi: An Ethnographic Study of a Traditional Domain in Eastern Sumba.*
        Verhandeling van het Koninklijk Instituut voor Taal-, Land-, en Volkenkunde
        no. 93. The Hague: Martinus Nijhoff.
Fowler, Roger
    1985 Power. In Teun A. van Dijk, ed., *Handbook of Discourse Analysis. Volume
        IV, Discourse Analysis in Society*, pp. 61–82. New York: Academic Press.
Fox, James J.
    1971 Semantic Parallelism in Rotinese Ritual Language. *Bijdragen tot de Taal-
        Land-, en Volkenkunde* 127:215–255.
    1973 On Bad Death and the Left Hand. In Rodney Needham, ed., *Right and Left:
        Essays on Dual Symbolic Classification*, pp. 342–368. Chicago: University of
        Chicago Press.
    1974 Our Ancestors Spoke in Pairs: Rotinese Views of Language. In Richard Bau-
        man and Joel Sherzer, eds., *Explorations in the Ethnography of Speaking*,
        pp. 65–85. Cambridge: Cambridge University Press.
    1975 On Binary Categories and Primary Symbols. In Roy Willis, ed., *The Inter-
        pretation of Symbolism*, pp. 99–132. London: Malaby Press.
    1977a *Harvest of the Palm: Ecological Change in Eastern Indonesia.* Cambridge,
        MA: Harvard University Press.
    1977b The Comparative Study of Parallelism. In Cornelius H. Schooneveld, ed.,
        Roman Jakobson: Echoes of his Scholarship, pp. 59–90. Lisse: De Ridder
        Press.
    1980a Introduction. In James J. Fox, ed., *The Flow of Life: Essays on Eastern
        Indonesia*, pp. 1–18. Cambridge, MA: Harvard University Press.
    1980b Models and Metaphors. In James J. Fox, ed., *The Flow of Life. Essays on
        Eastern Indonesia*, pp. 327–333. Cambridge, MA: Harvard University Press.
Fox, James J. ed.
    1980 *The Flow of Life: Essays on Eastern Indonesia.* Cambridge, MA: Harvard
        University Press.
    1988 *To Speak in Pairs: Essays on the Ritual Languages of Eastern Indonesia.*
        Cambridge: Cambridge University Press.
Frake, Charles O.
    1977 Plying Frames Can be Dangerous: Some Reflections on Methodology in Cog-
        nitive Anthropology. *Quarterly Newsletter of Institute for Comparative Hu-
        man Development.* 1(3): 1–7.
    1980 *Language and Cultural Description.* Stanford, CA: Stanford University Press.
Frankenberg, Ronald, ed.
    1988 "Gramsci, Marxism and Phenomenology: Essays for the Development of
        Critical Medical Anthropology." Special Issue of *Medical Anthropology Quar-
        terly* (n.s.) 2(4): 323–464.
Friedrich, Paul
    1979 *Language, Context and the Imagination.* Stanford, CA: Stanford University
        Press.
    1986 *The Language Parallax: Linguistic Relativism and Poetic Indeterminacy.* Aus-
        tin: University of Texas Press.
    1989 Language, Ideology and Political Economy. *American Anthropologist* 91(2):
        295–312.
Geertz, Clifford
    1980 *Negara: The Theatre State in Nineteenth Century Bali.* Princeton, NJ:
        Princeton University Press.

→ 1983a Centers, Kings and Charisma: Reflections on the Symbolics of Power. In *Local Knowledge: Further Essays in Interpretive Anthropology*. pp. 121–146. New York: Basic Books.

1983b Blurred Genres: The Refiguration of Social Thought. In *Local Knowledge: Further Essays in Interpretive Anthropology*, pp. 19–35. New York: Basic Books.

Giddens, Anthony
1979 *Central Problems in Social Theory: Action, Structure, and Contradiction in Social Analysis*. Berkeley: University of California Press.

Goffman, Erving
1974 *Frame Analysis*. New York: Harper and Row.
1981 *Forms of Talk*. Philadelphia: University of Pennsylvania Press.

Gossen, Gary
1984 [1974] *Chamulas in the World of the Sun*. Prospect Heights, IL: Waveland Press

Grainger, Roger
1974 *Language of the Rite*. London: Dalton, Longman, and Todd.

Gramsci, Antonio
1971 *Selections from the Prison Notebooks*. London: Lawrence and Wishart.

[Gronovius, D.J. van den Dungen]
1855 Beschrijving van het eiland Soemba of Sandelhout. *Tijdschrift voor Nederlandsch Indie* 17:277–312.

Gumperz, John
1982 *Discourse Strategies*. New York: Cambridge University Press.

Habermas, Jürgen
1984 *The Theory of Communicative Action*. 2 vols. Trans. Thomas McCarthy. Boston: Beacon Press.

Halliday, Michael A. K.
1978 *Language as Social Semiotic*. London: Longman.

Hangelbroek, H.
1910 *Soemba: Land en Volk*. Assen: G. F. Hummelen. (Cited in Needham 1983.)

Hanks, William
1984 The Evidential Core of Deixis in Yucatec Maya. In J. Drogo, et al, eds., *Papers from the 20th Regional Meeting of the Chicago Linguistics Society*, pp. 154–172. Chicago: Chicago Linguistics Society.
1987 Discourse Genres in a Theory of Practice. *American Ethnologist* 14(4): 668–692.

Hardeland, A.
1858 *Versuch einer Grammatik der Dajackschen Sprache*. Amsterdam: F. Muller.

Haripranata, H.
1984 *Ceritera Sejarah Gereja Katolik Sumba dan Sumbawa*. Ende, Flores, Indonesia: Arnoldus.

Harris, Roy
1984 The Semiology of Textualization. *Language Sciences* 6(2): 271–286.

Heider, F.
1958 *The Psychology of Interpersonal Relations*. New York: John Wiley and Sons.

Hill, Jane
1985 The Grammar of Consciousness and the Consciousness of Grammar. *American Ethnologist* 12(4): 725–737.

Hobsbawm, Eric
1983 Introduction. In Eric Hobsbawm and Terence Ranger, eds., *The Invention of Tradition*, pp. 1–14. London: Cambridge University Press.

Hoekstra, Pieter
1948 *Paardenteelt op het Eiland Soemba.* Batavia: John Kappee.
Hoskins, Janet
1983 Paths to Riches and Renown: Kodi Spirit Worship and Feasting. Ph.D. Diss. Department of Anthropology, Harvard University.
╲ 1985 A Life History from Both Sides: The Changing Poetics of Personal Experience. *Journal of Anthropological Research* 41(2): 147–169.
1987 The Headhunter as Hero: Local Traditions and their Reinterpretation in National History. *American Ethnologist* 14(4): 605–622.
1988 Etiquette in Kodi Spirit Communication: The Lips Told to Speak, the Mouth Told to Pronounce. In James J. Fox, ed., *To Speak in Pairs: Essays on the Ritual Languages of Eastern Indonesia,* pp. 29–63. Cambridge: Cambridge University Press.
1989 On Losing and Getting a Head: Warfare, Exchange and Alliance in a Changing Sumba, 1888–1988. *American Ethnologist* 16(3): 419–440.
1989 Dead Bodies as Text: Augury and Violence in an Eastern Indonesian Sacrificial Complex. Unpubl. ms.
Hymes, Dell
1972 Models of the Interaction of Language and Social Life. In Dell Hymes and John Gumperz, eds., *Directions in Sociolinguistics,* pp. 35–71. New York: Holt, Rinehart and Winston.
1974 *Foundations in Sociolinguistics.* Philadelphia: University of Pennsylvania Press.
1981 *"In vain I tried to tell you": Essays in Native American Ethnopoetics.* Philadelphia: University of Pennsylvania Press.
Irvine, Judith T.
1979 Formality and Informality in Communicative Events. *American Anthropologist* 81(3): 773–790
1989 When Talk Isn't Cheap: Language and Political Economy. *American Ethnologist* 16(2): 248–267.
Jakobson, Roman
1966 Parallelism and its Russian Facet. *Language* 42(2): 398–429.
1980 Metalanguage as a Linguistic Problem. In *The Framework of Language,* pp. 81–92. Ann Arbor: University of Michigan Press.
Jakubinskij, Lev
1979 [1923] On Verbal Dialogue. *Dispositio* 4(11–12): 321–336.
James, William
1911 On Some Mental Effects of the Earthquake. In *Memories and Studies.* New York: Longmans, Green.
Kapita, Umbu Hina
1976a *Masyarakat Sumba dan Adata-Istiadatnya.* Waingapu: Gereja Kristen Sumba.
1976b *Sumba dalam Jangkauan Jaman.* Waingapu: Gereja Kristen Sumba.
Keeler, Ward
1986 *Javanese Shadow Puppets, Javanese Selves.* Princeton, NJ: Princeton University Press.
Kern, W.
1956 *Commentaar op de salasilah van Koetai.* Verhandelingen van het Koninklijk Instituut voor Taal-, Land-, en Volkenkunde, no. 19. s'Gravenhage: Martinus Nijhoff.
Krusemann, J. D.
1836 Beschrijving van het Sandelhout Eiland. *de Oosterling* 2:63–86.

Kruyt, Albert
    1901 Het Wichelen in Midden Celebes. *Tijdschrift der Bataviaasch Genootschaap voor Taal- Land- en Volkenkunde* 44:85–96.
    1922 De Soembaneezen. *Bijdragen tot de Taal- Land- en Volkenkunde* 78: 466–608.
Kuipers, Joel C.
    1982 Images of Life and Death: Textiles in Sumba, Indonesia. *Discovery* 16(2): 18–20.
    1984a Matters of Taste in Weyéwa. *Anthropological Linguistics* 26(1): 84–101.
    1984b Place, Names and Authority in Weyéwa Ritual Speech. *Language in Society* 13(3): 455–466.
    1986 Talking About Trouble: Gender Differences in Weyéwa Speech Use. *American Ethnologist* 13(3): 448–462.
    1988 The Pattern of Prayer in Weyéwa. In James J. Fox, ed., *To Speak in Pairs: Essays on the Ritual Languages of Eastern Indonesia*, pp. 104–128. Cambridge: Cambridge University Press.
    1989 "Medical Discourse" in Anthropological Context: Views of Language and Power. *Medical Anthropology Quarterly* 3(2): 99–123.
Langer, Suzanne
    1942 *Philosophy in a New Key*. New York: Pelican Books.
Laufer, G. and A. Kraeff
    1960 *The Geology and Hydrology of West- and Central- Sumba and Their Relationship to the Water Supply and the Rural Economy*. Bandung: Pusat Djawatan Geologi.
Lears, T. J. Jackson
    1985 The Concept of Cultural Hegemony: Problems and Possibilities. *American Historical Review* 90:567–593.
Leon-Portilla, M.
    1969 *Precolumbian Literatures of Mexico*. Norman: Oklahoma University Press.
Levinson, Stephen
    1983 *Pragmatics*. Cambridge: Cambridge University Press.
Lévi-Strauss, Claude
    1969 *The Raw and the Cooked*. New York: Harper and Row.
Lukes, Steven
    1979 Power and Authority. In Tom Bottomore and Richard Nisbet, eds., *History of Sociological Analysis*, pp. 631–676. New York: Basic Books.
Lutz, Nancy
    n.d. Adat and Resistance in Adonara, Eastern Indonesia. Unpubl.
Lyons, John
    1977 *Semantics*. Vols. 1–2. Cambridge: Cambridge University Press.
Marcus, George
    1986 Contemporary Problems of Ethnography in the Modern World System. In James Clifford and George Marcus. eds., *Writing Culture: The Poetics and Politics of Ethnography*, pp. 165–193. Berkeley: University of California Press.
Marvin, Carolyn
    1984 Constructed and Reconstructed Discourse: Inscription and Talk in the History of Literacy. *Communication Research: An International Quarterly* 11(4): 563–594.
McCanles, Michael
    1982 Machiavelli's Principe and the Textualization of History. *Modern Language Notes* 97(1): 1–18.

McKinnon, Susan Mary
1983 Hierarchy, Alliance and Exchange in the Tanimbar Islands. Ph.D. diss. University of Chicago.
Meijering, M. et al.
1927 Tot dankbarheid genoopt: Gedenkboek ter gelegenheid van den 25-jarigenzendingsarbeid op Soemba van wege de Gereformeerde Kerken in Groningen, Drente, en Overijssel. Kampen: J. H. Kok.
Mertz, Elizabeth
1985 Beyond Symbolic Anthropology: Introducing Semiotic Mediation. In Elizabeth Mertz and Richard Parmentier, eds., Semiotic Mediation: Sociocultural and Psychological Perspectives, pp. 1–19. New York: Academic Press.
Metzner, Joachim
1977 Pemiliharaan Ternak di Daerah Agraria Pulau Sumba Dan Masalah Peceklik Musiman. Kupang, Timor, Indonesia: Biro Penelitian, Universitas Nusa Cendana.
Middleton, John ed.
1967 Magic, Witchcraft and Curing. New York: The Natural History Press.
Mitchell, David
1970 Wanokalada: A Case Study in Local Administration. Bulletin of Indonesian Economic Studies 6(2): 76–93.
Needham, Rodney
1967 Percussion and Transition. Man 2:606–614.
1980 Principles and Variations in the Structure of Sumbanese Society. In James J. Fox, ed., The Flow of Life: Essays on Eastern Indonesia, pp. 21–47. Cambridge, MA: Harvard University Press.
1983 Sumba and the Slave Trade. Working Paper no. 31, Melbourne: Department of Anthropology, Monash University.
1987 Mamboru. Oxford: Oxford University Press.
O'Barr, William
1982 Language Strategy in the Courtroom. New York: Academic Press.
Ochs, Elinor
1979 Transcription as Theory. In Elinor Ochs and Bambi B. Schieffelin, eds., Developmental Pragmatics, pp. 43–72. New York: Academic Press.
1988 Culture and Language Development. Cambridge: Cambridge University Press.
Olson, David R.
1977 From Utterance to Text: The Bias of Language in Speech and Writing. Harvard Educational Review 47:257–281.
Ong, Walter
1982 Orality and Literacy: The Technologizing of the Word. New York: Methuen
1984 Orality, Literacy and Medieval Textualization. New Literary History 16(1): 1–12.
Ono, Akiko
1976 Clan and Village in Western Sumba. Minzokugaku Kenkyu 40:299–326.
[Onvlee, Louis; Enos Boeloe and S. D. Mbili, eds.]
1938 Li'i kira ndaa ndiki, Li'i ndandi ndaa ngero. Batavia: G. Kolff and Co.
1970 Kira Ndandi Bo'u. Jakarta: Lembaga Alkitab Indonesia.
Onvlee, Louis
n.d. Lessen Wewewas. (unpublished manuscript).
1929 Palatalisatie in eenige Soembaneesche dialecten. In Bataviaasch Genootschaap van Kunsten en Wetenschappen, comp. [Lembaga Kebudayaan Indo-

nesia] *Feestbundel uitgegeven door het Koninklijk Bataviaasch Genooschaap van Kunsten and Wetenschappen bij gelegenheid van zijn 150 jarig bestaan 1778–1928*, Vol. 2, pp. 234–245. Weltevreden: Kolff & Co.

1950 Over de mediae in het Soembanees en Sawoenees. In Ronkel, Philippus Samuel van, comp. *Bingkisan Budi. Een bundel opstellen aan Dr. Philippus Samuel van Ronkel door vrienden en leerlingen angeboden op zijn tachtigste verjaardag, 1 Augustus 1950*, pp. 215–234. Leiden: A. W. Sijthoff's Vitgeversmaatschappij.

1973 *Cultuur als Antwoord*. Verhandeling van het Koninklijk Instituut voor Taal-Land- end Volkenkunde, no. 66. The Hague: Martinus Nijhoff.

1980 The Significance of Livestock on Sumba. In James J. Fox, ed., *The Flow of Life: Essays on Eastern Indonesia*, pp. 195–207. Cambridge, MA: Harvard University Press.

Pandey, Triloki
1972 Anthropologists in Zuni. *Proceedings of the American Philosophical Society* 116(4): 321–337.

Parmentier, Richard J.
1987 *The Sacred Remains: Myth and History in a Belauan Polity*. Chicago: University of Chicago Press.

Peirce, Charles Sanders
1974 *Collected Papers*, vols 1 and 2. Cambridge, MA: Harvard University Press.

Pfeiffer D. and P. Meiser
1968 Geologische, Hydrologische Und Geoelektrische Untersuchungen Auf Der Insel Sumba (Indonesien). *Geologische Jb.* 86:885–918.

Phillips, Nigel
1981 *Sijobang: Sung Narratives of West Sumatra*. Cambridge: Cambridge University Press.

Pigeaud, Th. G. Th.
1967–1970 *Java in the Fourteenth Century: A Study in Cultural History*. 5 vols. Koninklijke Institut voor Taal- Land- en Volkenkunde Translation Series no. 4. The Hague: Martinus Nijhoff.

Popesko, Peter
[1970] *Atlas of Topographical Anatomy of Domestic Animals*, Vol. I. Trans. R. Getty. Philadelphia: W. B. Saunders.

Pratt, Mary Louise
1977 *Toward a Speech Act Theory of Literary Discourse*. Bloomington: Indiana University Press.

Prins, A. H.
1916 Memorie van overgave betreffende het bestuur der afdeeling Soemba, Juni 1916. Unpubl. archival material. Amsterdam: Instituut Voor De Tropen, Afd. Handschriften.

Renard-Clamagirand, Brigitte
1988 Li'i Marapu: Speech and Ritual Among the Wewewa of West Sumba. In James J. Fox, ed., *To Speak in Pairs: Essays on the Ritual Languages of Eastern Indonesia*, pp. 87–103. Cambridge: Cambridge University Press.

Ricoeur, Paul
1976 *Interpretation Theory: Discourse and the Surplus of Meaning*. Fort Worth: Texas Christian University Press.

1981 The Model of the Text: Meaningful Action Considered as Text. In John B. Thompson, ed. and trans., *Hermeneutics and the Human Sciences*, pp. 197–226. Cambridge: Cambridge University Press.

Riekerk, G.H.
    1936 Bestuursmemorie van den controleur van West Soemba. Van 10 April 1933
        tot en met 22 Juli 1936. Unpubl. Archival Material.
Roos, Samuel.
    1872 Bijdrage tot de Kennis van Taal, Land en Volk op het Eiland Soemba. *Ver-
        handeling van het Bataviaasch Genootschap van Kunsten en Wetenschappen*
        36:1–125.
Russell, Bertrand
    1950 *Mysticism and Logic*. New York: Norton.
Sacks, Harvey, Emanuel Schegloff and Gail Jefferson
    1974 A Simplest Systematics for the Organization of Turn-taking for Conversation.
        Language 50:696–735.
Saussure, Ferdinand de
    1959 [1916] *A Course in General Linguistics*. Ed. Charles Bally and Albert Seche-
        haye, trans. Wade Baskin. New York: McGraw-Hill.
Schegloff, Emanuel
    1982 Discourse as an Interactional Achievement: Some Uses of "uh-huh" and
        Other Things That Come in Between Sentences. In Deborah Tannen, ed.,
        Analyzing Discourse: Text and Talk, pp. 71–93. Washington, DC: George-
        town University Press.
Schiffrin, Deborah
    1987 *Discourse Markers*. Cambridge: Cambridge University Press.
Sherzer, Joel
    1983 *Kuna Ways of Speaking*. Austin: University of Texas Press
Silverstein, Michael
    1976 Shifters, Linguistic Categories and Cultural Description. In Keith Basso and
        Henry Selby, eds., *Meaning in Anthropology*. Albuquerque: University of
        New Mexico Press.
    1981 The Metaforces of Power in Traditional Oratory. Unpubl. ms.
    1984 On the Pragmatic 'Poetry' of Prose: Parallelism, Repetition, and Cohesive
        Structure in the Time Course of Dyadic Conversation. In Deborah Schiffrin,
        ed., *Meaning, Form and Use in Context: Linguistic Applications*, pp. 181–
        199. Washington DC: Georgetown University Press.
    1988 The Indeterminacy of Contextualization: When is enough enough?
        Unpubl. ms.
Shuy, Roger
    1976 The Medical Interview: Problems in Communication. *Primary Care* 3(3):
        365–386.
Tambiah, Stanley Jeyaraja
    1985 *Culture, Thought and Social Action: An Anthropological Perspective*. Cam-
        bridge, MA.: Harvard University Press.
Tannen, Deborah
    1986 Introducing Constructed Dialogue in Greek and American Conversational
        and Literary Narrative. In Florian Coulmas, ed., *Direct and Indirect Speech*,
        pp. 311–332. Amsterdam: Mouton de Gruyter.
    1987 Repetition in Conversation: Toward a Poetics of Talk.
        Language 63(3): 574–605.
Tanz, Christine
    1980 *Studies in the Acquisition of Deictic Terms*. Cambridge: Cambridge University
        Press.

Tedlock, Dennis
    1983 *The Spoken Word and the Work of Interpretation.* Philadelphia: University of Pennsylvania Press.
Traube, Elizabeth
    n.d. Order and Events: Cultural and Historical Perspectives on Indigenous Responses to Colonialism. Unpubl. ms.
    1980 Mambai Rituals of Black and White. In James J. Fox, ed., *The Flow of Life: Essays on Eastern Indonesia*, pp. 290–314. Cambridge, MA: Harvard University Press.
    1986 *Cosmology and Social Life: Ritual Exchange among the Mambai of East Timor.* Chicago: University of Chicago Press.
Turner, Victor
    1961 *Ndembu Divination: Its Symbolism and Techniques.* Rhodes Livingston Paper no. 31. Lusaka: Rhodes-Livingston Institute.
    1975 *Revelation and Divination in Ndembu Ritual.* Ithaca, NY: Cornell University Press.
Tyler, Stephen
    1986 Post-Modern Ethnography: From Document of the Occult to Occult Document. In James Clifford and George Marcus. eds., *Writing Culture: The Poetics and Politics of Ethnography*, pp. 122–140. Berkeley: University of California Press.
    1987 *The Unspeakable: Discourse, Dialogue and Rhetoric in the Post-Modern World.* Madison: University of Wisconsin Press.
Urban, Greg
    1986 Ceremonial Dialogues in South America. *American Anthropologist* 88(2): 371–386.
    1987 On the "Psychological Reality" of the Text. Upubl. ms.
Van Gennep, Arnold
    1908 Essai d'une théorie des langues spéciales. *Revue des Etudes Ethnologiques et Sociologiques* 3:327–337.
Van Wouden F. A. E.
    1968 *Types of Social Structure in Eastern Indonesia.* Trans. Rodney Needham. Koninklijk Instituut voor Taal-, Land-, en Volkenkunde, Translation Series no. 11. The Hague: Martinus Nijhoff. Originally published in Dutch in 1935.
Veen, H. van der
    1965 *The Merok Feast of the Sa'dan Toraja.* Verhandelingen van het Koninklijk Instituut voor Taal-, Land-, en Volkenkunde, no. 45. The Hague: Martinus Nijhoff.
Volosinov, V. N.
    1973 *Marxism and the Philosophy of Language.* Trans. Ladislav Matejka and I.R. Titunik. New York: Seminar Press.
Waitz, E.W.F.J.
    1933 Bestuurs-Memorie Van Den Gezaghebber Van West Soemba, 1933. Unpubl. archival material. Amsterdam: Instituut Voor De Tropen, Afd. Handschriften.
Whorf, Benjamin Lee
    1956 Some Verbal Categories in Hopi. In *Language, Thought and Reality*, ed. John Carroll, pp. 112–124. Cambridge, MA: MIT Press.
Wielenga, D. K.
    1911–1912 Soemba: Reizen Op Soemba. *De Macedonier* 15:303–308, 328–334, 16:144–150
    1916–1918 De Zending Van De Gereformeerde Kerken. Voor Zendingstudiekrin-

gen. Soemba. 1. Historie. *De Macedonier* 20:137–146, 161–169, 201–214, 225–237, 299–309, 332–339, 353–359, 21:3–11, 33–43, 77–83, 107–112, 129–136, 170–177, 204–210, 239–246, 269–272, 299–309, 359–367, 22:16–22, 33–40, 76–80, 110–117, 145–151, 172–178, 235–239, 270–275, 298–305.

Wijngaarden, J. K.
1893 Naar Soemba. *Mededeelingen Van Wege Het Nederlandsche Zendelinggenootschap* 37:352–376.

Witkamp, H.
1912–1913 Een Verkennignstocht Over Het Eiland Soemba. *Tijdschrift Van Het Koninklijk Nederlandsch Aardrijkskundig Genootschap* 29:744–775; 30:8–27; 484–505; 619–637.

Woodbury, Anthony
1985 The Functions of Rhetorical Structure: A Study of Central Alaskan Yupik Eskimo discourse. *Language in Society* 14(2): 153–190.

Worsley, P. J.
1972 *Babad Buleleng—A Balinese Dynastic Genealogy*. Bibliotheca Indonesica 8. The Hague: Martinus Nijhoff.

Wurm, S. A. and S. Hattori, eds.
1983 *Language Atlas of the Pacific Area. Part II: Japan area, Taiwan (Formosa), Philippines, Mainland and Insular South-East Asia* (Pacific Linguistics C-67). Canberra: Australian Academy of the Humanities, in collaboration with the Japan Academy.

Wurm, S. A. and B. Wilson
1983 *English Finderlist of Reconstructions in Austronesian Languages (Post Brandstetter)*. 2nd ed. Pacific Linguistics Series C. Canberra: Research School of Pacific Studies, The Australian National University.

Zuckerkandl, Victor
1973 *Man the Musician*. Vol. 2: *Sound and Symbol*. Princeton, NJ: Princeton University Press.

Zurbuchen, Mary Sabina
1987 *The Language of Balinese Shadow Theatre*. Princeton, NJ: Princeton University Press.

Index of Names

Index of Subjects

University of Pennsylvania Press
CONDUCT AND COMMUNICATIONS SERIES

Erving Goffman and Dell Hymes, Founding Editors
Dell Hymes, Gillian Samkoff, and Henry Glassie, General Editors

Erving Goffman. *Strategic Interaction*. 1970
William Labov. *Language in the Inner City: Studies in the Black English Vernacular.* 1973
William Labov. *Sociolinguistic Patterns.* 1973
Dell Hymes. *Foundations in Sociolinguistics: An Ethnographic Approach.* 1974
Barbara Kirshenblatt-Gimblett, ed. *Speech Play: Research and Resources for the Study of Linguistic Creativity.* 1976
Gillian Sankoff. *The Social Life of Language.* 1980
Erving Goffman. *Forms of Talk.* 1981
Dell Hymes. *"In vain I tried to tell you": Essays in Native American Ethnopoetics.* 1981
Dennis Tedlock. *The Spoken Word and the Work of Interpretation.* 1983
Ellen B. Basso. *A Musical View of the Universe: Kalapalo Myth and Ritual Performances.* 1985
Michael Moerman. *Talking Culture: Ethnography and Conversation Analysis.* 1987
Dan Rose. *Black American Street Life: South Philadelphia, 1969–1971.* 1987
J. Joseph Errington. *Structure and Style in Japanese: A Semiotic View of Linguistic Etiquette.* 1988
Charles L. Briggs. *Competence in Performance: The Creativity of Tradition in Mexicano Verbal Art.* 1988
Joel C. Kuipers. *Power in Performance: The Creation of Textual Authority in Weyewa Ritual Speech.* 1990

This book was set in Linotron Electra. Electra was
originally designed for the Merganthaler Linotype
Company by W. A. Dwiggins in 1935. Designed as a book
typeface, Electra retains some of the characteristics of
oldstyle types but has modern serifs that give the typeface a
light contemporary look.

Printed on acid-free paper.